Explore the World

NELLES GUIDE

EGYPT

Author:
Eva Ambros

D1579854

*An Up-to-date travel guide with 145 color photos
and 21 maps*

**Third revised edition
1999**

Dear Reader: Being up-to-date is the main goal of the Nelles series. Our correspondents help keep us abreast of the latest developments in the travel scene, while our cartographers see to it that maps are also kept completely current. However, as the travel world is constantly changing, we cannot guarantee that all the information contained in our books is always valid. Should you come across a discrepancy, please contact us at: Nelles Verlag, Schleissheimer Str. 371 b, 80935 Munich, Germany, tel. (089) 3571940, fax. (089) 35719430, e-mail: Nelles.Verlag@T-Online.de

Note: Distances and measurements, including temperatures, used in this guide are metric. For conversion information, please see the *Guidelines* section of this book.

LEGEND

▪ Public or Significant Building	Jirza Place Mentioned in Text	▨ National Border	
▪ Hotel	⇥ International Airport	═ Throughway	
▪ ○ Shopping Center, Market	⇥ National Airport	═ Principal Highway	
✝ ☪ Church, Mosque		═ Main Road	
✳ Place of Interest	\ 13 / Distance in Kilometers	═ Other Road	
⤓ Beach	**Nagb Ghūl** 861 Mountain Summit (Height in Meters)	── Railway	
◡ Water source, Well		── Ferry	
		26 Route Number	

EGYPT
© Nelles Verlag GmbH, 80935 Munich
   All rights reserved

Third Revised Edition 1999
ISBN 3-88618-158-8
Printed in Slovenia

Publisher:	Günter Nelles	**Translation:**	Christiane Banerji, Chase Stewart
Managing Editor:	Berthold Schwarz		
Project Editor:	Eva Ambros	**Cartography:**	Nelles Verlag GmbH
English Edition		**Color Separation:**	Priegnitz, Munich
Editor:	Chase Stewart	**Printed By:**	Gorenjski Tisk

TABLE OF CONTENTS

THEBES: CITY OF A HUNDRED GATES

FROM LUXOR TO THE NUBIAN TEMPLES

CORAL REEFS AND WONDROUS MOUNTAINS

FEATURES

GUIDELINES

LIST OF MAPS

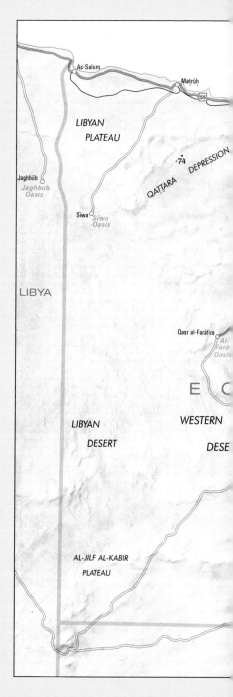

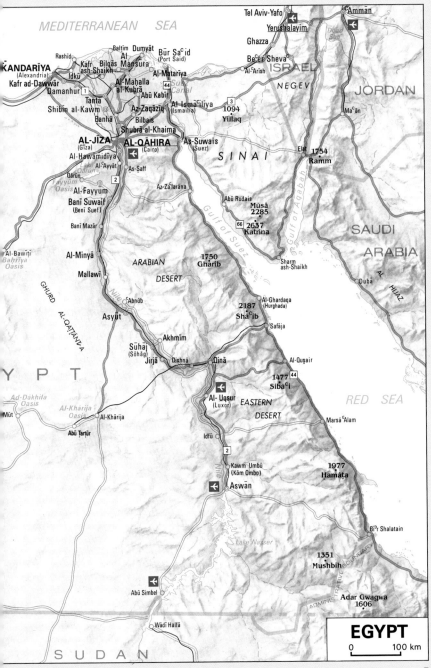

Tel Aviv-Yafo
Yerushalayim
Ghazza
Beʿer Sheva
ʿAmman

Rashīd
Baltīm   Dumyāt
Al   Būr Saʿīd
ʿKANDARĪYA   Kafr   Bilqās   Mansūra   (Port Said)
(Alexandria)   ash-Shaikh
Idkū
Kafr ad-Dawwār
Damanhūr   Al-Mahalla   al-Kubrā   Abū Kabīr
Tanta   Az-Zaqāzīq   Al-Ismaʿīliya   (Ismailia)
Shibīn al-Kawm   Banhā   Bilbais   1094   Yíllaq
Shubrā al-Khaima
AL-JĪZA   AL-QĀHIRA
(Gīza)   (Cairo)   As-Suwais   (Suez)   Elat   1754   Ramm
Al-Hawāmidīya
Al-ʿAyyāt
Qārūn   As-Saff   S   I   N   A   I
Al-Fayyūm   As-Ṣaff
Fayyum   Oasis   Az-Zaʿfarāna
Banī Suwaif   Abū Rudais   Mūsā   2285
(Benī Suef)
Banī Mazār   66   2637   Katrina
Al-Bawīṭī   Sharm   ash-Shaikh
Baḥrīya   Oasis   ARABIAN   1750   Ghārib
Al-Minyā
Mallawī   DESERT   Al-Ghardaqa   (Hurghada)
GHURD   2187   Shaʿib
ʿAbnūb   Safāja
Asyūt
Akhmīm
Sūhaj   (Sōhāg)   Qinā   Al-Quṣair
Jirja   Dishnā
1477   44   Sibaʿi
Al-Uqsur   (Luxor)   EASTERN   DESERT   Marsā ʿAlam
Ad-Dākhila   Oasis
Mūt   Al-Khārija   Oasis   Al-Khārija
Abū Tartūr   Idfū
Kawm ʿUmbū   (Kōm Ombo)   1977   Hamāta
Aswān
Biʾr Shalatain
Lake Nasser
1351   Mushbih
Abū Simbel   Adar Gwagwa   1606
Wādī Halfā

ISRAEL
NEGEV
JORDAN
Maʿān
SAUDI
ARABIA
AL HIJAZ
Dubā
RED   SEA
EGYPT
0   100 km

Gulf of Suez
Gulf of Aqaba
Suez Canal

Y   P   T
S   U   D   A   N

A GIFT OF THE NILE

When viewed from the air, Egypt is an impressive sight which calls to mind Herodotus' poetic metaphor for the ancient country: "Egypt is truly a gift of the Nile." This is a 35,000-square-kilometer river oasis, shaped like a long-stemmed flower, in the midst of the desert that covers most of Egypt's one million square kilometers.

For more than half of its 6,671-kilo-meter-long journey to the Mediterranean, the "Great River," as the Nile was known to the ancient Egyptians, carves a channel straight through the largest desert area in the world; the subtropical dry belt between the Atlantic coast and central Asia.

Preceding pages: The Great Sphinx of Giza with the Khafre Pyramid. Young women at a banquet (Tomb of Nahkt, Thebes West). Water-seller. Above: Egypt's lifeline – the Nile. Right: Canals flow through many villages.

To the west, the Sahara borders the Nile Valley, with the flat waves of the limestone massif of the Libyan Desert and the tablelands of Nubian sandstone. To the east, the Arabian Desert swells into a granite mountain range that marks the eastern edge of the African continent, and extends across the fault trough of the Red Sea into the southern Sinai. It is into this vast, 400-meter-high plateau that the River Nile gradually cut its valley over many thousands of years: a veritable Garden of Eden in the middle of the barren desert.

The intensively farmed river oasis is a narrow strip of fertile land on each side of the river, which runs for 900 kilometers between Cairo and Aswan and which is never more than 20 kilometers wide. Only in the Delta, where the Nile once divided into seven branches (today there are only two), does the fertile area grow to an impressive 25,000 square kilometers.

The longest river in the world begins its course in the rain-rich heart of Africa,

in Burundi to be specific, with the headwaters of the Kagera and other rivers. They flow through Lake Victoria and Lake Albert and then become the Mountain River (Arabic: *Bahr al-Jabal*) that irrigates the swamps of Sudan.

In the northern swamplands of southern Sudan it is joined by the Gazelle River (Arabic: *Bahr al-Ghazâl*), the Giraffe River (Arabic: *Bahr az-Zarâfa*) and the Sobat River, and is thenceforth called the White Nile.

In Khartoum it meets with the Blue Nile, and a little further on with the Atbâra River, before ploughing through the Sahara for the final 3,000 kilometers. Between Khartoum and Aswan the granite barriers of six cataracts, two of which have now disappeared into the waters of Lake Nasser south of Aswan, represent major obstacles to its flow.

The pulse of Egypt's main artery is the summer flooding, started by the monsoon rains in the Abyssinian highlands. They quickly turn the Blue Nile and the Atbâra into turbulent and muddy masses of water which pour into the main river in the Sudanese Nile Valley.

Since the construction of the new High Dam, however, the flooding in Egypt reaches only to the giant lake reservoir which is dammed to the south of Aswan. Until 1968, the water level would begin to rise every year in July, and soon afterwards the waters would spill over their banks; the entire fertile area would be flooded, leaving only the higher-lying villages emerging from the waters like little island fortresses. The fields would only begin re-emerging after the peak had been reached in September, signaling the moment to sow grain for the next harvest.

Over thousands of years the "Black Lands," as the Pharaohs called Egypt, were formed wherever the floods deposited their silt, the 10- to 12-meter-thick layer of fertile black earth, alongside which the infertile, rainless desert abruptly begins. Together, the fertility of the banks of the Nile and the protection of the desert provided the ideal geo-

15

graphical conditions for the development of one of the oldest civilizations known to mankind.

For thousands of years the fate of the country depended on the flooding of the Nile: people worried about whether the floods would be too great or whether they might not come at all. And even when the waters came regularly, the extent of the rise varied a great deal, and this ultimately determined the size of the next harvest.

Until the 20th century, the system of basin irrigation of the ancient Pharaohs was used. The land was divided into wide basins, bordered by dams, which were filled for about 45 days by a complex network of canals during the flooding. After that, seeds were sown in the wet silt and were later harvested without need for further watering.

Above: Wooden ploughs are rarely seen nowadays. Right: The donkey is still an important means of transportation for the fellahs.

The irrigation of higher-lying fields, or even the watering of the fields throughout the year, was possible only by using water-drawing and levering implements, sometimes still seen in use today, in particular in Upper Egypt.

The oldest of these levers is the *shadûf*, a branch which is used to lift a bucket of water using a lump of clay as a counterweight. The famous *sâqîya* was probably introduced from Persia: an animal drives a horizontal cog wheel which moves a second vertical wheel to draw water. The fellahs also make use of the *tanbûr*. This is a cylinder with a spiral passage inside which is used to raise water by "cranking" it from one level to another (see photo p. 17).

Major improvements in irrigation techniques first came about when Muhammad 'Alî introduced cotton growing to the region in 1820. Because basin irrigation allows for only a single harvest, a series of dams, weirs and large canals was built, and finally, in 1902, the first Aswan Dam was constructed to make

sufficient water available all the year round, thus enabling a second – or even a third – harvest. The construction of the Aswan High Dam marks the end of a process of development which finally freed Egypt from its millenia-long dependence on the flooding of the Nile.

Today, the green and fertile fields that can be seen throughout the year are ordered according to culture and crop rotation plans laid down by farming co-operatives. Since President Mubarak officially rescinded the socialistic land reforms of the Nasser era (which were no longer observed anyway), there are once again large landowners whose holdings far surpass the maximum 100 *feddân* (42 hectares) a farmer was formerly allowed to own. Almost all farmers belong to one of the 5,000 cooperatives which organize the buying of seed, machines and fertilizers, and which are also responsible for selling the crops.

The entire fertile area, inasmuch as it is not settled, is used for agriculture. The most important crops here are grains, such as wheat, millet, rice and maize, clover, vegetables, sugar cane and cotton. Fruit and olive plantations are mainly concentrated in the Fayyûm area and in the Delta. But Egypt's "tree of life," the date palm, is found everywhere. One palm tree can provide an annual crop of 60 to 100 kilograms of the sweet fruit. In addition, dried palm fronds are used to make simple furniture, fruit crates, fencing and enclosures.

Almost all the vegetation in the area consists of useful crops, and most livestock consists of beasts of burden. In the Nile Valley tractors have by no means replaced the traditional camels (which in Egypt are mainly dromedaries), donkeys and water buffalo. Because there is scarcely any pasture land, livestock breeding plays only a minor role in Egypt. For this reason the country's biblical "fleshpots" are nowadays filled mainly with chickens. Or with doves, for which beautiful towers are built all over the country, be they clay-colored sugarloaf towers or whitewashed dove castles.

THE EMPIRE OF THE PHARAOHS

"The Egyptians, ... more than any other people, cultivate the memory of the past, and have more knowledge of history than any people I have ever met during my travels." This observation was made by the Greek writer Herodotus in his *Histories.*

The "Father of History," as Herodotus is often called, traveled through Egypt in the fifth century B.C., and afterwards described the culture, history and geography of the Land of the Nile to his contemporaries. He had every reason to be impressed by the Egyptians' knowledge of history; they were able to give him not only the names and length of the reigns of their kings – beginning with Menes, "the oldest mortal king of Egypt" – but also told him many other details of their long history. Just how much history was recorded is revealed by the fact that at the time of Herodotus' writing, 2,500 years had already passed since the rule of Menes.

But where did the priests of the great temples, whom Herodotus named as his sources of information, get their knowledge from? The ancient Egyptians had no system of written recorded history in the Western sense. However, in the temple archives, annals and lists were preserved in which historical events, names, reigns, even the dates of birth and death of individual Pharaohs, were recorded chronologically.

These royal papyri were some of the most important sources for Manetho, a high priest from Heliopolis who wrote a three-volume history of Egypt at the beginning of the third century B.C. This work has served as a great aid to researchers, even though only excerpts of it have been preserved. Even the modern

Right: The enigmatic smile of a Pharaoh (detail of a statue of Ramses II in the Temple of Luxor).

division of the Pharaohs into 30 dynasties dates back to Manetho.

But this bureaucratic bookkeeping never interfered with the mythical conception of history that the ancient Egyptians maintained, which claimed that at the beginning of all time a dynasty of gods ruled the land, and that an eternal world law, the *Maat,* governed all history. Cosmic order, justice and truth were the basic values of this Maat, and it was the king's duty to guarantee its continuing application; only the king alone understood the legalities of the Maat, and only he could maintain the order of the world through the correct performance of certain rituals.

In this way the god-kings became the center of creation for the peoples of ancient Egypt; a view which finds visible expression in the enormous pyramids of the Old Kingdom.

Egypt before the Pyramids

The reference in the Lists of Kings to Menes (c. 3050 B.C.) as the first king of the First Dynasty and as the founder of the state appears, in the light of modern research, to be an almost arbitrary caesura. The First Dynasty was preceded by a long – albeit mostly unwritten – history, during which the foundations of Egyptian civilization were laid.

Evidence shows that the mountain areas bordering the Nile Valley and the neighboring desert had already been settled by the Paleolithic Age, but it was only in the sixth millenium B.C. that the far-reaching change from a hunter-gatherer culture to a settled way of life took place. The increased desiccation of the Sahara, which at one time offered far better living conditions, compelled the nomadic inhabitants of North Africa to move to the oases and the fertile Nile Valley, where they settled.

Archeological research covering a period of more than 2,000 years has re-

vealed little more than isolated individual settlements, cemeteries and artifacts. But around 3500 B.C., in the whole of the Nile Valley from the Delta to Nubia, a unified culture spread whose centers, probably independent city-states of sorts, had many contacts with one another. Trade relations even existed with the Middle East and Mesopotamia.

Around 3050 B.C., these separate entities joined together to become a unified state, although the exact sequence of events is hotly contested. The old theory of the Two Kingdoms, suggesting that a mainly nomadic federation of clans from Upper Egypt conquered the settled farmers of the Delta area, would seem not only to explain many Egyptian cultural phenomena; it would also be confirmed by the Egyptians' own view of historical events. They describe the birth of their state in terms of "the unification of the Two Lands," and attribute this event to their founder, King Menes.

What really happened will probably never be known, but it seems that legend has projected a long and gradual evolutionary process onto the figure of a single cultural hero who personifies the beginning of the glorious history of the Land of the Nile.

The mythical portrayal of a centralized state as having been born through the unification of two constituent kingdoms highlights one of the characteristics of ancient Egyptian thinking: the perception of the created world and its phenomena in terms of dualities; dualities that merge together into an ordered whole.

This dual paradigm pervaded not only mythical-religious life, but political life as well. Take, for example, the various emblems of the rulers, presenting everything in twos: whether it be the two different forms of the crown to represent the different landscapes – the high tiara crown for Upper Egypt and the flat crown for the Delta; or the two scepters, the crook and the flail; the title of "King of Upper and Lower Egypt" which the Pharaohs carried to the end of Egypt's antiquity; or even the pair of deities asso-

ciated with the king, who join the emble-matic plants of the two lands, the lotus and papyrus.

The true "father of the Pharaonic king-dom," though, was the Nile, which trans-formed the infertile desert along its banks into a Garden of Eden, and which pro-vided the people there with everything they needed to live. But long-term plan-ning was required if the waters of the river were to be used effectively. Dams and canals were needed to irrigate the fields, to serve as protection against floods, and as reservoirs in case the floods did not come at all. Political unifi-cation was thus born of the organization of water distribution.

The geographical makeup of the Nile Valley naturally required an extensive administration, and for this to function properly, writing had to be developed. A calendar was introduced that fixed the number of days of the year at 365.

Above: At the Mycerinus Pyramid. Right: The Alabaster Sphinx in Memphis.

The Time of the Pyramids

The protected location and the lucky circumstance that there was no equally matched state in the immediate vicinity allowed life in the Land of the Nile to proceed peacefully for more than 1,500 years. During the first two dynasties (c. 3050-2715 B.C.) the empire was consoli-dated and the groundwork was laid for the first cultural golden age, the era of the Old Kingdom (c. 2715-2192 B.C.).

This was the age of the pyramid builders, the god-kings who, with their awareness of the afterlife, would have gigantic tombs built for themselves in which they would reign, immortal, for all time.

The first Pharaoh to have his tomb built in monumental dimensions is also considered to have been the founder of the Old Kingdom. He was King Djoser (c. 2697-2677 B.C.), who built the Step Pyramid of Saqqâra. Even though hardly any historical information regarding his reign, which lasted for two decades, has been passed down through the ages, his enormous tomb stands as a stone symbol of a tempered and powerful state, with the divine king at its apex.

The center of the empire was Memphis, the "City of the White Walls," which lies at the point where the Nile Valley and the Delta meet, and is said to have been founded by Menes. The step pyramid was built within sight of the city, and its beauty and perfection was praised by pilgrims throughout Egyptian history. Even more honors were heaped on its brilliant architect, Imhotep: posterity not only considered him to be the "Opener of the Stone," but also regarded him as a physician, a wise man, and even as a god of healing.

The Fourth Dynasty, which lasted from about 2641 to 2521 B.C., saw the beginning of the age of the pyramid builders, whose mighty tombs rise up like abstract stone mountains on the edge of the western desert near Cairo. The most famous of these structures are the pyramids of kings Cheops, Khafre and Mycerinus near Gîza, but the first real pyramid can be traced to Snefru, founder of the dynasty.

There is relatively little information regarding the Fourth Dynasty as a whole, but Herodotus reported that Cheops and Khafre were terrible despots who mercilessly exploited their subjects for the construction of their pyramids and forced them to work. Cheops was supposed to have been such a dreadful man that "when he was in need of funds he took his own daughter to a bordello and ordered her to earn a certain sum of money there."

Such negative images have survived to the present day, most of which were probably based on the monumental size of the two great pyramids; unsurpassed feats of building. Yet in reality the construction of these huge monuments was the concern, perhaps even the *raison d'être*, of a whole nation that placed its

own hopes for eternal life in the immortality of its god-kings. The mortuary cult of the deceased king was the national cult of an era in which the people saw their Pharaoh as a divine incarnation. So the pyramids are not to be seen as a memorial to a tyrannical age, but rather as an expression of the religious feeling of a strong community.

The first signs that a change in the perception of the world had come about came at the pinnacle of this sacred absolutism. This new perception did not altogether strip the god-king if his divine role, it rather placed him the position of following in the shadow of the gods. The almighty Pharaoh, the "Great God," henceforth called himself the "Son of Ra," making it clear that he now felt himself subordinate to the will of the divine father, the sun god Ra.

With the beginning of the Fifth Dynasty (c. 2521-2359 B.C.), the triumphal march of the cult of the sun reached its high point. Not far from the royal pyramids, which in the meantime had taken on more modest dimensions, temples to the sun god were erected; walled courtyards appeared with obelisk-like cult pillars at their centers. Here sacrificial offerings were made in the open air to the sun god Ra, the creator of all life, so that he could receive his gifts directly with his rays.

Scholars have long puzzled over the background of this religious change, which may have been associated with the increasing influence of the sun priests. But whatever happened, a far-reaching change in consciousness, which has been aptly described as "the birth of the individual," almost certainly lay behind it: suddenly, the Pharaoh is presented in writings as a human being, as an affable and caring ruler. And even public officials take on personal contours when they proudly recount stories of their lives in their biographies.

Ultimately, though, the seed of political decline lay in this new self consciousness. The individual power of high officials, who were becoming ever more powerful in their inherited fiefs in the provinces, increasingly paralyzed the central administration. And when the country suffered a terrible famine which lasted for almost 20 years shortly after the end of the 64-year reign of King Pepi II (c. 2259-2195 B.C.), the whole of the state structure disintegrated, and power fell completely into the hands of individual regional princes.

With this, the conception of the world of an entire people was shattered. The pain to the individual on suffering the loss of all previously held values is reflected in the outstanding works of literature which were written in the era after this so-called First Intermediate Period (c. 2192-2040).

In the face of anarchy, chaos and famine, many could not hold themselves

Right: Depiction of King Sesostris I wearing the crown of Lower Egypt.

back from bitterly reproaching the god of creation, and in their resignation many even longed for death. In this climate of scepticism, many questioned whether life had any point at all, and even doubted whether there was life after death. And such sentiments culminated in this unusual call to enjoy this life: "Make of this a good day and do not weary of it! Lo, no one is able to take his goods with him! Lo, none who departs this life comes back again!"

The Middle Kingdom (2040-1781 B.C.)

Around the year 2040 B.C., the Theban regional prince Mentuhotep II succeeded in reuniting the country politically. His powerful reign was the starting point for a new golden age of Egyptian culture, the era of the Middle Kingdom, which was regarded by the ancient Egyptians as the classical period of their history. At that time, Thebes began its rise to becoming one of the most famous cities of the ancient world, for Mentuhotep II made his residence, present-day Luxor, into the new capital.

In Karnak the first sacrificial altars were erected to Amen. This was the beginning of a huge imperial shrine to the god who would become fused with the sun god Ra and would become the King of the Gods of the Egyptian pantheon. In the Dair al-Bahrî basin the founder of the Middle Kingdom built a royal tomb of a completely new design: a terraced temple which towers above a rock tomb deep in the mountain.

Even after Amenemhet I (1991-65 B.C.), the first king of the following Twelfth Dynasty, moved the political center to the area near Memphis, Thebes continued to be an important religious center, and Amen-Ra remained the god of protection of the dynasty. King Amenemhet I finally succeeded in winning back the loyalty of the once powerful re-

gional princes to the royal house and in establishing a centralistically-ordered political system based on the model of the era of the pyramids.

The conscious associations with past greatness can also be seen in the pyramids which he and his successors had built near Dahshûr, Lisht, Al-Lâhûn and Hawwâra. Yet it seems almost symbolic that the royal tombs were now built from mud bricks and no longer from massive stone blocks. Even though the shape had been revived, the contents had become different.

The First Intermediate Period had seen a spiritual change, the importance of which has been compared to that of the Renaissance in the West. Personal initiative and responsibilty had taken over from blind devotion to the god-king. Religious feeling was now directed toward the gods and no longer toward the Pharaoh; and so the hope for life after death was now turned toward Osiris, and pilgrimages were made to the religious center of the god at Abydos. Now everyone,

no longer just the king, could identify with the god and have a part in the resurrection after death which was ritually enacted in the annual mystery plays of Abydos.

Under the rulers who followed, all of whom were called Amenemhet or Sesostris, the reins were pulled still tighter. The state became absolutist, even totalitarian. A well-organized bureaucracy spread its finely-spun net of rules and regulations over all areas of life. Those who tried to escape to the oases or to the desert were threatened with incarceration in "the great prison" and with hard labor. The growing resistance to such oppressive state power finally led to the decline of the Middle Kingdom in the Thirteenth Dynasty.

The Pharaohs of the Twelfth Dynasty were the first to make imperialistic claims and to extend the territory of Egypt in the south to the other side of the Second Cataract. Their military campaigns to Palestine were initially intended to protect their allied trade towns.

But the Middle East moved ever closer to the center of events. This fact can be impressively seen in the story of a harem official named Sinuhe, one of the most popular literary works to survive from the Middle Kingdom, which contains a vivid description of Syria.

So it was from the Middle East that the first foreign rulers of Egypt came, the *Hyksos,* the "Rulers of the Foreign Lands" as they were most often called. Around 1650 B.C., when the Land of the Nile was weakened by the relentless struggles for supremacy of the Thirteenth Dynasty, the Asian troops of the Hyksos arrived in the Delta with their new miracle weapons, horses and carriages, and founded an empire whose area of influence at its height reached from Palestine to Nubia.

For 108 years, from their capital Auaris in the eastern Delta, they ruled over their empire which was administered by kings and vassals. And once again it was Theban princes who reunited Egypt and brought about a new golden age.

The New Kingdom:
A Golden Age

With Ahmose, who freed Egypt from the Hyksos, a new era of incomparable cultural blossoming began, reflected above all in the grandiose temples of Luxor, and the refined art and literature of the Eighteenth Dynasty (c. 1550-1292 B.C.). Yet the time of foreign rule had not disappeared without trace: if the collapse at the end of the era of the pyramids had primarily affected the individual, now the whole society was changed. Inherent necessity and *Zeitgeist* would be the modern expressions to explain how the god-king now became a warrior hero on the chariot, his successes supported by

Right: Amenhotep, son of Hapu, the brilliant architect of King Amenhotep III.

an enormous professional army. For if the debacle of the Hyksos period was not to be repeated, he would have to be able to maintain military strength in the Middle East.

And so, weapons bared, Egypt entered the international scene under the guidance of Thutmose I (1504-1492 B.C.). The stage was Syria-Palestine, and the opponent was the Mitanni Empire on the Upper Euphrates and its vassals. What began as a demonstration of power was completed under Thutmose III (1479-25) in 17 military campaigns: Egypt's supremacy over the Orient.

Now "beneath the sandals of the Pharaoh" was an empire which stretched from deepest Sudan to Syria. Immeasurable riches flowed into the country – war booty, tribute and trading goods. From Nubia came caravans loaded with gold, ivory and precious woods, and accompanied by exotic animals; valuable cedar wood was taken from Syria-Palestine, along with horses, weapons and raw materials such as silver, lapis lazuli and rock crystal. Incense and myrrh were the most important products of the legendary Land of Punt, which is thought to have been in the area of Sudan and Ethiopia. Cretan traders brought weapons and vessels from their homelands to the Nile. Many foreign and exotic things came to Egypt from other lands; even gods were "imported" from Asia.

The capital of the empire was now Thebes, and its spiritual center was the temple of Amen-Ra in Karnak. It was this god who had given the Pharaohs victory over the foreign lands, and in gratitude the most valuable offerings were made to him, and new temples and estates were dedicated to him.

Near Amen, but hidden in a valley in the western mountains, the Pharaohs now built their tombs. Their mortuary temples honored Amen above all. But despite the fact that – or perhaps because of it – the Pharaoh was now more human than ever

before, he emphasized his divine heritage all the more.

The first royal personage to portray this descendence from Amen-Ra in pictures was a woman. Hatshepsut (1479-57 B.C.) was the daughter of Thutmose I and the wife of Thutmose II, after whose death she became regent in place of her stepson, who was still a minor. But she soon donned the double crown herself and ruled Egypt for about 20 years – a period of peace brought to an end by her heir, Thutmose III.

Thutmose III not only embarked on his own military campaigns, he also waged war with the memory of his hated stepmother, who had withheld the throne from him for so long. He had her name hacked out of all her buildings and monuments, and in Karnak he even had her large obelisk walled in.

When peace was finally achieved in Asia in the middle of the Eighteenth Dynasty, an increasing opposition became apparent between the Amen priesthood and the Royal Court. This was to have

grave consequences. The war years had brought about a situation in which the king had relied more on his officers and his liberal advisors than on his more conservative priests and public servants. And when Amenhotep III (1392-53 B.C) married Tiyi, a commoner, it was regarded as an attack both on dogma and religion. The break, however, did not come until the reign of his son Amenhotep IV (1353-37 B.C.), whose intention was a total reform of the country through a religious revolution.

The belief in a single god, the sun god Aton, alongside whom no other gods were allowed to be worshiped: this was the radical declaration of the new king, who no longer called himself *Amenhotep*, "Amen is Pleased," but now took on the name *Akhnaton*, or "Splendor of Aton." On the altar of his new religion the king sacrificed not only the old gods along with their priesthood, but also time-honored traditions and values. The images of the new style of art, which sometimes seem to be almost scurrilous,

reflect his uncompromising rejection of convention.

Far away from Thebes and Amen, Akhnaton founded a new residence for his god, the huge temples, villas and palaces of which sprang up in the shortest time. Yet the city of Akhet-Aton, "Horizon of Aton," no more survived its founder than did his new monotheistic teachings.

After the death of Akhnaton, the priests of Amen regained their earlier influence, and under Tutankhamen (1333-24 B.C.) the country returned once again to its old order. Behind the Boy King, already crowned at the age of nine, stood his generals: Ay and Horemheb, who succeeded him to the throne after his early death and who completed the restoration.

With them, military men came to power. This was the Nineteenth Dynasty,

Above: Nefertari, the wife of Ramses II.
Right: The ruins of Tanis, Delta residence of the kings of the Twenty-first Dynasty.

from which one of the most famous kings of Egypt came: Ramses the Great (1279-13 B.C.) – a king among kings, who showered his country over almost 67 years of rule with countless buildings and statues, and yet of whom history really knows very little. Ramses had himself celebrated as a great warrior hero in all of his temples. Yet the much celebrated Battle of Qadesh against the new powers of the Middle East, the Indo-Germanic Hittites, was a poetic triumph rather than a military one. In the long run it could be considered a diplomatic success through the later peace pact and treaty of alliance, which sanctioned Egyptian supremacy over the important trading towns of the eastern Mediterranean.

His wonderful new capital in the eastern Delta, Piramesse – the Biblical "Raamses" – also remained the political center of the Twentieth Dynasty, with which the great period of the New Kingdom ended. The migrations of the time threatened Egypt from outside; the tribes of the Libyans in the east and of the Indo-Germanic groups in the west. At home, power struggles and economic crises weakened the country. There was only one further Pharaoh of any measurable strength, Ramses III (1189-58 B.C.), but under his heirs, all of whom bore the name of Ramses, central rule finally collapsed once and for all.

Once again the country was divided: this time into a "Divine State of Amen," established by the newly powerful high priests of Thebes in Upper Egypt; and a secular kingdom in the Delta area which was ruled by the kings of the Twenty-first Dynasty from their residence in Tanis (1080-946 B.C.). When Northern Egypt finally disintegrated into a myriad of individual principalities ruled by Libyan descendents, the time was ripe for a reorganization of the country. And this time again the unifiers of the empire came from the south, not from Thebes but from far away Napata in Nubia.

The Late Period
(713-525 B.C.)

With the Nubian rulers of the Twenty-fifth Dynasty (713-656 B.C.) the stylish finale of the so-called Late Period began. It was a period of nostalgia for past greatness and of attempts to evoke it again through the revival of old values. In all areas a return to ancient traditions can be found; whether in religion, in the arts or in ideals. This attitude has often been denigrated as being nothing more than archaism and imitation. But probably this has served as the indispensible foundations upon which the Late Period once again created wonderful works of art of technical perfection.

Centuries of Egyptian colonial rule had Egyptified Nubia to the extent that the new rulers had come as liberators and not as conquerers. But the glorious days of the great power of Egypt had gone forever. The invasions of the Assyrians – historically only one violent episode which effected the change in power to the

Twenty-sixth Dynasty (664-525 B.C.) – were a warning to the Pharaonic empire. Psamtik I (664-610 B.C.), whose residence was in the Delta city of Sais, could ensure the autonomy of the country once again, but the maelstrom of political change which was shaking the Middle East would also soon affect Egypt.

With foreign policy in the meantime completely in shambles, the successors of Psamtik could offer no resistance to the expanding Persian Empire. When Egypt was made a province of the Persian king Kambyses' empire (525-404 B.C.), it suffered a blow from which it never recovered. The great war between Athens and Persia into which Egypt was drawn pointed the way to Egypt's future fate. The brief independence under native rulers from the Twenty-eighth to the Thirtieth Dynasty (404-342 B.C.) brought a ray of light, but after the second Persian occupation, in the year 332 B.C., the Land of the Nile welcomed the Macedonian Alexander the Great as a liberator.

WORSHIP OF THE GODS AND BELIEF IN THE AFTERLIFE

In classical antiquity the Egyptians were considered to be "the most devout people in the world," and the Land of the Nile was regarded as one great temple: the "temple of the world." There was good reason for this impression, for Egypt was filled with temples built side by side. Since the time of the New Kingdom these temples had become veritable fortresses which towered over the towns like castles.

Generally surrounded by high, white-washed mud brick walls, the stone temples themselves could not actually be seen by the local people; for the sacred area was a place under a powerful taboo, and only the king and the priests were allowed inside. The simple believers had to stop at the tall pylon, a huge gate tower, the gateway of which was enclosed by heavy double gates of bronze or other metal. The only place where one could usually come close to one's god was in the forecourt laid out as a garden in front of the pylon.

But on feast days the great gates were thrown open and the gods were brought out in processional barques which were carried by the priests on their shoulders like litters. Part of the procession of the god's statue, which was usually hidden in a wooden shrine, was the ceremonial visit to other shrines and chapels. Considerable distances were covered on these occasions. The goddess Hathor, for example, was carried 160 kilometers every year in a great procession that traveled south to the temple of her husband Horus in Edfu.

Pilgrims from the whole of Egypt came to the great state festivals, such as the Feast of Opet which was celebrated in Thebes. Thousands of believers lined the banks of the Nile waiting for the convoy of the ships of the gods, and they filled the processional streets. When the holy barques containing the statues of the gods appeared, the people threw themselves to the ground, praying and singing praises. Some of them hopefully awaited the decision of an oracle; for everyone could expect divine guidance on the processions if he placed *ostraka* (clay or limestone fragments) in the path of the procession on which he had written his urgent questions regarding the future and the past.

The divine reply was expressed in specific movements of the religious symbol, which might bring to light a theft, give consent to a wedding or advise against undertaking a planned journey. In this way the god, whose temple could never be entered, was nevertheless present for each and every person, and therefore had a direct effect on the life of the individual. The great religious events for the people were the festivals, and there were many of these held during the course of the year.

The complex ritual, carried out three times daily in temples throughout the country, was not a part of a communal worship; it was not a celebration of the coming together of man and god. It was, rather, a service centered exclusively on the gods, which was intended to pacify and satisfy them. Early in the morning the high priest of the temple awoke the god's statue, greeted it, cleaned, anointed and dressed it, sang hymns and prayers and brought it rich offerings of food and incense. In this way the gods could be made to accept their religious representations – the temple reliefs as well as the statues, which were often made of precious metals – as earthly bodies and to live in them.

The presence of the gods in the temples of the Land of Egypt brought divine blessings to the country, protecting the universe from ever present danger

Right: The Temple of the Dead of Ramses III stands before the hills of Thebes West.

and ensuring its daily renewal. Only in this way could the constant battle between good and evil, truth and lie, justice and injustice be won; in short, the struggle between the cosmic order *Maat*, called into existence by the God of Creation, and the forces of chaos, which could be tamed and put to positive use.

The Temple as the Cosmos

The official temple cult guaranteed, in its magical way, the continuation of the created world; a world which was symbolized by the architecture of each and every temple. While at the beginning of Egyptian history temples were built of perishable materials, of wood, rush matting, reeds and mud bricks, by the era of the pyramids a "process of petrification" had set in.

The symbolic language of architecture was intended to be eternal, and it could only be so if the microcosm, that is to say, the temple, were built of eternal materials. And so the columned halls are veritable thickets of stone plants, while the ceiling of the temple is the symbol of heaven, and is therefore decorated with astronomical pictures or stars. The temple floor represents the earth or, where it was covered with silver, as inscriptions describe, it represents water, from which the plant columns grow. Countless relief cycles on the walls fill this stone cosmos with life, not by describing the world between heaven and earth in pictures, but by the representation of important ritual and sacrificial scenes.

According to dogma, only the king himself was allowed to perform these rites by virtue of his divine office. But usually, because there were so many of these holy sanctuaries, his magical presence alone had to suffice. And so, wherever the Pharaoh is portrayed performing multifarious sacrificial fuctions on the walls of temples, it was, in fact, normally the priesthood who carried out these ritual duties and who directed the religious ceremonies in his place.

Myths which Explain the World

One of the tasks which the Pharaoh could not delegate to his priests was the foundation of a temple, for this was equivalent to the creation of a world. The Egyptians believed that each temple embodied the mythical place where the world began, the so-called primeval hill. This was the first island to rise from Nun, the primeval waters which were the very quintessence of primeval chaos, and from there the history of the creation of the universe took its course. Every year nature confirmed this myth when high-lying land and villages protruded from the flood waters of the Nile like so many islands.

The creation of the world is told in almost every temple in the country in a different way. In Hermopolis, for example, the story is that Thot, the ibis-headed god

Above: The king greets Amen's divine barque. Right: The tomb owner and his wife hunting birds.

of wisdom, laid the primeval egg on the primeval hill, from which the sun god emerged.

In Heliopolis, the center of worship of the sun god Ra, a god called Atum stood at the beginning of creation. The first gods which he created were Shu, the god of the air, and Tefnut, the goddess of moisture. Their children were Geb and Nut, earth and heaven, whom their father Shu separated by lifting the goddess of the sky, Nut, high above the prostrate body of the earth god Geb. In contrast to the creation myths of all the other peoples of the world, the Egyptians saw the sky as female and the earth as male. In this way they explained the sun's new appearance each day on the horizon: it was reborn every morning from the womb of the goddess of the sky, through whose body it had journeyed during the night.

The most important myth from the time of the Pharaohs, the Osiris myth, is centered on the four children of "mother sky" Nut: the god-pairs of Isis and Osiris, and Nephthys and Seth. In hazy prehis-

torical times Osiris ruled over Egypt as a benevolent king. He gave his people laws and taught them to work the fields and to honor the gods. But his brother Seth envied his power and plotted a conspiracy against him. The attack on Osiris succeeded and his dead body was thrown into the Nile.

Only after a long search and much confusion did Isis find the body of her husband in Byblos, an Egyptian colony in the Lebanon, where it had been washed ashore. From there she returned it to Egypt, where she magically brought him back to life through a ritual dirge. Together they had a son, Horus, who was heir to the throne. But from now on Osiris himself reigned over the Kingdom of the Dead.

Horus's revenge on Seth – the personified battle between Order and Chaos – is the theme of various myths, all of which naturally end with the victory of Horus. Just as the annual flooding of the Nile represented the reality of the myth of creation for the Egyptians, the kingdom of

Horus was also a reality: during his lifetime each Pharaoh was regarded as an incarnation of Horus, and was only identifed with the King of the Afterlife, Osiris, after his death.

Life after Death

Two natural phenomena appear to have served the Egyptians as both the image of life after death and proof that it existed: the growth and decay of plants, which "die" at the end of the cycle of growth, but which reawaken to a new life the following spring; and the course of the sun, which goes down in the west every evening but rises anew in the morning.

Against this background, human death was understood to be only the threshold to another life, as a transitional state, albeit one which contained many hidden dangers. Numerous precautionary measures and rites were required in order to prevent the deceased from being eternally damned on his way to the world on

31

the other side (or once he had arrived there), or from suffering a second – and therefore final – death.

The most important thing was always the construction and furnishing of a grave. The scenes and inscriptions, magically brought to life through special rites, were supposed to guarantee the owner of the tomb eternal care in the afterlife. All the goods which were placed in the tomb along with the deceased had one predominant purpose: to provide the person departing this world with everything he might wish for in the next. He would want to eat and drink, and to amuse himself with games and hunting, and he would want to live on in the circle of his family. He would also want to maintain his social standing in the afterlife, and so gladly had himself portrayed according to his rank and dignity. The logical consequence of believing in life after death

Above: The god Anubis performing rites on a mummy. Right: Funeral scene (tomb of Ramose, Thebes West).

as merely being a continuation of earthly existence was the realization that the corpse would have to be protected from the natural process of decay.

The mummification of the corpse was performed in an embalming tent especially erected in the vicinity of the tomb. Embalming began with the extraction of the brain and the entrails, which were stored in the tomb in four vessels or *canopi*. The heart was usually left in the body, which was dried for 70 days in sodium salts, after which it was wrapped in linen bandages soaked in resin. Now the burial ceremonies could take place, one of the most important of which was the "Opening of the Mouth," a rite which was meant to revive the mummy and enable it to take nourishment.

The services of the dead, which were carried out either by the eldest son of the deceased or by contracted priests of the dead, share certain similarities with the temple cult. Incense was burned, prayers were recited and ritual offerings of food were placed before the statue of the dead person. In this statue the *Ka* of the deceased could take residence and accept the offerings.

It is difficult to explain exactly what the Egyptians meant by "Ka." It seems to have described a life force, physical as well as psychic; an elemental characteristic of existence common to gods and humans. This applies also to the concept of *Ba*, which is akin to our idea of the soul as the immaterial, immortal essence of the human being. The Ba symbolized the wish of the deceased to be able to move freely between heaven and earth, and is therefore represented in the form of a bird with a human head.

The third of these concepts of the soul, which are so difficult for us to concretely conceive of, but by which the Egyptians meant the whole person and not only a spiritual part of him, is the *Akh*: the transfigured spirit provided with everything, in which the dead person wanted to trans-

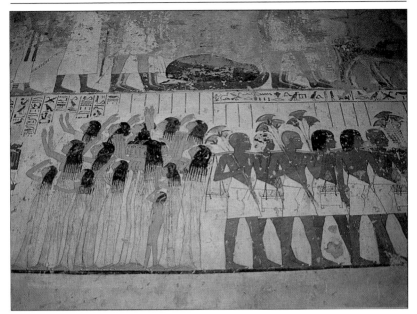

form himself and whose power even the living feared.

During the age of the Pharaohs, however, before the deceased was allowed to enter the abodes of the blessed dead, he or she had to give an account of his life before the court of Osiris. In the form of a negative confession of sins he declared his righteousness. The 125th chapter of the *Book of the Dead* – sayings on papyrus which were placed in the tombs of the deceased – contains a catalogue of all the sins which the dead person could guarantee that he had *not* committed.

The dead person's honesty was tested on the divine scales, on one side of which the heart of the deceased was placed, and on the other side of which a small statue of the Maat was placed as a counterbalance. Only then could it be established whether the dead person belonged to the "Glutton," a terrible demon with the head of a crocodile, or to the Abodes of the Blessed. But where were these Abodes of the Blessed; where was the place in which the dead lived on?

The Egyptians had a complicated answer to this apparently simple question. Although at certain times various images of the other side were preferred, the various conceptions of the afterlife were never mutually exclusive. Next to the idea that the deceased lived in his tomb on earth, the idea existed of another sphere, either in the underworld or in heaven.

On the one hand the Kingdom of the Dead was simply the "Beautiful West," where the sun went down every night, but it was also the *Dat,* an enormous underground cave through which the sun god traveled at night in his barque. The royal *Books of the Underworld* of the New Kingdom portray this nocturnal journey on the large river of the Dat, whose inhabitants are brought light and nourishment by the sun god. The heavenly sphere was personified by the goddess Nut, whose embrace brought the dead back to life, just as the sun and the stars were reborn from her every day and every night.

33

EGYPT'S GREAT GODS

The Egyptian pantheon is made up of hundreds of gods and goddesses which were worshiped in the form of fetishes, animals, plants, people and half men-half animals. The early peoples experienced divine power in the strength and particular abilities of animals (e.g., strength in battle, speed, the ability to fly). But the beginning of the period around 3000 B.C. saw a "humanization" of the gods. Yet the old symbols were still adhered to, and so the god Horus, for example, might be portrayed as a falcon or a falcon-headed man. Alongside their many gods the Egyptians also had an abstract concept of the Divine: the one and nameless God who created the world.

AMEN – His name means "The Hidden One." He was originally the god of wind, invisible, but his influence was omnipresent. His blue skin and high crown of feathers symbolize the element air. Usually portrayed as a man, he could, however, also take on the form of his holy animals, the ram and the goose. In Thebes, his center of worship, this "King of the Gods" was worshipped with his wife **Mut** and his son, the moon god **Khonsu**.

ANUBIS – "He Who is in the Bandages of the Mummy" is one of the most common names for the jackal-headed god who watches over the mummification of the deceased.

KHNUM – The ram-headed god is the Lord of the Sources of the Nile, which spring from the first Nile cataract – according to the Egyptians' mythical concept of the world. As a god of creation, he makes people out of clay and forms their bodies on the potter's wheel. In his center of worship on the Elephantine Island he was worshiped together with the goddesses **Satet** and **Anuket**.

Right: The goddess Hathor. Far right: Horus, the falcon god.

HATHOR – The goddess of love, dance and music, identified with Aphrodite by the Greeks. The Egyptians called her "Mistress of Heaven," emphasizing her maternal role, they portrayed her with the attributes of a cow (horns, ears). In the Theban necropolis she was revered as a goddess of death and as a tree goddess who provided food and shade.

HORUS – The falcon who flies up to heaven and whose wings span the earth like the sky was called "The Distant One." The great lights in the sky, the sun and the moon, are his eyes. In the myths surrounding Osiris, Horus is the son of Isis and Osiris. After he had punished Seth, the murderer of his father, he became king of Egypt.

ISIS – The loving sister-wife of Osiris is the embodiment of a mother and goddess of protection. As such she is usually portrayed in human form with the horns of a cow. She also carries the hieroglyph of a throne on her head which is used to write her name. The images which show her nursing the young Horus in her lap are regarded as direct precedents of the Christian Madonna pictures. In the cult of the dead she plays the part of a mourner with her sister **Nephthys**.

MAAT – The goddess with a feather in her hair is the personification of the universal law, which meant truth, justice and order to the ancient Egyptians.

NUT – The goddess of the sky and mother of Osiris is often portrayed as a woman whose body is decorated with stars or suns and floats above the earth as a great protecting and luminescent firmament. Every night she swallows the sun as it prepares to set on the western horizon, and after its long nocturnal journey through her body, it is born again from her lap in the morning.

OSIRIS – Murdered by his jealous brother Seth and brought back to life by his wife Isis, Osiris is the symbol of hope, resurrection and eternal life. As the lord of the afterlife he is portrayed as human,

but in the form of a mummy. His crown of corn, decorated with feathers, and his skin, frequently green in color, refer to the fact that his fate was often identified with the cycle of the harvest and the renewed growth of the plants.

PTAH – In the course of history the Lord of Memphis and patron of artisans and artists became a universal divinity. Legends tell how he created the world with "heart and tongue," the forces of understanding and of the word of creation. Ptah is always portrayed as a man, dressed in tight robes and a cap. The triad of Memphis is formed by Ptah, the god of the lotus blossom, **Nefertem**, and the lioness **Sekhmet**, revered as a goddess of war and – the reverse of her bloody wild nature – as goddess of healing.

RA – Ra is the sun itself, which shines daily in the sky and which is honored as creator and guardian of the world. He often appears, fused with Horus as **Ra-Harakhti** (Ra-Horus on the Horizon), as a falcon-man with a huge sun disk on his head. The center of worship of Ra was

On, the sun city of Heliopolis. In Thebes he was fused with Amen and became the "King of the Gods" Amen-Ra. For awhile he was elevated by the religious reformer Akhnaton to the position of sole god of Egypt who went by the name of **Aton**, portrayed by the abstract shape of the disk of the sun with hands of rays.

SETH – The god with a donkey-like head is revered as "Lord of the Desert and the Storm." Having murdered his brother Osiris, he is regarded as being the symbol of evil while playing an important part in the eternal battle for cosmic order. Temple drawings show him either as a man with the head of a crocodile or else completely in the shape of a crocodile, whose powers one tried to curb by making sacrifices.

THOT – The god of writing and wisdom is portrayed as an ibis-headed man or in the form of his holy animals, the ibis and the baboon. As "Lord of Time" he is associated with the moon, and for this reason carries a moon crescent and disk on his head.

35

PICTURES FOR ETERNITY

The vast majority of the Pharaonic works of art that we admire today belong to the realms of the sacred; to the tombs and temples. As testimonials to a religious style of art they can only truly be understood when seen in their proper context. In marked contrast to the art of the Christian West, the sacred cycles of paintings and sculptures were not created to be looked at; they were neither devotional pictures nor catechisms, neither glorifications of belief nor memorials, rather, they were magical symbols in the cult of the dead and of the gods, which had lives of their own achieved through magic ritual.

In this way, the luxurious tables richly laden with food depicted on the murals could become true food for the dead through the invocations of the priests, and the statues served the gods as well as the dead as real bodies, into which they could slip in order to accept sacrifices and rites.

Egyptian style is deeply rooted in these concepts. The individual figures and objects are at the same time universally valid symbols of the things they portray; pictures for eternity which were intended to represent the essence, the typical characteristics of that which is portrayed, and not the individual person or unique thing itself. When reduced to their common denominator, the portraits become pictorial signs, hieroglyphs. In sculpture as well as in pictures, normalized types are represented which have specific meanings. Thus, the scribe sitting with legs crossed stands for all officials or the sacrificing king as the guarantor of divine world order.

Formally, too, this love of artistic abstraction leads to an artificial reduction to the essence, to clear and simple lines. The result of this conscious concentration on pure form is seen nowhere as clearly as in the severe monumentality of the pyramids of the Old Kingdom.

In the portrayal of the human figure, a strict canon of proportion developed from this striving for the eternally valid norm. Squares and a right-angled axial system were used as an aid, into which the body was incorporated without any regard for naturalistic movements or rotations. The implications of this can best be seen in the reliefs and paintings: reality was portrayed as it is per se, and not as it appears at any given moment. In order to portray the essence of an object or figure, its characteristic individual parts were joined together in a "montage," combined in a whole which appears almost magical.

The result of this – from the point of view of our own ideas on perspective – was an inorganic fusion of ground plans and elevations, and of frontal and profile views. For example, a sacrifical table was always portrayed with its top upright, above – and not upon – which the sacrificial offering of food was heaped.

If the intention was to portray allegories of human beings or objects and not their true images, the portrayal of time and space was also seen from the point of view of eternity. Thus, for example, no specific hunting expedition was being depicted in a painting of the tomb owner who is shown harpooning a hippopotamus; much more than this, a scheme had been formulated which would be valid for all time, and which would guarantee repeated joyous hunting in the afterlife. That the theme of hunting additionaly incorporated the concept of the destruction of evil – which in the tomb served as a magic symbol to ward off evil – once again shows just how dominant magic was in the expression of the arts.

Just as no specific point in time is fixed, the site where the scene is taking

Right: Bas-relief on one of the gilded shrines of King Tutankhamen.

36

place is not clearly fixed either. There is neither an illusionary region, nor an identifiable background. In the horizontal strips of pictures, the so-called "registers" which adorn the walls of temples and tombs, the essential elements are arranged before a background void of form.

If a subject consists of more than one motif, such as the cycles of planting and harvesting which were so important for the physical well-being of the dead, the time sequence is portrayed through the simple juxtaposition of individual scenes. Thus, the events can be simply read as a continuous story in pictures.

It is quite likely that this strict artistic convention may have arisen from the synthesis of a religiously inspired method of portrayal and, simultaneously, from a childlike perception of the world (something that was common to all other early cultures). However, the fact that this convention was adhered to for more than 3,000 years reflects a conscious decision founded in belief.

Within the framework of this canon a stylistic development can be traced running parallel to the history of each period, with its golden age followed by decay. Exceptions to the rules, secondary scenes in which artistic imagination seems to have developed freely, can frequently be found, but at only one time did artists manage to truly break free of it. The art of the era of Akhnaton comes close to the portrayal of single moments in time. In it we find a greater richness of movement and even the first hesitant signs of a spatial perspective in art for this world, which is also conscious of the beauty of the transiency.

Ancient Egyptian artists of all epochs, however, were concerned with creating a symbiosis between religious conviction and the ideal of beauty – an aesthetic concept which meant perfection – and which to our eyes seems to have been frequently achieved. It is an art in which form and content have not been separated – and perhaps this is why it says so much to modern people.

37

ANTIQUITY AND CHRISTIANITY

A new era began for Egypt, and for the entire ancient world, with Alexander the Great. The Persian Empire, the leading power of its day, broke up under the onslaught of the Hellenic troops, and Egypt was one of the first stages of their inexorable victorious campaign.

Alexander remained in Egypt for only half a year, but he used this time to reorganize the administration, to found a city, Alexandria, and to move to the temple of Amen at the oasis of Sîwa. There he was recognized as the son of Amen, a distinction which gave his expansionist politics throughout the world a kind of divine justification, and which legitimized him as an Egyptian Pharaoh. In the spring of 331 B.C., Alexander resumed his march eastwards. He was never to see the Land of the Nile again.

When the Macedonian Empire was divided up after Alexander's death (323 B.C.), commander Ptolemy I received Egypt. For the next three centuries the Ptolemaic dynasty ruled the country from its capital Alexandria. The Greek rulers, all of whom bore the name of Ptolemy and who saw themselves as legitimate descendents of the Egyptian Pharaohs, respected the old religion and brought about a period of bustling building activity throughout the country. Political strategy may very have led them to adopt this attitude, as well as the Hellenistic ideal of the fusion of Greek and Oriental features.

The most important rulers were without doubt the first three Ptolemies; for under their rule Egypt became an empire again. The Ptolemaic Empire stretched from Libya to Asia Minor and from Ethiopia to the islands of the Aegean. Alexandria now became the spiritual center of the Eastern Mediterranean region.

Right: In the ruins of the Roman theater in Alexandria.

An academy for the most eminent scholars of the time, the Museion, and the great library were built. The famous lighthouse – one of the Seven Wonders of the World – was erected on the island of Pharos, and on the island of Philae and in Edfu great temples dedicated to Isis and Horus were built.

But trouble was brewing amongst the people. The Greek rulers cut themselves off from the native Egyptian people; mixed marriages were forbidden, the people were suffering under high taxation. In spite of various reforms, the tension which had been mounting since the time of Ptolemy IV (221-205 B.C.) was discharged again and again in uprisings throughout Egypt.

Within the royal household there was no peace either. Bloody power struggles for the throne dominated domestic politics until the last days of the Ptolemaic Dynasty, which was becoming ever more dependent on the expanding Roman Empire. Before Egypt sank into the complete obscurity of a Roman province, though, it rallied once more to a grandiose finale, the radiant focal point of which was the "Queen of Queens," Cleopatra VII (51-30 B.C.).

Clever, ambitious and seductive: this is how the last Ptolemaic ruler was described. Her long-range goal was to see to it that Egypt once more became a great power in the Orient. To succeed at this, however, she needed the agreement of Rome, which she first achieved through a liaison with Caesar.

After Caesar's death she ensnared the new strong man of the empire: Mark Antony. When they married, in 36 B.C., Cleopatra's imperial dreams seemed close to realization. But then Rome became aware of this dangerous opponent in the East. Octavian, the adopted son of Caesar, went into battle against Antony and Cleopatra. The Roman victory in the Gulf of Actium in the year 31 B.C. was decisive. Cleopatra and Antony fled to

Alexandria, where they committed suicide a year later. The new ruler of Egypt was Octavian, the future Augustus Caesar. Egypt now became a Roman province subject only to the Roman emperors.

Egypt: A Roman Province

Like the Ptolemies, the Roman emperors, who ruled from 30 B.C. until A.D. 395, portrayed themselves as descendents of the Pharaohs. They respected religious traditions and had temples built in their names all over the country. But what appears as tolerance and care is revealed on closer examination to be sober tactics of appeasement. Nothing was allowed to disturb the most effective possible exploitation of the country, a country which played a significant role as the great bread basket of Rome.

A viceroy administered the rich province of Egypt for the emperor, who regarded it as his personal possession. Indeed, without imperial approval no Roman senator was even allowed to enter the country.

The strict racial discrimination which had been given up gradually during the Ptolemys' rule was revived and intensified. The Romans pursued a policy of inflexible apartheid, which made any social advancement impossible for the native Egyptian population. The non-Egyptian population (Greeks, Romans and Levantines), on the other hand, enjoyed significant privileges. This, coupled with the worsening economic situation of the oppressed and exploited Egyptians, led to renewed uprisings, which brought the people no real improvement of their situation.

In this climate of social conflict and the most bitter injustice, the comforting message of Christianity was able to spread quickly. In the belief in a God who accepts the poor and the oppressed, and who even gave himself up as a sacrifice to save the world, life suddenly acquired a new meaning.

ЈѠѦ ПІРЄЧТѠмХ   ПЄТРОС   ѦNѦРІѦС   ІѦКѠВ

ѦВВѦ ѦNТѠNІОС   ѦВВѦ ѦNТѠNІОС nЄμ ѦВВѦ ПѦүлЄ   ѦПѦ NОΥ

The Copts

The beginnings of the Christianization of Egypt are obscure, but legend tells how the evangelist Mark converted the Egyptians to Christianity. The name "Copt" for the Egyptian Christians comes from the Arabic *Qubtî,* which at the time of the Arabic victory meant nothing more than "Egyptian." Only when the majority of the Egyptian population had converted to Islam did this term refer to Christians alone.

The capital, Alexandria, became the spiritual center of early Christianity, and by about the year 200, the most important theologians of the Oriental Church taught there. It was at this time that the terrible persecution of the Christians by the Roman emperors also began. The height of these dreadful massacres was seen during the rule of Emperor Diocletian, who had thousands of Christians put to death in the arena of Alexandria. In memory of this era of martyrdom, the beginning of the Christian Era according to the Coptic calendar is even today based not on the year of Christ's birth, but rather on the year A.D. 284; the first year of the rule of Emperor Diocletian.

Emperor Constantine's Edict of Tolerance, which was promulgated in the year 313, brought about a turn in events. Now that the Christians in the whole Roman Empire could openly worship, the great period of the Egyptian Church began. Its universal importance was based on two overriding factors: Alexandrine theology, which for a time even attained a dominant roll in the imperial church; and monasticism.

The roots of the Egyptian monastic movement are strictly bound up with the oppressive political situation in the country. Many people fled into the solitary desert, where they were able, despite deprivation, to live freely and to follow their beliefs.

Above: Scenes from the life of Saint Anthony. Right: A church in the Wâdî an-Natrûn.

St. Anthony is seen as the father of Egyptian monkhood, and of Christian monasticism in general. He was born around the year 250 in central Egypt. His way of life, from his period as a hermit in extreme asceticism to being the teacher of a loose community of hermits, was a model for countless believers. The pains and sorrows of his mystical search for God, the "Temptations of St. Antony," are among the most popular themes of Christian art.

At the beginning of the third century, there were colonies of hermits such as that of St. Anthony all over the land. These hermits only rarely came together for communion or for instruction from their teacher.

The idea of joining in monastic communities and of living together in the spirit of Christianity goes back to St. Pachomius (c. 290-346). Schooled in pious asceticism, as a young man Pachomius became the leader of a group of hermits. With them he founded his first monastery, in about A.D. 320, in Tabennese, north of Thebes. On the basis of the rules he devised for the monks, which ordered every detail of communal life, nine monasteries and seven convents quickly sprang up.

One of the most sparkling personalities of these first monastic societies was the Abbot Shenute of Sohâg (333-451). His inflexible fanaticism demanded of his monks and of himself the most extreme exercises in belief. Again and again he formed armies and led iconoclastic attacks on "pagan" temples.

It was also Abbot Shenute who made the language of the common people, Coptic (as this last stage in the ancient Egyptian language is known), the official language of the Church. Now numerous religious texts and literary works were no longer written in Greek, but rather in the Coptic language. However, the Greek alphabet was retained for the sake of simplicity.

During Shenute's long life – he died at the ripe old age of 118 – the deep-reaching theological disputes of the early Christian era came about, which would eventually lead to the first great schism in the Church. The controversies were not untainted by political considerations, either, and many an argument made by the patriarchs of the Egyptian Church was aimed, however indirectly, at Roman sovereignty. Since the division of the Roman Empire, in A.D. 395, Egypt had belonged to the Eastern Roman Empire, the old Byzantium. But even if the ruling powers had changed, the exploitation of the people by the foreign rulers remained the same.

The Foundation of the Coptic Church

The questions which were at the center of theological disputes of the time were not much different from those that are still asked today: Was Jesus Christ a mortal man? Was he an angel? Or was he

Above: Coptic monk.

indeed God? Behind the attempt to precisely define Jesus' human or divine nature was the question of salvation, which affected everyone.

The early Christian community had believed that salvation would take place in the immediate future: they thought that Jesus Christ would return again very soon after his death in order to establish the Kingdom of God on Earth. When this expectation was not fulfilled, however, they began to understand that salvation had, in fact, already taken place: the death and resurrection of Christ was the salvation in which each individual took part through the sacraments. Therefore the Kingdom of God came to mean a more general end of the world, and was reformulated to mean an afterlife in paradise which awaits the dead after the Last Judgment.

But if the salvation of mankind through Jesus Christ had already come about, was he not then indeed a god?

How could he have lived as a man and died as a man? Or was it not possible that he was both man and god?

At the Fourth Council of Chalkedon, in the year 451, a decision was reached: the teaching of Jesus's dual nature, Dyophysitism, was elevated to Church dogma. This teaches that both a human and a divine nature co-existed in Jesus Christ. In order to explain Jesus' humanity, his death on the cross, his resurrection and his salvation, both are required, but the two natures are not mixed as one. The Alexandrians, however, refused to give up their Monophysitism; the belief that Jesus had only one, indisoluble nature which was divine and human at the same time. It was, after all, traditional to Egyptian thinking that a god could take on human form.

The Oriental Church split over this dissent regarding the question of the nature of Jesus, and the year 451 saw the foundation of an independent Coptic Church, which is still the largest Christian community in the Orient.

UNDER THE BANNER OF ISLAM

In the year 570, in distant Mecca on the Arabian Peninsula, a man was born whose teachings would change the whole of the Orient – and thereby Egypt as well – within a period of only a few decades: Muhammad Ibn 'Abdallah, the Prophet of Islam. His teachings were not new, for he spoke of the same God who was worshiped by the Jews and the Christians whom Muhammad had met on his travels. What was new was that this time God had spoken directly to the Arabs through Muhammad, and to him, the last of his prophets, God had revealed the Holy Book of the Koran in the Arabic language.

The rise of Islam began in 622 with the emigration of the Prophet from Mecca (Arabic: *Hijra*) to the nearby town of Yathrib, which later became Medina. And only here did the religious leader also become a political leader, who, with his growing numbers of followers, would conquer the whole of central Arabia within a period of only 10 years. His descendents, the caliphs, would create an empire which stretched from the Hindu Kush to the Pyrenees.

The losers of the time were the former great powers of Byzantium and the Persian Sassanid Empire, which had managed to mutually wear each other down over the years through their endless struggling for hegemony. In their weakened condition, these once-powerful states quickly fell to the attacks of the zealous Muslims.

In the year 641, Byzantine Egypt fell into the hands of commander Amr Ibn al-'Âs' Arab troops. The native population had barely offered resistance against the invaders, for they brought with them longed for freedom from the Byzantine yoke. Egypt became a province of the caliphs' empire, and its history was now determined by Arabia. In the long term, the Arab invasion meant a deep caesura

in the development of the land of the Pharaohs, which had already entered a new cultural circle through its Christianization. It laid the foundations for the spread of Islam and of Arab culture in Egypt, even if it took centuries before the Coptic language died out and the Copts became a minority.

The power struggles that broke out over the succession to the Prophet, who died in 632, split the young Muslim community, and the dynasty of the Umaiyads came to the forefront as victors. They made Damascus their residence, and the Arabian Peninsula, with the exception of the holy cities of Mecca and Medina, once again sank into cultural insignificance.

The most important political objective of the Umaiyads had to have been the administrative consolidation of the conquered regions. But the social, religious and ethnic conflicts could not be checked for very long in such an enormous empire. The growing unrest was further fueled by their defeat by Charles Martel in 732, the first defeat of the usually victorious Muslim troops. In 750, the Umaiyads were finaly brought down in a bloody uprising, and Abû al-'Abbas became caliph.

The Abbasids
(750-1258)

The first century of Abbasid rule can also be regarded as the golden age of Islamic culture and the sciences. In their newly founded residence in Baghdad the caliphs rose to the height of their power, and their by far most famous representative, Hârûn ar-Rashîd (786-809), is remembered as the embodiment of a good and just ruler.

A constant source of trouble was, even during his own lifetime, the extreme centralization and the luxurious city life which the peasants of the conquered countries had to finance through drastic

increases in taxes. And so once again in Egypt the Copts rose up in revolts, the last of which was brutally quashed in 830 by Caliph Ma'mûn, one of Hârûn ar-Rashîd's sons.

Meanwhile, Islam had already spread throughout Egypt. Arabic tribes settled in the Nile Valley and many Christians were converted – whether it was because they wanted for once to belong to the ruling classes, or whether it was because they were convinced, as many were, that success could only be won through the grace of God, and that the triumphal march of Islam must therefore be an expression of God's will.

Inner-Islamic political conflict led, under Ma'mûn's follower Al-Mu'tasim (833-42), to a radical restructuring of the army: the caliph created a bodyguard answerable only to him, which he re-

Above: Prayer niche in the Mosque of Sultan Hasan, Cairo. Right: The owner of this house is proud of his pilgrimage to Mecca (mural near Kôm Ombo).

cruited from Turkish slaves and not from mercenaries. When soon afterwards the entire court of Baghdad moved to its newly built residence in Samarra, the Turkish soldiers seized their chance and, unofficially, the reins of power.

And so it was that, in the year 868, the Turkish Ahmad Ibn Tûlûn came to Egypt as military governor. He took advantage of the caliphs' troubled situation to make the Land of the Nile independent, and to found the Tulunid dynasty, which reigned from 868 to 905. The price of autonomy was the payment of large annual tributes, which had to be delivered to the caliph's court.

But, in spite of everything, Egypt's economic situation was so good that Ibn Tûlûn was able to build himself a splendid palace city on the Nile on the model of Samarra. However, with the exception of one famous mosque, all the magnificent buildings from his dynasty fell victim to the frenzy of destruction wrought by the Abbasid troops when they conquered Egypt again in 905.

The Fatimids
(969-1171)

At the beginning of the 10th century, a new Islamic power arose in North Africa, which reached its hands not only for the rich province of Egypt, but for the caliph's throne itself. The Fatimids, so called because they traced their origins to Fâtima, the daughter of the Prophet, were Shiites. And this meant that not only did they not accept the authority of the orthodox (Sunni) caliphs, but they also had their own mystically inclined interpretation of Islam.

After they had spread their rule from Tunisia to the far areas of the Maghreb, the troops of the Fatimid general Gôhar (Arabic: *Jawhar*) marched into Egypt in 969. In the same year, Gôhar began the construction of the new city residence Al-Qâhira (Cairo) into which its ruler, the

Shiite anti-caliph Al-Mu'izz would move four years later.

In 970, the foundations were laid of the High School of Islam, the Al-Azhar Mosque, in which, alongside the study of theology, subjects such as mathematics, astronomy and medicine would soon be taught.

The rule of the Fatimids brought about a radical economic and cultural rise in Egypt, which soon enabled it to become the strongest power in the entire Arabic world. Treaties with the rising Italian republics and the transfer of sea trading routes to the Red Sea turned the Land of the Nile into the epicenter of international trade. The luxurious court life of the Fatimids was praised by contemporary authors throughout the Orient, as was the splendor of their public festivals. Examples of the fairy-tale treasures amassed by the Fatamids can still be admired in museums.

By now completely caught up in their religious zeal, the Fatimid caliphs sent missionaries out into the whole world,

but their attempts at conversion were aimed only at their orthodox brother believers. Their intention was to convince them of the validity of the Shiite faith, rather than to convert others to Islam. Christians and Jews were able to rise to high positions under their rule, and Caliph Al-'Azîz was even married to a Christian.

This vivid atmosphere of tolerance was broken for a time, however, under the rule of Al-Hâkim (996-1021). Possessed by his incontrovertible religious ideas, the caliph created very strict – and sometimes incomprehensible – laws which led temporarily to the persecution of Jews and Christians. On one of the nocturnal rides he was known for taking he disappeared under mysterious circumstances. Some suspected that he had been murdered; others thought that he had simply been spirited away for a time, and that he would return one day in order to found a new world empire.

The beginnings of the decline of the Fatimid Empire could be seen under the

long rule of Al-Mustansir (1036-94). Uprisings by mercenary troops, the failure of the Nile floods and plague epidemics weakened the country. Only one further man was able to ensure peace and prosperity: the Armenian Badr al-Gamâli, who ruled Egypt from 1074 as Al-Mustansir's vizier.

At the same time, the situation along Egypt's borders began to heat up with the arrival of two feared enemies who established themselves in the immdeiate vicinity of the empire: the Turks, who as orthodox Sunnis had set themselves the task of waging a holy war against the heretical Fatimids, and the crusaders who conquered Jerusalem in 1099.

The situation finally came to a head when the crusaders advanced on Cairo in 1168. In their distress the Fatimids turned for help to the Turks, who came to Egypt with an army – and stayed. One of their

Above: The mosque of the Mameluke sultan Al-Mu'ayyad. Right: View of the mosque of Sultan Hasan and modern Cairo.

generals was the Kurd Saladin (Arabic: *Salâh ad-Dîn*), who made himself Sultan in 1171 and founded his own dynasty, the Ayyubids. With this, Egypt returned to the fold of orthodox Sunni Islam forever. The most impressive architectural symbol of this new era is the Citadel that Saladin had built as the Sultan's residence high above Cairo.

Saladin united Egypt and Syria soon afterwards, and turned all his strength on the Crusaders. In 1187, he won back Jerusalem and Palestine. Six years later he died in Damascus without having seen Egypt again.

The Crusades determined the policies of his heirs, the Ayyubids, who ruled the country from 1193 to 1250, and who tried again and again to live peacefully alongside the Crusaders. But even after the spectacular peace treaty between Sultan Al-Kâmil and Emperor Frederick II, fighting flared up again, and Egypt became the battleground of the Fifth and Sixth Crusades.

The Christian army had hardly been beaten back when the Ayyubid's own army attempted to seize power. And so it was that the last Ayyubid Sultan fell victim to his bodyguards, the Mamelukes, who took power themselves after the brief interregnum of the sultana, Shagarat ad-Durr.

The Mamelukes
(1250-1517)

Who were these Mamelukes who ruled Egypt for almost three hundred years? The Mamelukes had once been slaves (Arabic: *mamlûk*), usually of Turkish or Circassian origin, who had been bought as children to become the ruler's bodyguards. After their conversion to Islam they received military training and were freed. After this, a career in the army was open to them.

Once they had risen to power, two dynasties ruled in Egypt: the Bahrî-Mame-

lukes (1250-1382), named after their barracks on the Nile (Arabic: *bahr*, or "stream") and the Circassian Burjî-Mamelukes (1382-1517), who were stationed at the Citadel (Arabic: *burj*, or "tower").

The most famous of the Mameluke sultans were Baibars I (1260-77) and Qalâ'ûn (1279-90). Under their rule Egypt became a leading military power which succeeded in fighting off the Mongols and in driving the Crusaders out of Palestine. After the decline of Baghdad, which was destroyed by the Mongols, Cairo became the seat of the caliph and the spiritual center of Islam.

The era of the Mamelukes was an era of political upheavals and power struggles; of the dictatorship of an army which did not shrink from committing atrocities. But in the empire itself, peace and unity prevailed. The administration was orderly, and the economy and trade seemed to be blessed by a lucky star. The monopoly on the sea trading routes to India and China filled the coffers of the

customs authorities and founded the almost legendary riches of Cairo's bazaars. Now Egypt was the focal point of Arab culture, and it experienced a golden age of Islamic art and architecture. Splendid buildings and mosques were erected as a tribute to a capital which, much to the credit of the Mamelukes, had been made into the most beautiful city in the Arabic Orient.

The decline of this powerful epoch began with the discovery of the sea route to India in 1498, for with that the trading monopoly of the Mamelukes was broken. The truly deadly danger to their rule, however, threatened them from another direction altogether, for in the northeast of the Mamelukes' empire a new great power had arisen: the Ottoman Turks, who had now conquered the whole of Anatolia and Constantinople.

In 1516, the troops of the Ottoman Sultan Selîm marched into Syria and defeated the army of the Mamelukes in battle. And it was only one year later that they marched into Cairo.

FROM SULTAN SELÎM TO PRESIDENT MUBARAK

The victory of Sultan Selîm over Egypt made it a province of the Ottoman Empire – one of many, for at the beginning of the 16th century the Ottoman Turks were creating a huge empire for themselves which would remain intact, at least nominally, until the First World War. The darkest period of Egyptian history now began.

The sultan's governor showed little if any interest in the country, and the Mamelukes continued to occupy the highest administrative positions, not least because one of their military clans had supported the Turkish occupation. But to prevent them from gaining too much power, the sultan stationed additional regiments of janissaries, who also played a part in the never-ending power struggle.

When the plundering and robbing Bedouins, who to some extant were able to grasp power even in parts of Upper Egypt, arrived at the gates of Cairo in the 18th century, the Mamelukes took advantage of the chaotic situation to once again take power. A civil war, initiated by Turkish agents between the rival Mamelukes, was the direct result. Against this background, Napoleon Bonaparte's fleet arrived at the Mediterranean coast of Egypt on July 2, 1798.

The French Interlude

The French arrived with the intention of ending the regime of terror of the Mamelukes and of helping the Egyptian people to gain liberty, equality and fraternity. This was the expressed reason behind the invasion. But behind this ethical explanation were somewhat less honorable motives: Anglo-French rivalry, and

Right: Contemporary portrayals of two Mameluke beys.

the coveted Indian trade which the English had developed on the well-tried Egyptian route.

On July 21 of that year, Napoleon conquered the "best cavalry in the world," as the horsemen of the Mamelukes were called at the time. But less than two weeks later, on August 1, Admiral Nelson sank the French fleet in the bay of Abû Qîr to the east of Alexandria. With that, Napoleon's expedition was doomed to failure, even though a further three years would pass before the French finally capitulated.

The relatively brief interlude of the French occupation had a lasting effect on Egypt. Although the Napoleonic reforms were quickly abolished, they had nevertheless pointed the way to social and economic changes which would, to some extent, be realized in the following century. Even the rediscovery of ancient Egypt can be credited to Napoleon, who had brought a group of scholars to the Nile in his entourage. They produced a monumental work entitled *Description de l'Egypt*, a unique historical and geographical document. But the most significant consequence was that the strategic importance of Egypt became apparent again, and it became the focus of European colonial interests.

The end of French rule was brought about by an Anglo-Ottoman alliance of troops, who arrived in Egypt in 1801. As deputy commander of the Albanian unit a young man came to Cairo who would soon become very well known indeed: Muhammad 'Alî.

Egypt enters the Modern Age

Four years of chaos and anarchy followed the French withdrawal. The British-Turkish alliance had dissolved again quickly because of their opposing interests, and now everyone was struggling for supremacy over the Nile: the Mameluke beys, who fought each other and the

Ottomans, the British and, of course, the Ottomans, who wanted to rule their province once more themselves.

In the year 1805, as the domestic political situation in Egypt became steadily more dangerous, the Islamic spiritual leaders abrubtly appointed a man of their choice to be the new governor: Muhammad 'Alî, who was soon confirmed in office by the sultan in Istanbul. The newly appointed governor set about cold-bloodedly disposing of his opponents. First came the British in the Battle of Rosetta (1807). Four years later he rid himself of the rebellious Mamelukes whom he had invited to a banquet at the Citadel; only one of the 480 beys who had accepted his invitation is said to have survived the terrible massacre which had been planned for them.

Now the way was free for Muhammad 'Alî's unlimited rule. However, before he could lead the Land of the Nile to full independence he had to build up a strong, powerful and modernly-equipped army. This ambitious project provided him with the incentive to modernize and industrialize Egypt. He brought in European experts with whose help he founded schools and military academies.

With the introduction of cotton as an additional summer crop he planned to provide new sources of income for the state coffers. The division and allotment of land amongst the peasantry, the comprehensive renovation and extension of the irrigation system, and a state trade monopoly created the framework for the cultivation and export of cotton. With the profits from exports he financed the creation of a domestic industry which was first and foremost oriented towards the needs of the nation's army.

The glorious victories which his son Ibrahîm Pasha won with the Egyptian army seemed to justify Muhammad 'Alî's policies. But they also attracted the attention of the European powers, who had no desire to sit back and watch while a new empire came into being on the Nile. They maintained the upper hand: in 1841, Muhammad 'Alî was forced to

49

withdraw and drastically reduce his troops. In compensation, the Turkish sultan awarded him the hereditary title of viceroy, which remained in his family until the abolition of the monarchy in 1953.

The Dynasty of Muhammad 'Alî

The economic rise of Egypt, which had begun with Muhammad 'Alî, continued under his sons and descendants, but it was only under his grandson Ismâ'îl (1863-79) that Egypt entered the international arena once again. The glorious height of Ismâ'îl's rule was the opening of the Suez Canal, celebrated with pomp and ceremony in the year 1869. Yet this enormous project, which had been started 10 years before under the rule of his uncle Sa'îd, would soon lead Egypt yet

Above: In front of the well house of 'Abd ar-Rahmân Kathkûda (18th century) in Cairo's Islamic old town. Right: President Nasser, still revered by many.

again into complete dependence upon foreign countries.

Before that, the country experienced a unique, though short, rise in fortunes through the cotton boom which came about as a consequence of the American Civil War. In order to increase Egypt's competitiveness on the international market, Ismâ'îl devoted his energies to building up the nation's infrastructure: 13,500 kilometers of irrigation canals were dug, 1,460 kilometers of railway track were laid down, and some 8,000 telegraph lines were put up.

In order to finance all these investments – but also to finance his luxurious royal household – Ismâ'îl led the country almost to the brink of bankruptcy, aided by the extortionate conditions and crippling interest rates that had been forced upon him by his foreign creditors. He was forced to sell Egyptian Suez Canal shares to the English and, in 1876, he even had to accept British-French financial control over Egypt. Three years later, as a result of this economic debacle, Ismâ'îl was forced to abdicate in favor of his son Tawfîq.

In this climate, nationalistic movements rapidly gained increasing support. Slogans such as "Egypt for the Egyptians" show not only how weary the populace had become of constant foreign interference and of the rich foreign ruling classes, but they also reflected mounting criticism of the high-handed autocracy of the ruling house.

Dissatisfaction in the country grew noticeably until, in 1882, it inspired a military revolt led by Colonel 'Orâbî. Tawfîq, who feared for his office and his honor, asked the British for military support, which they guaranteed him immediately. After all, for them the debts they were owed by Egypt and the Suez Canal itself were at stake. Troops were sent to occupy Egypt temporarily as a protective force, landing in Alexandria in 1882. British troops remained there until the

revolution of the "Free Officers" some 70 years later.

British Colonial Rule

It was now the consuls general of Great Britain who steered the course of Egypt's government, which consisted of a shadow cabinet and a weak viceroy. As in India, in the interests of the English textile industry they perfected growing and transport methods, and the marketing of cotton. But they were not particularly interested in building up a domestic industry. And so the balance of payments improved, but the capital was concentrated in the hands of foreigners and a small Egyptian elite.

At the beginning of the First World War, England officially declared Egypt to be a British protectorate, and with that the Ottomans' rights to sovereignty were ended once and for all. Nationalist groups began to become hopeful again and, finally, on November 13, 1918, they sent a delegation (Arabic: *wafd*) under the leadership of Sa'd Zaghlûl to the British High Comissioner to demand Egypt's independence. It wasn't until three years later that England gave in to the massive pressure being exercised by the nationalists and allowed Egypt at first somewhat limited autonomy.

In 1922, one of Muhammad 'Alî's great-grandsons became King Fu'âd I of Egypt. One year later a new constitution was ratified which gave the monarch the calamitous right to dissolve parliament – a right which would determine the instability of Egyptian politics during the following decades. The great parliamentary opponent of the king was the Wafd, which had now become the most important party in the country and which, in 1924, provided Egypt with its first prime minister, Sa'd Zaghlûl.

For three decades Egyptian politics were shaped by the rivalries that existed between the Royal House, the Wafd and the British Consulate General – and nothing changed under King Faruk either, who succeeded his father Fu'âd to the throne in 1936. No government ruled the country for longer than 18 months, corruption and intrigue flourished everywhere, and when the king and the government led the badly equipped Egyptian troops into crushing defeat in the Palestinian war in 1948, tension reached the boiling point.

In Cairo, in January 1952, unrest broke out aimed initially at the British military presence. On July 23, 1952, came the upheaval: a bloodless coup in which the "Free Officers," led by Colonel Nasser (Gamal Abdel Nasser), took power.

The Revolution and its Sons

The revolution ended two thousand years of unbroken foreign rule in Egypt. King Faruk abdicated on July 26 in favor of his son, and one year later the Republic was declared. After a short period in office, Nasser took over the presidency from General Najîb – complete with dictatorial powers and supported by a united party.

Since the conclusion of the treaty which had agreed the British troop withdrawal, the carefully-directed rebuilding of the country had come to be regarded as the most urgent task in improving the living conditions of all Egyptians. The initial goals were to increase farming productivity, to build up a domestic industrial base, and to establish a functioning educational system and health service. But in order to achieve all this, Egypt would need foreign financial help and expertise. Yet this time no one wanted a return to dependence on foreign powers – a problem which also confronted other developing countries.

"Positive Neutrality" was the catchword in the foreign policy strategy which Nehru, Tito and Nasser developed to solve this problem. But Nasser's leading

role in the nonaligned movement did not fit easily into the political calculations of the West during the Cold War. And so the World Bank took back the credit it had already agreed to supply for the building of the Aswan Dam. Nasser's response came as a shock: he nationalized the most important international waterway, the Suez Canal, to finance the building of the dam with the income.

England and France, who still possessed the majority of the shares, hit back and, together with Israel, occupied the Suez Canal zone. But both superpowers were forced to retreat immediately – and Nasser celebrated his most glorious victory! With this triumph he had given not only the Egyptians but the whole Arab world a new national self confidence. And even after the failure of the experiment to form the United Arab Republic with Syria and Yemen (1958-61), Nasser remained the figurehead of pan-Arabic ideology.

Nasser's domestic political model was so-called "Arab Socialism," a third path between communism and capitalism, which was modeled on Tito's ideas. After initial economic growth, Egypt's structural and financial problems grew increasingly worse. After suffering catastrophic defeat in the Arab-Israeli War in June 1967, these problems were exacerbated by the deep disillusionment of the entire nation. In only six days almost the entire Egyptian air force had been destroyed, and the Israelis conquered the Sinai Peninsula and the Suez Canal. Nasser's star had faded – even if the Egyptians used mass demonstrations to prevent him from resigning at the end of the war. On September 28, 1970, he suffered a heart attack, three months before his life's work, the Aswan High Dam, was inaugurated.

Another member of the revolutionary council, Anwar el-Sadat, became president in 1952. One of his first spectacular acts in office was the expulsion in 1972

Right: Time still has not buried the traces of the war on the Sinai Peninsula.

of the Soviet advisors who had played such a significant role in Egypt in the preceding decade. With this move, Sadat introduced his new political concept: the *Infitâh,* the "opening up" to the West, was the means by which considerable financial help and private investment could be brought into the country, and by which the stagnating economy could be given a boost. Joy over the longed-for Western consumer goods was great, but the other side of the coin was a rapidly rising inflation rate caused by the colossal increase in imports.

His first political triumph abroad was the October War against Israel in 1973. Although he brought Egypt no victories, he did recuperate the territories lost in the previous war and made peace with Israel. It was, in fact, a double-edged peace, which isolated Egypt in the Arab world and lacked anything nearing unanimous support from the country itself. Some of his most bitter critics belonged to the orthodox Muslim circles from which his assassins came: on October 6, 1981, they

killed Anwar el-Sadat during a parade to celebrate the October War.

When Hosni Mubarak took the helm, he was more or less an unknown quantity, even though he had been vice-president under Anwar el-Sadat. He steered the same course as Sadat but, in addition, tried to relieve the economic and social problems caused by the politics of the Infitâh.

The return of the Arab League to its traditional seat in Cairo in 1989, without Egypt having to sacrifice the peace of Camp David, crowned his diplomatic efforts. The leading role Mubarak adopted was also seen in the anti-Iraq coalition during the Gulf War in 1991. This brought a reduction of about US \$35 billion to the national debt. Sweeping reforms along the path to a free market economy helped to reduce the country's unemployment rate to six percent, as well as to raise economic growth to five percent, well above the growth in population (two percent). The end of the tunnel now seems to be in sight.

BETWEEN ORIENT AND OCCIDENT

ALEXANDRIA

THE BEACHES

THE OASIS OF SÎWA

THE DELTA AND WÂDÎ AN-NATRÛN

ALEXANDRIA

"Alexandria is the pearl of the Mediterranean and the second capital of Egypt": this is the Alexandrians' enthusiastic verdict of their home town – and that of hundreds of thousands of others who flee each summer from the oppressive heat of Cairo to the long sandy beaches of this metropolis of six million people.

Despite unconfirmed reports of its death, Alexandria (Arabic: *Al-Iskandarîya*) is once again in the process of rising like a phoenix from the ashes; this time as a modern, cosmopolitan Arabic city unfolding along the Corniche, the 16-kilometer-long promenade on the sea. An impressive urban panorama opens up here: a chain of white tower blocks and hotels lines the bays from the city center all the way to Al-Montâza, the one-time summer residence of the king on the eastern edge of town. Only behind this modern façade – in the second row, so to speak – does the real city begin, with shops, offices, a university and residential areas. Here, the architecture often reflects that

Preceding pages: Felûkas, sailboats, can be seen everywhere on the Nile. The Eastern Harbor of Alexandria. Left: Colorful carpets are also made in Sîwa.

typical, if somewhat faded, glory of the *fin de siècle*, which is also found in the buildings in the city center around the Mîdân Sa'd Zaghlûl, as well as those on the Anfûshî promontory. Perhaps it is only here that traces of the Levantine character which made Alexandria what it once was – the cultural center of the Hellenistic world and of late antiquity – still remain.

An enormous industrial area forms a third zone. This stretches in a wide arc on the other side of the Mahmûdîya Canal, which joins the city with the eastern arm of the Nile of the Delta. Textile, food and chemical factories all contribute to the new economic rise of Alexandria, which has once again taken its place as the sight of one of the most important ports on the Mediterranean. Compared to the other cities of the Land of the Nile, Alexandria is young, relatively speaking, of course. Alexander the Great founded the city on the Mediterranean in 332 B.C., on his way back from the oracle of Zeus-Amen in Sîwa. It looked out onto the new world: his Greek-Hellenic empire which was in the process of being formed. But Alexander would never see the most famous of the cities he founded. Soon after his death it became the capital of Egypt, and the splendid residence of the Ptolemaic dynasty.

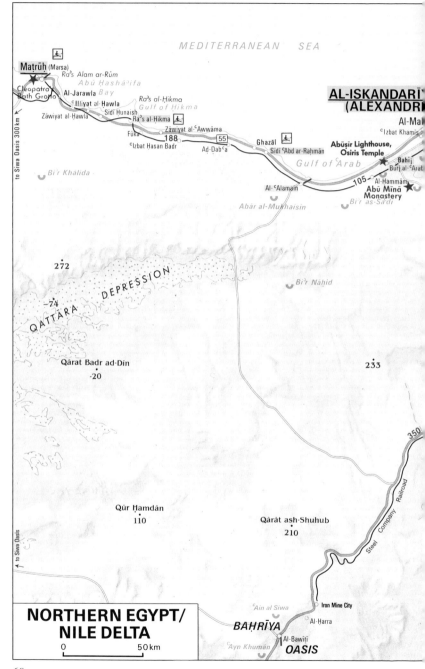

MEDITERRANEAN SEA

Maṭrūḥ (Marsa)
Ra's Alam ar-Rūm
Abū Ḥashā'ifa Bay
Cleopatra
Bath Grotto
Al-Jarawla
cIlliyat al-Ḥawla
Ra's al-Ḥikma
Gulf of Ḥikma
Zāwiyat al-Ḥawla
Sīdī Hunaish
Ra's al-Ḥikma
Fūka
Zāwiyat al-cAwwāma
188   55
cIzbat Ḥasan Badr
Ghazāl
Ad-Dabca
Sīdī cAbd ar-Raḥmān

AL-ISKANDARĪ
(ALEXANDRI
Al-Ma
cIzbat Khamīs

Abūṣir Lighthouse,
Osiris Temple
Gulf of Arab
Bahij
Burj al-cArat
105
Al-Ḥammām
Abū Mīnā
Monastery
Bi'r as-Sacdī

Bi'r Khālida

Al-cAlamain
Abār al-Mukhaisin

272

QATTĀRA   DEPRESSION

Bi'r Nāhid

-74

Qārat Badr ad-Dīn
-20

233

350

Qūr Ḥamdān
110

Qārat ash-Shuhub
210

Steel Company Railroad

to Siwa Oasis 300 km

to Siwa Oasis

cAin al Siwa
Iron Mine City

**NORTHERN EGYPT/
NILE DELTA**

BAḤRĪYA
Al-Ḥarra
Al-Bawiṭī
cAyn Khumān   OASIS

0   50km

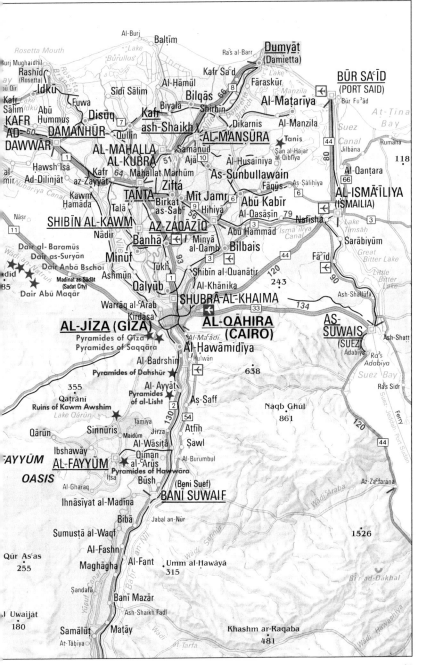

Rosetta Mouth

Al-Burj
Balṭīm
Lake 'Burullus'
urj Mughaidhil
Ra's al-Barr
Dumyāṭ (Damietta)
Rashīd (Rosetta)
Idkū
'ū Qīr
Kafr Sa'd
Fāraskūr
BŪR SA'ĪD (PORT SAID)
Sīdī Sālim
Al-Hāmūl
Bilqās
Al-Maṭariya
Būr Fu'ād
At-Ṭīna Bay
Kafr Sālim
Abū Hummus
Fuwa
Kafr ash-Shaikh
Biyala
Shirbīn
Dikarnis
Al-Manzila
Suez Canal
Rumāna
KAFR AD-DAWWĀR
DAMANHŪR
Disūq
Quīlin
AL-MAṢŪRA
Tanis
San al-Hajar al-Qiblīya
Rashīd

Al-Qanṭara
118
al-mir Mubārīya Canal
Hawsh Īsā
Ad-Dilinjāt
AL-MAHALLA AL-KUBRĀ
Kafr az-Zayyāt
Samanūd
Ajā
Al-Husainīya
'As-Sunbullawain
Fāqūs
As-Sālihīya
AL-ISMĀ'ĪLIYA (ISMAILIA)
Nāṣr
Kawm Hamāda
Mahallat Marhūm
Zifṭā
TANṬĀ
Birkat as-Sab'
Mīt Jamr
Hihiyā
Abū Kabīr
Al-Qasāṣīn
Nafishā
Ismā'ilīya Canal
Isma'ilīya Canal
Lake Timsāh

SHIBĪN AL-KAWM
Nādir
AZ-ZAQĀZĪQ
Abū Hammād
Sarābiyūm
Great Bitter Lake
Dair al-Baramūs
Dair as-Suryān
Dair Anbā Bschoi
Banhā
Minyā al-Qamh
Bilbais
Fā'id
Little Bitter Lake
'did
'85
Madīnat as-Sādāt (Sadat City)
Dair Abū Maqār
Minūf
Ashmūn
Tūkh
Shibīn al-Quanāṭir
Al-Khānika
120
243
Ash-Shallūfa

Qalyūb
Warrāq al-'Arab
Kirdāsa
SHUBRĀ AL-KHAIMA
134
AS-SUWAIS (SUEZ)
AL-JĪZA (GIZA)
Pyramides of Gīza
Pyramides of Saqqāra
AL-QĀHIRA (CAIRO)
Al-Ma'ādi
Al-Hawāmidīya
Ash-Shatt
Adabīya
Ra's Adabiya
Al-Badrshīn
Hulwān
Suez Bay
Pyramides of Dahshūr
638
Ra's Sidr
355
Al-'Ayyāṭ
Pyramides of al-Lisht
As-Saff
Naqb Ghūl
861
Qaṭrāni
Ruins of Kawm Awshim
Lake Qārūn
2
54
120
Qārūn
Sinnūris
Tāmiya
Maidūm
Jirza
Atfīh
Ṣawl
FAYYŪM
Ibshawāy
Al-Wāsiṭā
Qīmān al-'Arūs
Al-Burumbul
Az-Za'farāna
AL-FAYYŪM
Pyramides of Hawwāra
Itsa
Būsh
AL-OASIS
Al-Gharaq
(Beni Suef)
BANĪ SUWAIF
Ihnāsīyat al-Madīna
Bība
Jabal an-Nūr
1526
Sumusṭā al-Waqf
Al-Fashn
Qūr As'as
255
Al-Fant
Umm al-Hawāyā
315
Bi'r ad-Dakhal
Maghāgha
Ṣandafā
Banī Mazār
l Uwaijāt
180
Ash-Shaikh Fadl
Samālūṭ
Maṭāy
At-Ṭābīya
At-Ṭarfa
Khashm ar-Raqaba
481

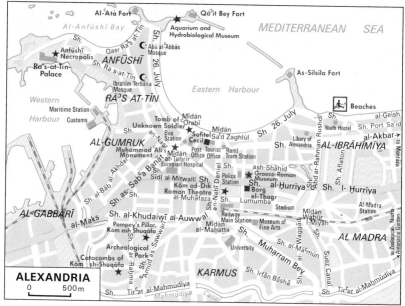

Authors of antiquity described ancient Alexandria as a wonderful city with many green parks, a grid of streets through which the cool north wind could blow, and an imposing administrative quarter, the *Regia*, with a palace, official buildings, theaters and the *Museion*, the famous academy with the largest library in the world at the time. Protected by an enormous outer wall, the residential quarters were grouped around Regia: to the east was that of the great Jewish community; to the west that of the Egyptians, with the *Serapeum*, where the Egyptian-Greek god Serapis was worshiped. But the heart of the city was the unique double harbor, which could be approached from any wind direction. The *Heptastadion*, a 1300-meter-long artificial dam which divided the natural harbor basin, also served as a bridge to the island of Pharos. There, in 280 B.C., Ptolemy II had the famous lighthouse built which

was later to become one of the Seven Wonders of the World.

Alexandria's Golden Age was the Hellenistic epoch, but even when the Roman troops invaded Egypt it remained the most important city in the Mediterranean area, second only to Rome itself. Its decline only came with the Arab conquerers in A.D. 641, who moved the capital to Cairo and the harbor to Rashîd (Rosetta), 50 kilometers away.

It was not until the beginning of the 19th century that Alexandria was awakened like a Sleeping Beauty by Muhammad ʿAlî, who made it into a Levantine metropolis for the second time. Its unique Oriental-European character has been immortalized in the works of Lawrence Durrell and Constantine Kavafis. The capricious ethnic mix of its inhabitants has dispersed since the days of President Nasser, but some Greeks have remained.

Ancient Alexandria has long since disappeared; its remains lie buried under the modern buildings of the city center or sunken in the sea. Lost forever are the

Right: The Qâ'it Bey fortress today stands on the site of the Pharos lighthouse.

900,000 scrolls of the Alexandrian library, which contained all the accumulated knowledge of the time. In 48 B.C., during Cleopatra's battles for the throne, the great Museion library burned down, and in 391 A.D., the smaller "daughter library" in the Serapeum was destroyed when Christianity was elevated to the state religion.

In regard to the many sites of archeological excavations, more and more attention has recently been paid to underwater finds. Pharoanic pillars, statues and building elements have been discovered in the sea around the Eastern Harbor; presumably including parts of the destroyed lighthouse.

There are future plans for the resurrection of the famous library of Alexandria, which it is hoped will be brought back to life through the help of an enormous international project. Millions of writings, books, maps and multimedia products are to be assembled here in order to make Alexandria a world center of science and culture once again.

The City Center and Anfûshî

The center of the city lies between Mîdân al-Mahatta (Station Square) and the Eastern Harbor, which is used today as a yachting and fishing port. The cape of **Anfûshî** separates the Eastern Harbor from the international Western Harbor. It follows the course of the Ptolemaic Heptastadion, which alluvial deposits have widened over the centuries, and which, with the one-time island of Pharos, has become a wide settlement of the old town quarter of Anfûshî.

A good starting point for a sightseeing tour is the central **Mîdân Sa'd Zaghlûl**, the wide square on the Corniche, to the west of which rises the **Hotel Cecil**, steeped in tradition. A walk to Anfûshî will take you first past the ancient columned semicircle of the **Monument to the Unknown Soldier** on the Mîdân 'Orâbî, which leads onto Liberation Square, **Mîdân at-Tahrîr**, at one time the center of the city. The lively streets around the square, with its bronze **eques-**

trian statue of **Muhammad 'Alî**, are still a busy shopping quarter.

From about the middle of the Corniche you can see the **Mosque of Ibrâhîm Terbâna** in the background. Many columns and stone blocks from ancient buildings were reused in its construction in the 17th century.

Not far from this is the imposing **Abû al-'Abbâs Mosque**, which was erected in 1943 on the site of an older building over the grave of a 13th-century saint. Its filigree façade and the four cupolas ornamented with geometric stone carvings are particularly impressive.

At the end of the great arc which the Corniche makes around the Eastern Harbor rises the striking landmark of **Fort Qâ'it Bey**. The Mameluke sultan built it in the 15th century. Until the year 1326, the legendary lighthouse still stood here. It is worth taking a sightseeing tour to the

Above: Everyday life in the streets of Alexandria. Right: The mighty Mosque of Abû al-'Abbâs.

castle just to see its renovated rooms and the wonderful view from its battlements. In the **Hydro-Bioligical Museum** located next door, the underwater world of the Mediterranean and the Red Sea can be admired.

The **Royal Palace of Ra's at-Tîn** is situated at the western tip of Anfûshî. Built by Muhammad 'Alî as the Alexandrian residence of the Egyptian rulers, it was here that the last ruler of his dynasty, King Faruk, signed his abdication declaration on July 26, 1952. Unfortunately, its 300 lavishly-furnished rooms are not open to the public.

Also worth paying a visit to is the **Necropolis of Anfûshî**, which has two interesting tombs which are painted in the mixed Egyptian-Greco style of the second century B.C. In the anterooms, which branch off from a communal atrium, there are wall paintings imitating marble and alabaster tableaux in the style of Pompeian wall decorations, while Egyptian motifs are portrayed in the burial chambers.

Today, Alexandria's true historical treasures are mostly to be found in the **Museum of Greco-Roman Antiquities**. The museum is located in the south of the city center on Sh. al-Hurrîya, close to the excavation site of Kôm ad-Dîk. The museum's displays provide a unique insight into the history of the city and its surroundings. Among them is the famous collection of *Tanagra* figurines, charming small clay figures from the Greek period.

In 1964, in the **Kôm ad-Dîk** area, Polish archeologists discovered a wonderfully-preserved **Roman theater**, of a kind never found before in Egypt. It has seating for about 800 spectators in its 12 marble semicircular rows.

The most important archeological site in Alexandria is the **Kôm ash-Shuqâfa**, the "hill of potsherds" in the southwest of the city. This was once the most important place of worship of the Greco-Egyptian god Serapis. Only a few statues, sphinxes and mud bricks survived the iconoclasm of the partiarch Theophilos

(A.D. 391). Today, only the 27-meter-high **Pompey's Pillar** of red granite remains as a landmark of the Serapis temple. This pillar was probably erected in honor of Emperor Diocletian in the year 297 A.D. Its present name is due to Pompey's tomb, which was believed to have been here.

A few hundred meters further south you come to the **Kôm ash-Shuqâfa Catacombs**, an unusual example of a Roman burial ground from the first and second centuries A.D. A spiral staircase leads down to the three floors of the underground chambers. The burial chamber itself is decorated in a fascinating combination of Egyptian architecture and motifs contaning Greco-Roman stylistic elements.

It is also worth seeing the beautifully-painted **Tomb from Tigrane Pasha Street**. This grave site was discovered during construction work on the above-named street, and was brought to the grounds of the Alexandrian catacombs, where it was re-erected.

THE BEACHES

Alexandria's beaches begin on the other side of the Eastern Harbor, almost in the center of the city itself, and extend eastwards in a chain of bays beyond the city limits. As in Italy, many beaches have changing cubicles on them and have been made into swimming areas. But the similarity ends there. Egyptian beach life revolves around relaxing by the water: people enjoy the sea, picnic with their families, play ball and chat. Swimming is of secondary importance, indeed, many Egyptian women will not even change into a bathing suit.

The most beautiful beaches can be found on the outskirts of town. Little **Montâza Bay** was very poular with the khedives and kings of the 19th and 20th centuries, who built their summer residence in the middle of a well-kept park

Above: The wondrous royal castle on Montâza Bay. Right: Picking dates at the Sîwa Oasis.

with shady palm groves. "Alexandria's Neuschwanstein," with its playful architecture, is a fine Neo-Renaissance **castle**. Unfortunately, its interior rooms are not open to the public.

The **Palestine Hotel** was built next to the castle during the Nasser era. Its functional, rather than beautiful, architecture is compensated for by its wonderful setting, directly on the bay.

Next to Montâza Bay, **Ma'mûra Beach** stretches for kilometers to **Abû Qîr**, which is famous for its excellent fish restaurants – and for Napoleon's defeat at the hands of Admiral Nelson – but which otherwise has little of interest to offer sightseers.

West of Alexandria, a 300-kilometer-long white sandy beach stretches to **Matrûh**, along which more and more resorts and holiday villages are built every year. In winter these places seem like ghostly abandoned film sets. The coastal road offers only an occasional view of the sea because it runs some distance from the water and is often hidden behind high sand dunes. Tempting as it might seem, you should never swim off the lonely open beaches: in many places there may still be unexploded mines from the Second World War.

Coming from Alexandria, you first drive past the international Western Harbor, and unattractive residential and industrial areas. The resort of 'Agamî lies only 16 kilometers away. In recent years it has become the Marbella of the Egyptian Mediterranean coast. Beautiful and clean beaches can be found to the west of Al-Alamayn at **Sîdî 'Abd ar-Rahmân**, **Ra's al-Hikma** and **Matrûh**. The busy town of Matrûh lies sheltered by cliffs on a wide lagoon with quiet sandy beaches. A particular attraction is **Cleopatra's Bath**, a grotto in the chalk cliffs of the coastal strip on the western tip of the lagoon.

Most famous of all are the picturesque bays to the west of Matrûh, with their snow-white limestone cliffs and their fine sand. Although many buildings have sprung up there in the last few years, '**Ubayyad Beach** and '**Agîba Bay** should not be missed.

FROM ALEXANDRIA TO THE SÎWA OASIS

The coastline to the west of Alexandria is not only of interest to those on a beach holiday. Forty-eight kilometers from the city, at **Abûsîr** on the Mediterranean, you will find the ancient *Taposiris Magna,* a **Roman lighthouse** which is supposed to be a copy of the famous Pharos of Alexandria. The Roman town saw its golden age in the first century A.D. as a harbor for nearby Abû Mînâ, a Christian place of pilgrimage. Unfortunately, it has been almost completely destroyed. Only the ruins of the Roman **Osiris Temple** have been partly preserved: an outer wall of limestone blocks and the pylon towers, from which you have a wonderful view of the sea.

Almost opposite, a road forks to **Burj al-'Arab**, a one-time holiday resort which the British built around 1920 in the style of a medieval fortress. Via neighboring **Bahîj** you reach the modern monastery and the ruins of **Abû Mînâ**, one of the most important places of pilgrimage in the early Christian era. Today, the remains of the **Burial Church** built on the grave of the martyr Menas (died A.D. 296) can be seen. It can be reached by means of 30 marble steps. Directly to the east was the **Great Basilica**. To the west was a **baptistery**. All around were houses and accomodations for the pilgrims who came from as far away as Cologne for the healing waters of Abû Mînâ. In the ninth century the town was destroyed by Bedouins, and in 1300 it was abandoned completely. The foundation stone of the new monastery near the ruins, was laid on Nov. 27, 1959, by the Coptic Patriarch Cyril VI, who is buried in a side chapel of the monastery church.

About 60 kilometers further along the coastal road you will reach **Al-'Alamain**.

It is famous for the battles between Rommel's Africa Corps and the finally victorious Allied troops under Montgomery in the 1942. Three **Military Cemeteries** and a small **Military Museum** comemmorate the 80,000 soldiers who died in these battles.

Matrûh, capital of the western border province of the same name, makes a good base for a visit to the **Sîwa Oasis**, which lies a full 300 kilometers away and has somewhat stronger economic links with the Nile Valley ever since the government built an asphalt road. The oasis stretches for 80 kilometers in a depression area in the Libyan plateau – a virtual paradise with its 300,000 date palms, lush fruit and vegetable fields, its 300 springs and small saphire-blue lake. Thanks to its isolated position, many of the old traditions have been retained, and even the language of the primarily Berber population has survived.

Sîwa, the capital of the oasis, has a picturesque, but for the most part abandoned, old town, **Shalî**, where mud brick buildings climb the slopes of the hills. Part of the area's forlornness has to do with its remote geographical location, not far from the Lybian border. Until the 19th century the center of the oasis lay further west at the fortress of **Aghurmî**. There you can still see the remains of a **temple** from the Twenty-sixth Dynasty. This is where the famous Oracle of Zeus-Amen, where Alexander the Great was inaugurated as an Egyptian Pharaoh, is said to have been located.

The **Rock Tombs of Jabal al-Mawta,** 1.5 kilometers northeast of Sîwa, which were constructed in the later Pharaonic period, served as air-raid shelters during World War II. The most beautiful paintings are to be found in the tombs of Niperpa-Thot, Si-Amen and Mesu-Isis.

Right: Dair as-Suryân, one of four left-over desert monasteries in the Wâdî an-Natrûn, still inhabited by monks.

THE DELTA AND THE WÂDÎ AN-NATRÛN

The triangle of the Nile Delta is fed by a complex network of canals and by two of the arms of the Nile which flow into the Mediterranean at Dumyât (Damietta) and Rashîd (Rosetta). Almost parallel to these are two highways which lead straight through the Delta: the *Route agricole*, from Cairo via the great provincial capital of Tantâ to Alexandria; and the route via Al-Mansûra to Dumyât which branches off at Tantâ.

As in ancient Egyptian times, the eight provinces of modern Lower Egypt still form the economic center of the country. In addition to the large fertile area, on the borders of which intensive land reclamation projects have been carried out, several industrial centers have sprung up around the city conurbations and in the newly-founded desert towns. But the economic efficiency of the Delta has also been responsible for the destruction of almost all the ancient sites: through the irrigation of the fields, the rise in the water table, through industrialization, and, last but not least, through the use of the mud brick ruins as fertilizers. For this reason, the Delta has little more than complex ground plans and stone blocks to offer the archeological lay person.

But there are some interesting **desert monasteries** at **Wâdî an-Natrûn** on the western border of the Delta, about halfway along the desert highway from Cairo to Alexandria. This 30-kilometer-long and eight-kilometer-wide depression takes its name from 10 salt lakes which dry up almost completely in summer, leaving salt and sodium deposits.

Wâdî an-Natrûn has developed since the fourth century into one of the most important monastery centers of the Land of the Nile. Four of the 50 original monasteries set up by colonies of hermits can be seen even today. But in the last few years the monastery communities have

experienced a revival, to the extent that many of the old buildings are being restored and extended. The monks welcome visitors and are happy to show people around the monastery areas.

The oldest of the four monasteries is the **Dair al-Baramûs**, which lies furthest north. This is the so-called Roman Monastery, which was, according to an old legend, founded by the sons of Emperor Valentinian, Maximus and Domitius, at the end of the fourth century. Destroyed in Bedouin attacks in the fifth century, it was rebuilt as a fortress in the ninth century.

Further south lies the **Dair as-Suryân**, built in the eighth century by a rich Syrian-Nestorian trader, who founded it for his fellow believers. This monastery is famous for its collection of Syrian writings from the 10th century, most of which are now in the Vatican Museums and in the British Museum in London. The main church of the monastery, with its beautiful frescos and stucco work, dates back to the 10th century.

Neighboring **Dair Amba Bshoî** was founded in about the year 400, but only a well remains from this time. Of its five churches and chapels, the **Titular Church** from the ninth century is the most important. You can get an excellent view of the whole complex and the surroundings from the **peel** (12th century). The monastery became important for being the domicile of the Coptic Patriarch Shenuda III for years. It is being renovated on a large scale at present.

Dair Abû Makâr, the southernmost monastery, is the most important of the four. It is reached by a different branch of the desert road. This modern four hectare monastery complex with mostly new buildings is a popular place of pilgrimage which traces its origins to a monastery, and to the grave of St. Macarius in the fourth century. The **Church of St. Macarius** is worth a visit, with its richly carved iconstasis from the fifth/sixth centuries. Also interesting are the chapels of the old fortified tower, in particular the **Chapel of St. Antony** with its beautiful frescos.

69

ALEXANDRIA

The area code for the entire region is 03

Arrival

Some international **airlines** fly directly to Alexandria. Egypt Air has several flights daily from Cairo to Alexandria.

The *Federal Arab Land Transport Company* and the *West Delta Bus Company* operate hourly **train** and **bus** services between Alexandria (bus station: Md. Sa'd Zaghlûl) and Cairo (bus station: Abd al-Munîm near the Ramses Hilton). Tickets for the *Super Jet Company's* luxury buses should be booked well in advance at the ticket-office in the bus station. **Group taxis** for Alexandria leave Cairo from the Mîdân al-Quâlî taxi stand.

Accommodation

Although Alexandria offers a great variety of hotels in all categories, it is advisable to book in advance during peak season (July-August). Budget hotels and guest houses often close from October to May.

All hotels on the Corniche face the sea; in the Eastern Harbor area the Corniche is called Sh. 26th July, whereas its eastern section up to Montâza Park is called Sh. al-Geish.

Central accommodation, mostly with a view of the sea, can be found around Mîdân Sa'd Zaghlûl and Raml Station.

LUXURY: **Sheraton Montaza**, Al-Montâza, tel. 5480550, 5481220, fax. 5401331; **Helnan Palestine**, Al-Montâza tel. 5474033, 5473500, fax. 5473378; **Ramada Renaissance**, 544 Sh. al-Geish, tel. 5483977, 5490935, fax. 5497690; **Sofitel Cecil**, Md. Sa'd Zaghlûl tel. 4834856, 4837173, fax. 4836401.

MODERATE: **Alexandria Hotel**, 23 Md. an-Nasr, tel. 4837694/-97, fax. 4823113; **Delta**, 14 Sh. Champollion, Mazarita, tel. 4829053, 4825630, fax. 4825630; **El-Haram**, 162 Sh. al-Geish, tel. 5464059, fax. 5464578; **Maamura Palace**, Al-Ma'mûra, tel. 5473108, 5473383, fax. 5473108; **Mecca**, 44 Sh. al-Geish, tel. 5973925/-35, fax. 5967935; **Metropole**, 52 Sh. Sa'd Zaghlûl, tel. 4821466/67, fax. 4822040; **Plaza**, 394 Sh. al-Geish, tel. 5878714/15, fax. 5873599; **San Giovanni**, 205 Sh. al-Geish, tel. 5473585, fax. 5464408; **Windsor**, 17 Sh. ash-Shuhadâ', Raml, tel. 4808123, fax. 4809090.

BUDGET: **Borg el-Thagr**, Sh. Safîya Zaghlûl, Raml, tel. 4924519; **Corail**, 802 Sh. al-Geish, tel. 5480996, fax. 5407746; **Gordon**, 19 Md. Sa'd Zaghlûl, tel. 4827054; **New Capri**, 23 Sh. al-Mîna ash-Sharqîya, Raml, tel. 809310, 809703; **Holiday**, 6 Md. 'Orâbî, tel. 801559, 803517; **Swiss Cottage**, 347 Sh. al-Geish, tel. 5875886, fax. 5870455; **Nobel**, 152 Sh. al-Geish, tel. 5464845, 5463374, fax. 5457488; **Philip**, 236 Sh. 26th July, tel.

4829620. **Union**, 164 Sh. 26th July, tel. 4807771, fax. 4807350.

YOUTH HOSTEL: **Youth Hostel**, 13 Sh. Port Said, Shatbî, tel. 5975459.

Restaurants

Alexandria is a gourmets' paradise for seafood and fish dishes. In addition to the restaurants in luxury hotels we can recommend: *FISH:* **Tikka Grill**, Sh. 26th July; **Mustafa Darwish**, Sh. 26th July, Raml; **El-Saraya**, Saba Pasha, Sh. al-Geish; **San Giovanni**, 205 Sh. al-Geish; **International Seafood Restaurant**, 808 Sh. al-Geish, Al-Montâza; **Taverna Beach**, Montâza Bay; **Zephyrion**, Abû Qîr (east of Alexandria); **Sea Gull**, Sh. 'Agamî, Al-Maks (suburb west of Alexandria).

ORIENTAL / INTERNATIONAL: **Athineos**, Md. Raml; **El-Ekhlass**, 49 Sh. Safîya Zaghlûl; **Sokrat**, Sh. Iskander al-akbar, Shatbî; **Taverna**, Raml Station (with an oriental snack-bar on the ground floor and small restaurant on the first floor).

CAFÉS: **Pastroudis**, 39 Sh. Al-Hurriya; **Trianon**, Md. Sa'd Zaghlûl.

Museums / Galleries / Gardens

Museum of Greco-Roman Antiquities, Sh. al-Hurrîya, open daily 9 am to 4 pm (closed Fridays from noon to 2 pm). Tickets are also valid for the necropolis of Anfûshî and Kôm ash-Shuqâfa.

Fort Qâ'it Bey, open daily 9 am to 2 pm.

Museum of Fine Arts, 18 Sh. Manasha, Muharram Bey, daily except Friday 8 am to 2 pm, European and Egyptian art of the 19th and 20th centuries.

Royal Jewellery Museum, 27 Sh. Ahmad Yahyâ, daily 9 am to 4 pm (closed Fridays from 11:30 am to 1:30 pm), royal jewelry from the dynasty of Muhammad 'Alî.

Antoniades Gardens are next to the **Nuzha Gardens** and the **Zoo**, Sh. Smûha.

Alexandria Nightlife

Nightclubs with music and belly dancing (dinner is obligatory!) are offered at the Montazah Sheraton, Plaza, Sofitel Cecil and San Giovanni hotels. The Ramada Renaissance Hotel has a discotheque (closed Mondays).

Tourist Information

The brochure *Alexandria by Night and Day* contains the most important addresses and tips; available at hotels or at the **State Tourist Office**. The main office is on Mîdân Sa'd Zaghlûl, Raml Station, tel. 805571. Office branches at the harbor (tel. 803494), airport and Misr Station (tel. 4925985). Don't expect too much from them.

Hospitals / Pharmacies

University Hospital, Shatbî, tel. 4201573; **Italian Hospital**, Al-Hadra, tel. 4221458.

24-hour pharmacy in the city center: **Sa'd Zaghlûl Pharmacy**, Md. al-Manshîya.

Transportation

Downtown traffic is dominated by the tram. From Raml Station (*Mahattit er-Ramleh* in Egyptian) in the city center, tram lines run to almost all important sights: **No. 15**: Raml Station – Sh. Ahmad 'Orabî – Anfûshî – Ra's at-Tîn; **No. 16**: Raml Station – Md. at-Tahrîr – Pompey's Pillar; **No. 14**: Raml Station – Md. at-Tahrîr – Main Station – Zoo. Buses **No. 220, 720** and **725** run along the Corniche to Al-Montâza (the bus stop in the city center is Md. Sa'd Zaghlûl).

Excursions

The following places are suitable for half-day or full-day tours from Alexandria (or can be combined to suit individual tastes and wishes):

To the West: The beach resorts of 'Agamî (23 km) and Sîdî Krair (34 km), the Roman ruins of Abûsîr (48 km), the monastery of Abû Mînâ (74 km), the military cemeteries of Al-'Alamain (104 km), and the beaches of Al-'Alamain and Sîdî 'Abd ar-Rahmân (133 km).

To the South: Desert monasteries in Wâdî an-Natrûn (120 km; at present only with military escort).

To the East: Rashîd (40 km), has lovely residential houses dating from the town's golden age as an Ottoman Mediterranean port.

BETWEEN ALEXANDRIA AND MATRÛH
Transportation

By Air: Egypt Air flies from Cairo to Matrûh once a week.

By Rail: Daily trains connecting Alexandria with Matrûh stop at Al-'Alamain and Sîdî 'Abd ar-Rahmân. From Cairo there is a train with sleeping car to Matrûh every second day.

By Bus / Group Taxi: From Alexandria (bus station: Md. Gumhûrîya) the *West Delta Bus Company* runs several buses daily to Matrûh. The group taxi stand is next to the bus station. From Cairo (bus station: Md. at-Tahrîr) there is one direct bus to Matrûh daily. 'Agamî is best reached from Alexandria with the city buses No. 455 and 460.

Alternative transportation is available with group taxis.

Accommodation

'AGAMÎ: *MODERATE:* **Agami Palace Hotel**, Bitash Beach, tel. 4330230, fax. 4309364; **Hannoville**, Hannoville Beach, tel. 4303258; **Summer Moon**, Bitash Beach, tel.4330834.

BUDGET: **Costa Blanca**, Hannoville Beach, tel. 4303112; **New Admiral**, Hannoville Beach, tel. 4303038; **Minas**, 'Agamî Beach, tel. 4300150.

AL-'ALAMAIN: *LUXURY:* **ATIC Hotel**, 15 km east of Al-'Alamain, Alexandria-Matrûh Road km 90, tel. 950717, fax. 950718; **Al-'Alamein**, Sîdî 'Abd ar-Rahmân, tel. 4921228, fax. 4921232.

MODERATE: **Resthouse**, at the English military cemetery, Alexandria-Matrûh Road km 105, tel. 4302785, 4301649.

MATRÛH: *MODERATE:* **Beach House Hotel**, situated near the beach, 934011, fax. 933319; **Beau Site**, Sh. ash-Shâti', tel. 932066; **Riviera Palace**, Sh. Alex, Market Area, tel. 933045, 935136; **Rommel House**, Sh. al-Gala'a, tel. 935466; **Semiramis**, Sh. al-Corniche, tel. 934091.

BUDGET: **Arous el-Bahr**, Sh. al-Corniche, tel. 932419/20; **Shâti'el-Gharam**, Lido Area, tel. 934387; **Reem**, Sh. el- Corniche, tel. 933605.

YOUTH HOSTEL: **Youth Hostel**, 4 Sh. el-Gala'a, tel. 932331.

Tourist Information

Matrûh Tourist Office, tel. 932055.

SÎWA OASIS
Arrival

Foreigners no longer need a visa in order to visit Sîwa. On the other hand, rules and regulations are subject to sudden change in Egypt, so you should really check with one of the state-run tourist bureaus. The oasis can be reached with a group taxi or by bus from Matrûh. A bus commutes once a day from Alexandria: it leaves from the bus station at Md. al-Gumhûrîya.

Accommodation

VERY SIMPLE HOTELS: **Arous el-Waha**, at the entrance to Shalî; **Cleopatra**, **Medina Hotel**, **Sîwa Hotel** in the center of Shalî.

Please Note: In spite of the rising number of tourists visiting Sîwa, it remains one of the more undisturbed areas of Egypt. Please make sure your clothing covers legs and arms.

DELTA AND WÂDÎ AN-NATRÛN
Arrival

The *East Delta Bus Company* connects Cairo with the larger Delta towns; buses run anywhere from every 15 minutes to once every hour. Departure from Cairo: Al-Qulâlî Bus Station west of the train station. Group taxis to the Delta leave from Md. Ahmad Hilmî. The overland buses operating the regular route between Cairo and Alexandria via the Alexandria Desert Road stop at the Wâdî an-Natrûn Resthouse (depending on current security regulations) on request. The nearby monasteries can be visited by taxi.

Accommodation

MODERATE: **Wâdî an-Natrûn Resthouse** (3-Star), Alexandria Desert Road km 120. It is also possible sometimes to find accomodation in the guest houses of the monasteries. Please make note of the fact that the monasteries are closed to visitors on Christmas, Easter and Coptic holy days.

PYRAMIDS, CHURCHES AND MOSQUES

**CAIRO / OLD CAIRO
ISLAMIC OLD TOWN
PYRAMIDS OF GÎZA
NECROPOLIS OF SAQQÂRA
MEMPHIS**

CAIRO

The famous Arab traveler Ibn Battûta called 14th-century Cairo "the mother of all cities" – a distinction which still applies to the modern capital of Egypt. For Cairo is not only the largest city in Africa and the intellectual center of the Arab world, it is also an unbelievable symbiosis of all conceivable modern ways of life. The dark side of this sparkling microcosm cannot be overlooked, of course, but the joy of life and unshakable humor of the inhabitants of this metropolis cannot be destroyed, even under the difficult conditions of a hopelessly overpopulated city.

Cairo has many faces. There is the hectic, loud, giant city – a megalopolis which has merged into the cities of Gîza and Shubrâ al-Khaima, both of which have more than a million inhabitants, and a series of suburbs and satellite towns to form Greater Cairo. Just how many people really live here no one knows for sure; 13 million, 15 million – or more? The figures vary. The only thing you can be sure about is that the high birth rate combined with the immigration of people

Preceding pages: In front of the pyramids of Gîza. Left: The Al-Hâkim Mosque, an 11th-century relic in the old town of Cairo.

from the countryside increases the population of Cairo by tens of thousands every year. The result of this is a unique density of population; in some of the poorer quarters there are more than 100,000 people per square kilometer.

The cityscape of Greater Cairo is dominated by faceless new buildings of the kind that are to be found all over the world. Yet around the Mîdân at-Tahrîr and along the banks of the Nile the modern architecture gains a more cosmopolitan feel. Hotels and government and office buildings grow increasingly taller, forming an impressive skyline. The somewhat American character of this bustling metropolis is highlighted by the evening glow of colorful neon signs and the wide freeways with their bold, high bridges.

But alongside this there is a completely different Cairo: a city of cupolas and minarets, where colorful bazaars stretch along the clay-grey confusion of streets between the old city gates of Bâb al-Futûh and Bâb Zuweila. Here it seems as if the modern age has yet to arrive. If not for the occasional motorized vehicle trying to makes its way through the overcrowded shopping streets, a person could almost believe that he had been picked up on a flying carpet and transported back to the Middle Ages.

75

Al-Qâhira:
A Thousand Years of History

In 1969, Cairo's 1,000th birthday was celebrated – a modest claim which only one of the oldest cultures on earth can allow itself to make. While Al-Qâhira, the namesake of modern Cairo, was actually founded in the 10th century, there is a long and glorious history of other famous towns that stood on on the site long before that. Its geographically and politically convenient situation, linking the Nile Valley and the Delta, was responsible for the foundation of the very first capital of Egypt at this location. **Memphis**, residence of the Pharaohs on the west bank of the Nile, is Cairo's oldest and most important ancestor. Many other cities would follow.

The history of the modern Nile metropolis began with the establishment of **Babylon**. Not the famous city on the Euphrates River, but a Greek settlement on the east bank of the Nile which Emperor Augustus made into a garrison for his legions in 30 B.C. From the fourth century onwards mainly Christians lived in this Babylon, and wonderful churches were built within the Roman fortress walls. When the Arab commander Amr Ibn al-'As conquered Egypt in 641, his troops set up camp near Babylon. And from this army encampment the first Arab city on the Nile arose. The capital of the new Islamic province was then called **Fustât**, "the camp."

In the centuries which followed, the history of the Egyptian capital was written at the courts of distant Islamic rulers. It was the Turkish governor Ahmad Ibn Tûlûn who freed the country again and built himself a new seat of government to the north of Fustât. His city, **Al-Qatâ'i'**, was to be the splendid symbol of the sovereignty of Egypt, experienced for a short

time under the Tulunid Dynasty (868-905). But the Abbasid caliphs did not want to relinquish control of the rich province of Egypt, and 40 years later the interlude of the renegade emir was over. Al-Qatâ'i' was destroyed, but the great mosque remained unharmed, and still today testifies to the splendor of Tulunid buildings.

In the year 969, the Fatimid commander Gôhar conquered all of Egypt for his caliph, Mu'izz li-Dîn-Illah, and laid the foundations for a new town: **Al-Qâhira**, "The Victorious," named after the planet Mars (Arabic: *Al-Qâhir),* which could be seen in the sky at the time of the city's founding. And so it was born: the "mother of all cities," the symbol of the Tales of a Thousand and One Nights. The site of today's great bazaar quarter, Khân al-Khalîlî, was where the Cairo of the Fatimids (969-1171) stood, a forbidden city whose palaces were only intended for the caliph, his court and his soldiers; the ordinary people lived further south in Fustât, where a colorful Oriental life developed amidst the bustle of narrow streets and covered markets.

Only when Saladin seized power, in 1171, were the gates of Al-Qâhira thrown open to everyone, and around this center the splendid old town of present-day Cairo developed. It was also Saladin who built the Citadel which today is one of the emblems of Cairo, with its alabaster Mosque of Muhammad 'Alî. Fustât's heyday came to an abrubt end in 1168, when the crusaders advanced on Cairo from Jerusalem and Fustât was burned down – out of fear that it would be impossible to defend it. It never recovered from this catastrophe.

During the Mameluke era, which lasted from 1250 to 1517, Cairo's star shone brighter than ever. The sultans, always fond of ostentation, made huge profits in their trade with Asia and decorated their capital with the most beautiful buildings. Contemporary authors all

Right: Modern life has also brought heavy traffic to the Nile island of Al-Gazîra.

praised the beauty and riches of the city, the splendor of its mosques, palaces and gardens. The classical appearance of the city, with its hundreds of cupolas and minarets, dates from this otherwise very martial era.

With the Turkish invasion of 1517, Cairo became nothing more than an insignificant provincial capital. Many traces of the Turkish rulers can be found in the architecture of the city, but by and large these traces are unimportant.

The new rise in fortunes began with Muhammad 'Alî (1805-48). His Alabaster Mosque in the Citadel was only the beginning. The construction of the Suez Canal completely changed the face of Cairo. Muhammad 'Alî's grandson Ismâ'îl, as ostentatious as any Mameluke sutltan, wanted to present the illustrious guests at the inauguration celebrations in 1869 with a glittering metropolis. And so, in a great flurry of activity, new neighborhoods were built in the European style. A wide ceremonial street led to Gîza and the pyramids, and to the

Mena House Oberoi Hotel. Another led straight through the old town to the Citadel. And, finally, the new Opera House (which burned down in 1971) was to provide a stylish setting for the first performance of Giuseppe Verdi's opera *Aida*, which was commissioned especially for the occasion. However, because the maestro could not meet the deadline, the Suez Canal was inaugurated with a performance of *Rigoletto* instead.

European style continued to characterize Cairo's architecture (and politics). A most beautiful European quarter was built by the Belgians in the colonial style before the gates of Cairo in Heliopolis. Quarters such as Zamalek, Dokkî (Arabic: *Duqqî*) and Garden City show where the Europeans preferred to live (and still do): on the island of Al-Gazîra or on the banks of the Nile. This area was later also chosen by President Nasser as the stage for the representative buildings of the young Arab Republic of Egypt, whose architectural symbol is the 187-meter-tall Cairo Tower.

SHUBRĀ

IMBĀBA

AZ ZAMĀLIK

BŪLĀQ

AL-AZBAKIYA AL-MŪSKĪ

National Circus

Shaharazad

AL- ʿAGŪZA

M. Benevolent Society Hospital

AL-GAZĪRA

El-Gezira Sporting Club

Agricultural Museum

AD- DUQQĪ (DOKKI)

Botanical Garden

Cairo Zoological Garden

Cairo University

AR-RŌDA

AL-GĪZA

Marriott Omar Khayyam

Ramses Hilton

Nile Hilton

Cairo Tower

Pharao Garden

Ramses II. Monument

Saʿd Zaghlūl Monument

Cairo Exhibition Ground, Opera

Mukhtar Museum

El Gezirah Sheraton

Le Meridien Le Caire

Fountain

Cairo University Hospital

Qasr al-ʿEini Hospital

Al-Manyal Palace

Midan Fumm al-Khalig

Nilometer

Coptic Mus.

Mâri Girgis

Roman Fortress

Helnan Shepherd

El-Nil

GARDEN CITY

Railway Station

Midan Ramsis

Victoria

Windsor

Ahmad ʿOrabi

Gamal ʿAbd an-Nasser

Tourist Office

National Egyptian Mus. M. Tal

Arab League

Midan at-Tahrīr

Central Government (Mugammaʿ)

American University

Anwar as-Sadat

Parliament

Maglis ash-Shaʿb

Saʿd Zaghlūl

As-Sayyida Zeinab

Ibn Tūlūn Mosque

Gayer-Anderson Museum

Zeinhum Gardens

TULŪL ZEINHUM

Aqueduct (Ruined)

OLD CAIRO

Amr Ibn al-ʿĀs

St. George
Abū-Serga
St. Barbara
Ben-Ezra Synagogue

Al-Fustāt

Remains of old wall Al-Fustāt

ABDĪN

AD-DARB AL-AHMAR

Mus. of Islamic Art

Ahmad Mahir

Abdīn Palace (Presidental Palace)

Bāb Zuweila

Al-Maridāni

Sultān Hasan Mosque
al-ʿAtabi

Ar-Rifāʿi

Blue Mosque

Bāb al-ʿAtabi

Salāh ad-Dīn

M an-Nasir

Muhammad ʿAli Mosque

Citadel

Al-Bāb al-Gadid

Military Nat. Museum

Joseph's Well

Gohara Palace

Tombs of the Mamelukes

CITY OF THE DEAD

Imām ash-Shafiʿi Mausoleum

Muhammad ʿAli Mausoleum

al-Qarāfa

al-Qadiriya

al-Aqmar
Beshtak Palace
M. an-Nāsir
Sultan
Qalāʿūn
Barsbey
Sayyidna al-Husein
Al-Azhar Mosque
Al-Ghūri Complex
Al Muʾayyad
Khan al-khalili

Police Station

Qaymās al-Ishaqi

CAIRO

0   500 m

Excursions in Cairo

"Cairo is heaven on earth for those who have eyes to see," an enthusiastic Arab poet once said of the capital of Egypt. But today noise, dust, smog, chaotic traffic and swarms of people are often all that the newcomer to Cairo can see, and many return home thinking "if it wasn't for the pyramids and the Egyptian Museum..." Yet Cairo has far more to offer.

An Oriental kaleidoscope awaits you if you are prepared to walk through the city with open eyes and no preconceptions. As paradoxical as it may sound, Cairo can – and indeed should – be discovered on foot. Only on foot will you discover delightful surprises on every street corner: booksellers with their wares broadly spread out on the pavement; a tea house with men in turbans lazily puffing hookahs and immersed in a game of dominoes out front; the countless colorful food stalls or the vegetable barrows with their carefully-stacked pyramids of oranges.

Flower sellers take advantage of the unavoidable traffic jams to sell aromatic jasmine blossom chains to car drivers, and no one is ever surprised about the number of travelers who only have one horse power moving through the middle of the city traffic.

A leisurely stroll is without a doubt the best and most charming way of discovering Cairo's city center; for this is the only way of getting a feel for the rhythm of this fascinating and contradictory city. The following sections show how you can combine such a stroll with visits to Cairo's sights, and historical and artistic treasures. Each one combines sights that are located in close proximity to one another, presenting them in the framework of a short – or at times somewhat longer – excursion that can pleasantly be undertaken in the city; either on its own, or in combination with another.

THE MODERN CITY CENTER

The absolute epicenter of modern Cairo is the spacious **Mîdân at-Tahrîr**, site of both the bus and underground railway junction and the first stop on a shopping trip along the main shopping streets, Sh. Qasr an-Nîl, Sh. Talaat Harb and Sh. at-Tahrîr.

Looking at the most important of Cairo's modern buildings from south to north, you will first notice a not particularly attractive but nonetheless striking arched grey highrise monstrosity, known as the **Mugamma'**. Fourteen stories of beaurocracy are hidden behind the uninviting façade of this city hall built during the Nasser period. Opposite, on the Sh. al-Qasr al-'Einî, is the **American University**, which is housed in a small 19th-century palace.

To the right, next to the Mugamma', a small colonial-style villa is tucked away on the Sh. at-Tahrîr. This is the former headquarters of the **Foreign Ministry**, which has moved to the square skyscraper next to the Press Center on the Corniche an-Nîl.

Opposite the ministry is the **Arab League Building**. As a sign of "the return of Egypt to the Arab fold," the one-time center of pan-Arabian politics has recently been given a new coat of paint. The complex of the **Nile Hilton Hotel** is next to it. This blue housing block from the 1950s is certainly no architectural jewel, but for Egyptians and visitors from all over the world it is an institution: a meeting place with a fine cosmopolitan atmosphere. The square of the flat annex not only houses the offices of a number of airlines, but also comprises a pleasant, shady green area with terrace cafés, a pizzeria and grills.

In the north of Mîdân at-Tahrîr is the classical building of the Egyptian Museum. A beautiful garden with ancient Egyptian statues and a pool with the emblematic plants of the Pharaohs – the

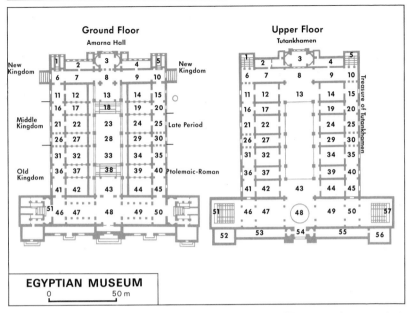

EGYPTIAN MUSEUM

0   50 m

lotus and papyrus – greet the visitor at the entrance to this unique collection of ancient Egyptian art.

The Egyptian Museum

A visit to this museum is an absolute must for every traveler through Egypt. It contains a fabulous treasure house of more than 120,000 objects. The sheer number of exhibits means that it is almost impossible to see everything in one visit. *The Official Catalogue of the Egyptian Museum* will serve as an excellent guide taking you through the main works of art in chronological order. It is necessary to get an additional ticket in order to visit the Hall of Mummies.

The **Ground Floor** rooms contain a great collection of ancient Egyptian sculpture and stonemasonry and, starting with rooms 43 and 47, lead clockwise through five millenia.

Right: The golden sarcophagus of Tutankhamen, a subject of intense contemplation.

The **Upper Floor** contains several almost perfectly preserved tomb finds. In addition, 11 royal mummies are on display here.

After President Sadat prohibited "visiting" the mummies on the grounds of piety in 1980, it took nearly 14 years before a new **Hall of Mummies** (Room No. 56) was set up. The remains of famous kings, such as Ramses II and his father Sethos, as well as the mummies of other kings and queens, are kept in the festively darkened room.

The **Treasures of Tutankhamen** are found in the galleries of the right wing and the side wing at the back. The tomb was discovered in 1922 by Howard Carter in the Valley of Kings. Of the more than 3,500 objects found in the tomb, 1,700 of them can be seen here. The most important of these are described briefly below.

The entrance to **Gallery 45** is flanked by two life-sized wooden statues of King Tutankhamen. These two figures, which are painted black and are partly gilded,

once stood guard in front of the wall leading to the burial chamber. In the center of the room is a gilded shrine, upon which the god Anubis rests in the form of a black jackal.

In **Gallery 40** you will find many beautiful chests and caskets of cedar wood, inlaid with ebony and ivory. A masterpiece of ancient Egyptian art work is a painted wooden chest which shows the Pharaoh hunting and in battle in a splendid chariot.

The left-hand display cases of **Gallery 35** house many statuettes of the king. These so-called *Ushebtis* were supposed to carry out the obligatory work in the realms of the blessed in place of the deceased. The small faience axes and baskets belong to them, too.

In **Gallery 25** you will find the beautiful thrones, the most famous of which is the Golden Throne with the portrayal of the royal couple under the sun's rays of Aton. It is wooden, overlaid with gold, and inlaid with semi-precious stones, glass and silver.

In **Gallery 9** stand three gilded ritual biers, each of which is flanked by divine animals in the form of a lioness, a cow and a fanciful creature with the head of a hippopotamus.

In **Gallery 4** you will find displays of jewelry and amulettes. The main exhibit in the room is the famous golden mask inlaid with lapis lazuli. It once covered the head of the royal mummy which lay in the 225-kilogram golden coffin (in the display case on the far right). This coffin was then placed inside two further coffins which fitted into each other (one of which is on the far left). The entrails of the king were buried in four small, beautifully worked coffins (in the display case on the right).

These miniature coffins were placed in the four ampulla cavities of the alabaster shrine in **Gallery 8**. The four kings' heads served as seals for the ampullae. This alabaster shrine was hidden in the gilded wooden shrine and was protected by the four goddesses Isis, Nephthys, Selkis and Neith. To the left of this you will find the king's chariots. Next to this are four golden wooden shrines which lead to **Gallery 7**.

These fitted inside one another, with the sarcophagus bearing the three coffins of the Pharaoh in the innermost one. The king's mummy itself still rests in the middle one of the three human-shaped coffins in the Valley of the Kings.

Other treasures that can be seen on the Upper Floor include:

– The burial treasures of Queen Hetepheres, mother of King Cheops (Fourth Dynasty) in **Gallery 2**.
– The burial treasures of the Kings' Tombs of Tanis (Twenty-first and Twenty-second Dynasties) in **Galleries 2** and **11**.
– The jewel room in **Gallery 3**, a fantastic collection of valuable jewelry from all epochs of ancient Egypt.
– The burial treasures of Juja and Tuja, the parents-in-law of King Amenhotep III (Eighteenth Dynasty) in **Room 13**.
– Burial gifts from the grave of Sennedjem from Dair al-Madîna (Twenty-ninth Dynasty) in **Room 17**.
– Papyri with religious texts and drawings in **Room 29**, as well as along the stairways to the upper floor.

Al-Gazîra and the West Bank

The island of **Al-Gazîra** can be easily reached on foot from Mîdân at-Tahrîr over the Tahrîr Bridge. A trip in a carriage or on a boat (stand and moorings on the Corniche) can be a pleasant alternative to walking.

Al-Gazîra Square (Mîdân al-Gazîra) is dominated by a **statue of Sa'd Zaghlûl**, founder of the Wafd party and the first prime minister of the independent monarchy. Directly behind it is the entrance to the new **Cultural Center**, built

Right: The Church of Al-Mu'allaqa. Far right: One of the mashrabîya windows at the Coptic Museum.

on the site of Cairo's old exhibition grounds. The centerpiece of the well-maintained park is the Oriental-style cupola of the **Opera House**, which was opened in 1988. Its rather pompous post-modernist beauty is the work, strangely enough, of a Japanese architect. Two of the former pavilions now house a small **Museum of Modern Art** and a **Municipal Gallery** for temporary exhibitions of the work of contemporary artists.

In the small park to the south of the island is the **Mukhtâr Museum**, which houses a collection of works by Egypt's most famous modern sculptor, Mahmûd Mukhtâr. The southernmost tip of the island is marked by the round tower of the **Sheraton Hotel**. The terrace café of the hotel offers a wonderful view of the Nile in general, and of the fountains in the middle of the river.

The landmark of the island is the 187-meter-high stylized concrete lotus blossom of the **Cairo Tower**. On a clear day a wonderful panorama of the city extends from the viewing platform and from the tower restaurant. At the foot of the tower is the **Pharaonic Garden**, a small park containing ancient Egyptian statues. Not far away the **Obelisk of Ramses II** stands directly on the Nile. On its southern side you will find the **Andalusian Garden**, laid out in the Moorish style, a favorite destination for the inhabitants of Cairo.

To the north of the Cairo Tower are the Al-Gazîra Club's sports facilities, which border on the district of Zamâlîk. This well-kept district is the preferred location of embassies and foreign missions. Apart from these you will also find a number of chic boutiques and the **Cairo Marriott Hotel** right on the Nile. The flat central building of the hotel was originally one of the palaces built for the inauguration of the Suez Canal. It is here that Emperor Napoleon III and Empress Eugénie were intended to find fitting accomodation for themselves.

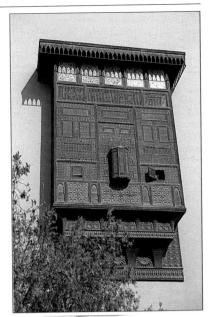

OLD CAIRO

Al-Gazîra and the west bank of the Nile have only been included in the city district of Cairo since the 19th century. Today, the districts of Imbâba, 'Agûza and Dokkî are located here. You can get to the west bank by taxi or on foot over one of the three bridges over the narow branch of the Nile.

The **Museum of Agriculture** (Sh. ad-Dokkî), which presents the history of Egyptian farming from Pharaonic times to the present day, the small **Botanical Gardens**, with their beautiful royal palm trees, and the **Zoo** (both Sh. al-Gîza) are all worth visiting. The Cairo Zoo perhaps has fewer species to offer the visitor than the many which are kept in European and American zoos, but the pretty park is an ideal place to escape from the noise and dust of the city.

It is here that the imperceptible transition from one large city to another takes place; the city border, once separating Cairo and Gîza, runs south of Cairo University, whose central building with its prominent cupola is visible from afar.

In the south of the city, across from the Nile island of Ar-Rôda, lies Old Cairo. This is the historical core of Cairo, where the first Arabic city in all Egypt was founded, **Fustât**, which arose alongside the Greco-Roman town of Babylon.

The walls of the Roman fortress of Babylon have been partially preserved, and surround Cairo's oldest quarter: the **Coptic Quarter**. The beautiful churches and the Coptic Museum, which are found in this section of Cairo, are among the most unusual places to visit in the otherwise Islamic city.

No overwhelming cathedrals await the visitor here, but rather somewhat smaller houses of God, which are enhanced, thanks to the darkness of their interiors, by an aura of mystical solemnity. Attending a church service here is a very special experience, indeed. The liturgy is similar to that of the Greek Orthodox Church, though it is recited in part in the ancient Coptic language.

The **Roman Fortress** once lay directly on the Nile, the course of which ran about 400 meters further east in ancient times. Harbors found six meters underground show that Babylon was once an important center of trade. The fortress itself dates back to the time of Augustus (30 B.C.). It was completely renovated under Trajan (98-117) and restored once more in the time of the Byzantine Emperor Arcadius (395-408).

The old entrance gate to the Coptic Quarter is opposite the Mârî Girgis metro station, several meters below street level. About 100 meters further south you come to two great round towers. And between them you will find the Museum Garden. Above the north tower rises the Greek Orthodox **Church of St. George** (19th century), of which the neighboring convent is also part. The ancient appearance

Above: The Ben Ezra Synagogue, built on the site of a 7th-century Christian church. Right: There is always time for a little chat between friends.

of the south tower of the fort can still be seen, though it has only been partly preserved. The solid towers, with their three-meter-thick walls, once stood 20 meters tall with a diameter of 33 meters. To the right of the south tower is the main entrance to one of the oldest and most beautiful churches in Cairo.

The Church of the Holy Virgin is called **Al-Mu'allaqa**, "The Hanging One" in common parlance, because it was built over the Roman southwestern gate. Nothing remains from the fourth century when it was founded, and only a few remains from its many renovations and restorations until the 18th century can still be seen. The church was given its present form in 1775. Already at its entrance you will be enchanted: the Baroque-style façade, with a wide stairway leading up to it, rises over a small palm garden. Behind the covered forecourt you come upon a pretty inner courtyard with a fountain.

Inside this splendid church, three arcades shaped from ancient white marble columns assymetrically divide the nave and the side aisles. As in all Coptic churches, the altar room is divided into three parts: the chapels of St. George (left), Jesus Christ (middle) and John the Baptist (right) are separated from the prayer room by a magnificent iconostasis of ebony, inlaid with ivory, from the 13th century. The icons above the iconostasis date back to the 18th century. In front of it is a dainty marble pulpit from the 11th century. You get to the chapel of Takla Hajmanot, one of the most famous Coptic saints (13th century) and to the baptistery along the right-hand aisle. You will find a wonderful view of the walls of the southern ramparts through a glass window in the floor.

Leaving the church, you can turn right from the small front garden and into the **Museum Garden**, where you will find some beautiful and unique objects on exhibit out of doors. The sixth-century

carved stone windows with portrayals of an elephant and a graceful gazelle are quite charming.

Even from the outside the **Coptic Museum** is a joy to behold, with its artfully elaborate dark brown *mashrabîya* windows and its polished walls. The rooms of the museum itself house a unique collection of Coptic art treasures which document the stylistic development from what were, at the beginning, Hellenic-Roman art forms to more Byzantine-influenced icon paintings, and later to ornamental art showing strong Islamic influences. The beautiful weavings that can be seen here represent a high point in Coptic art.

On the ground floor you will find individual, ornamental finds from buildings, tomb stelai and small funeral chapels. On the upper floor are examples of the famous Coptic cloths, and next to them fine wood and ivory carvings and different kinds of metal objects, pottery and glassware. The wonderful frescos, brought here from churches and tombs, and the collection of Coptic writings are also worth seeing.

From the Museum Garden, to the right of the ticket-office, a small alley leads into the Coptic Quarter. After a few paces you come to a second church, a visit to which should not be missed: the **Abû Serga Church**, dedicated to the martyrs Sergius and Bacchus. The present building dates only from the 10th and 11th centuries, and was erected under the Fatimids, but the founding of the church probably dates from the fifth century. Its spiritual roots can be traced even further back, for, according to legend, the Holy Family is supposed to have lived where the present-day crypt now disappears into the ground water.

The church's interior is dark and exudes an aura of mystery and secrecy. Its architecture is a classic example of an early Christian basilica, with a raised nave and two side aisles. The open framework of the roof, along with the galleries on the flat roofs of the side aisles and the arcades between the aisles, give the building a certain lightness. The high altar, which stands beneath a wooden cupola-shaped baldaquin, can be admired from the chapel of St. George to the left. The chapel to the right of the inner sanctum is dedicated to St. Michael. Here, too, the entire altar area lies behind the ebony wall of an iconostasis which is decorated with ivory incrustations and carvings.

If you turn right behind the Abû Serga Church, after only a few meters you will come upon the **Church of St. Barbara**, which dates back in its present form to the 10th and 11th centuries. Especially worth seeing in the three-naved basilica are the beautiful marble pulpit and the iconostasis with its ivory inlays.

To the right you will come to a most unusual feature of the Coptic Quarter: the **Ben Ezra Synagogue**. This was originally the site of the Church of St. Michael, which was founded in the seventh century but was destroyed in the 11th century under Caliph Al-Hâkim. In the 12th century, the Jews of Cairo rebuilt the house of worship and turned it into a synagogue. In 1984, a sensational discovery was made during renovation work on the building: a veritable treasure trove consisting of 200,000 parchment fragments with writing in Hebrew, Aramaic and Arabic. Scrolls with Old Testament texts are exhibited behind glass in precious silver cases in the chancel.

To the northeast of the Coptic Quarter lies **Fustât**. Little remains of this once thriving trading center which stretched from the banks of the Nile all the way to the heights of the Jabal al-Muqattam. Seven-storied houses, splendid mosques and an abundance of wares on sale reflected the richness of the city which overshadowed even Baghdad in its heyday. Founded in 641, Fustât was rebuilt after the great fire of 750 and became

Right: Through belly dancing, the Tales of a Thousand and One Nights come to life.

even larger and more beautiful than ever. However, after the city went up in flames for a second time in 1168, only the harbor area was rebuilt.

The only building left from Fustât's great past is the **Mosque of Amr Ibn al-'Âs**, which the conquerer of Egypt had built in 641. After being altered several times, the oldest Islamic building in Cairo was given its present appearance in 1798. The interior of the mosque is especially impressive: regular rows of seemingly endless white columns are grouped in four aisles around a square court. Many of the ancient marble columns were replaced by modern replicas in the course of the last restoration work carried out in 1986. The legendary columns that once stood next to the prayer niche were also removed at the time. It is told that Caliph Omar sent these columns flying through the air from Medina with a single crack of the whip.

Behind the mosque to the east you will find Cairo's potteries on the **ruins of Fustât**. Their smoking kilns evoke images of the burning city. Anyone with professional or even amateur interest in archeology can visit the excavations in Fustât. However, little more than ground walls and the remains of a highly developed irrigation system are to be seen. Interesting finds and beautiful handicrafts from Fustât can be admired in the Islamic Museum.

The only well-preserved building from the golden age of Fustât is the **Nilometer** on the southern tip of Ar-Rôda island. The well house, which has been restored several times, was constructed on the orders of the Abbasid caliph Al-Mutawakkil in 861. Its main purpose was to measure the exact height of the waters of the Nile. It wasn't until the construction of the Aswan Dam that the Nilometer become redundant. It is possible to inspect the inside of the Nilometer, but you will have to ask the guard to unlock the door for you.

THE ISLAMIC OLD TOWN

Of the three fairy-tale cities of the Islamic Orient – Cairo, Damascus and Baghdad – the Egyptian metropolis was the only one to remain undamaged by the devastation caused by Mongol attacks, and was therefore able to retain its medieval feel. But not only the buildings have been preserved, the atmosphere of that legendary time has also remained: with the colorful bustle of its markets; with people haggling in words and gestures; with quiet moments over a cup of Turkish coffee. Perhaps this is an ability which Middle Easterners have in particular – to preserve their society for centuries; an ability which is bound in with the consciousness that human beings are not the measure of all things.

But as splendid as the mosques and palaces of Islamic Cairo may be, many of them are threatened with falling into ruin. This state of affairs has come about in part due to the decades of neglect of the buildings, but also because of the damage suffered in the great earthquake that shook the region in October 1992. The densely-populated Islamic old town was one of the worst-hit quarters of the city. Added to that is the steadily rising ground water level which, since the construction of the Aswan Dam, has been putting more and more historical buildings into jeopardy.

The last comprehensive inventory of historical monuments considered to be worth protecting was carried out in the 1950s, but this list comprised only the monuments built before the 18th century. Since 1972, comprehensive restoration work has been underway, but the scope of restoration will now have to be considerably enlarged if Cairo's immense number of treasures of Islamic architecture is to be saved for posterity.

The centers with the most important sights are Fatimid Cairo with the Khân al-Khalîlî Bazaar, the Al-Azhar Mosque, the mosques between the city gates Bâb al-Futûh and Bâb Zuweila, and the area around the Citadel and the necropolis.

Khân al-Khalîlî Bazaar

The large bazaar quarter is located in the area where Al-Qâhira was founded as a Fatimid residence in 969. The most famous, but not the only *sûq*, as the bazaar is called in Arabic, is the Khân al-Khalîlî. Next to it is the *Sûq an-Nahâssîn*, the market of the coppersmiths who still make the minaret tips today. But the old bazaar divisions into wares and guilds are no longer so strictly adhered to. And so you will sometimes see a spice merchant next to a butcher, or a shoemaker in the middle of the cloth market.

The whole shopping paradise stretches in a maze of alleys on both sides of the busy main street Sh. al-Azhar. The real **Khân al-Khalîlî** begins opposite the Al-Azhar Mosque on the Mîdân Husein. A good point of reference, in case you

Above: Rest and relaxation in a coffee house. Right: The elaborately decorated minaret of the Mosque of Muhammad an-Nasîr.

should lose your way in the Khân al-Khalîlî, is the minaret of the **Husein Mosque** (closed to non-Muslims!), which is shaped like a pencil and can be seen for quite some distance.

The bazaar quarter takes its name from a high official called Al-Khalîlî, who some 600 years ago built a *khân* here, a combination of a warehouse and a hotel. Precious stones, silks and spices were the valuable trading goods of the time, but today you can buy anything you could possibly want. Although there are plenty of souvenirs on offer, the Khân al-Khalîlî is in no way a bazaar strictly for tourists. The inhabitants of Cairo still buy their jewelry here, and the neighboring **Sh. Muskî**, officially called Sh. al-Gôhar al-Qâ'id, is like one huge department store where you can buy everything from aluminium pots to bridal gowns.

A trip to the bazaar would not be complete without stopping off for a glass of sweet, hot *shay* (tea) or a cup of *ahwa* (coffee). The Khân al-Khalîlî offers plenty of opportunities for this. In the aracades opposite the Husein Mosque there are several cafés, some of which have a loggia on the second floor with a pleasant view of the wide square. The café on the fifth floor of the **Husein Hotel** (corner of Mîdân Husein and Sh. Muskî) offers a fantastic panorama. The entrance to the hotel is in the dimly-lit alley behind the arcades where Cairo's oldest coffee house, **Fishawi**, is also hidden. With its pompous but cloudy mirrors and its threadbare interior, it possesses all the charm of decaying splendor – a romantic setting, even if only at second glance.

The newest coffee house in the Khân al-Khalîlî is the exact opposite. It is nestled in a beautifully renovated medieval building where the Indian five star hotel chain Oberoi has created a stylish Oriental café. The café, which also has an exquisite restaurant, takes its name from Cairo's most famous man of letters, the Nobel Prize-winning author **Naguib Mahfouz**. Just follow the street which leads into the bazaar next to the Husein Mosque and you can't miss it.

Al-Azhar Mosque

Only a few buildings today reflect the splendor of the Cairo of the Fatimids. One of these is the **Al-Azhar Mosque**, founded in 970 by General Gôhar as a Friday mosque for the new official residence of Al-Qâhira. It soon became a center of Islamic scholarship. Initially a shelter for the Shiite beliefs practiced by the Fatimids, the University Mosque became the theological center of orthodox Sunni teachings after Saladin seized power. In the Western World, the Al-Azhar Mosque has sometimes been referred to as "The Vatican of Islam," in order to convey some idea of its importance in the world of Islam. Unlike the Pope, however, the Sheikh of Al-Azhar does not claim to be the final authority on all religious questions.

Until 1961, only a very limited course of studies could be pursued here: theology, the Islamic sciences, Islamic Law (Arabic: *Shar'îa*) and Arabic were the only subjects taught at the university. Today, there are additional faculties of trade, medicine, pharmacology, engineering, agriculture, the natural sciences and the arts. But even those who would rather choose a secular subject of study have to attend lectures and take exams in theology and Islamic law.

Over 100,000 students are taught by some 4,000 professors here. Since 1964, the doors of the Islamic University have also been open to women – both as students and as professors. The entrance requirement is generally a graduation certificate from one of the Al-Azhar schools that are scattered around the country. Foreign students begin their studies with a preparatory year in which they concentrate on Arabic, English and Islamic subjects.

Over the centuries, the Al-Azhar Mosque, which means "The Shining

89

One," has been renovated and rebuilt many times. A blueprint showing its ground plan and the individual phases of construction is displayed in the entrance area. From the mosque, which is dominated by three minarets, you walk through the **Barbers' Gate** (where the students' heads were once shaved).

To the left is the **Library**, with its 60,000 manuscripts. This was erected with the building on the right as a *madrasa* (mosque school) in the 14th century. Behind a portal with beautiful wood carvings the central court opens out. This dates from the 10th century Fatimid building. The decoration of the colonnade, with its medals and arched paneling, comes from the 12th century. The portal itself and the minaret above it were built by Sultan Qâ'it Bey (1469).

The covered prayer room, a giant columned hall, joins the court. The prayer

Above: Erecting a tent, as has been done for centuries. Right: The entrance to the mausoleum of Sultan Qalâ'ûn.

niche in the central nave marks the original division of the five-aisled hall as it was built by Gôhar. It was only in the 18th century that it was extended by a further four aisles to the east. Here you can still sometimes see students sitting in semicircles at the feet of their teachers, as has been done for almost a thousand years. Otherwise, today almost all the lectures take place in the modern university buildings.

Between Bâb al-Futûh and Bâb Zuweila

The most beautiful buildings in the heart of the bazaar quarters can all be found on the **Sh. Mu'izz li-Dîn-Illah**, once a majestic 15-meter-wide boulevard at the heart of the Fatimid's palace city. Taking the main street, **Sh. al-Azhar**, as a dividing line, you can stroll northwards to the Bâb al-Futûh. A second walk will take you from the Sh. al-Azhar through the cloth market and on to the Bâb Zuweila.

The **Madrasa of Sultan Ashraf Barsbay**, built in 1425, at the crossing of the Sh. Muskî and the Sh. Mu'izz li-Dîn-Illah, dominates the spice market, where today, as in ancient times, aromatic incense and exotic spices are offered for sale. Inside the somewhat dilapidated building, the blue and gold ceiling decorations, the inscribed friezes and the beautiful inlaid pulpit are well worth having a look at.

On the other side of the Sh. Muskî more profane attractions are bound to catch your eye. Here you join the maze of streets of the Khân al-Khalîlî, with their numerous jewelry shops, and, a few meters on, the polished copper and brass wares in the Coppersmiths' Bazaar can be seen. Soon afterwards, you come to an immense building complex with three cupolas and minarets.

The first building on the left is the **Mausoleum of Sultan Qalâ'ûn**, which the ruler had built, along with a madrasa and a hospital, in 1284 and 1285. Behind the monumental grey façade, the actual

beauty of which is easily overlooked, one of the most splendid Islamic buildings in Cairo is tucked away. A tall gate leads to a dark corridor which leads in turn, to the left of the entrance, into the inner courtyard of the madrasa, which has not been so well preserved. After a few steps you come to an atrium with four ancient pillars.

The entrance to the burial chamber itself is crowned by a pointed arch with wonderful ornamental plasterwork, and is closed by the latticework of a *mashrabîya* gate. This is one of the earliest examples of the kind of intricately carved wooden latticework found all over the Middle East as decorative architectural elements or as furniture ornamentation. Originally, such wooden lattices were used as air-permeable shades for keeping clay water jugs cool. This is where they take their name from: *mashrabîya* literally means "that which belongs to the drinking place."

Inside of the mausoleum is the largest mashrabîya wall in Cairo. Measuring 17

meters by four meters, it surrounds the sarcophagi of the Sultan and his son Muhammad an-Nâsir. The mysterious semi-darkness of the high, square room is emphasized by the kaleidoscopic effects of the stained-glass windows. The central cupola rises like a baldaquin above four pillars and four massive columns, the arcades of which are decorated with beautiful plasterwork and which join together to form a graceful octagonal ensemble. The walls are ornamentally lined with different colored marble panels, stone paneling with polychromatic inlays, and golden inscriptions. The prayer niche is inlaid with colorful, gleaming mosaics and divided by rows of alabaster pillars. The incredible diversity and beauty of the decoration in this mausoleum gives a good idea of just how splendid other Mameluke buildings must once have been.

Above: The bazaar, Cairo's traditional shopping center. Right: View over the Islamic old town, all the way to the Citadel.

The neighboring **mosque** was built by **Sultan Muhammad an-Nâsir**, son of Qalâ'ûn, in 1304. Unfortunately, its rooms are closed to the public, although the fine stonemasonry of the artistically ornamented minaret can be admired from the street.

Next to this is the **Tomb Mosque of Sultan Barqûq**, who was reburied by his son in a considerably larger mosque in the northern necropolis. Of special interest are the wonderful bronzework doors, the star patterns of which are partly inlaid with silver. In front of the restored mausoleum, which contains the grave of one of the daughters of the sultan, lies the madrasa, built on a cross-shaped ground plan. The attractive painted wooden ceiling of the main wing rests on four ancient porphyry pillars.

Opposite the mosque complex is the 14th-century **Palace of Amîr Beshtak**. This impressive building is one of the very few examples of Mameluke secular architecture and has only recently been beautifully restored. The entrance to the palace can be found on the neighboring side street.

The guard at the Beshtak Palace also has the key to the charming **Well House of 'Abd ar-Rahmân Kathkûda** (built in 1744), where the main street forks in a northerly direction. A *sabîl kuttâb*, as this combination of a public well (situated on the ground floor) and Koran school (on the upper floor) is called, was the most popular form of religious endowment in Ottoman times. The interior of the well house is decorated with blue Syrian tiles. Note the portrayal of the great mosque of Mecca with the black cube of *ka'aba* at its center.

The path to the Bâb al-Futûh continues to the left of the sabîl kuttâb. To the right of the second side street you will see the beautiful ornate façade of the **Al-Aqmar Mosque**, built in 1125. As one of the few preserved buildings from Fatimid times it plays a key role in Islamic art. All the

decorative elements of the façade were new creations which were to become part of the stonemasons' standard repertoire: ribbed shell niches with central medallions or small flanking pillars, texts from the Koran under the molding, and the stalactite paneling.

If you turn down the next (third) side street, after a short distance you will come to what is considered to be one of the finest private Ottoman-era residences in all Cairo: the **Beit as-Suheimî**, from the 17th century. Of all the rooms in the house, which are still partly furnished, the reception rooms, the harem and the baths are particularly interesting.

Back again on the main street, on your right you will see the striking minarets of the **Al-Hâkim Mosque** (built in 1013). The small ribbed cupolas introduced the style of minaret which would remain popular until early Mameluke times, and which were given the nickname "Fatimid pepper pots." Their solid trapezoidal foundations were only added later to strengthen them.

Restoration work carried out on the mosque was financed by an Ismailite sect from India, and, since its completion, the mosque of the Fatimid caliph once again shines in all its former glory. White alabaster paving stones cover the square of the broad courtyard which is bordered by aisles of covered arcades. You can get a good view of the mosque from the neighboring city wall, which you can access by climbing the steps at the Bâb al-Futûh, the "Gate of Conquests."

In 1087, Vizier Badr al-Gamâlî had a new and bigger city wall built around Al-Qâhira, the first monumental stone contruction of the Islamic era of Egypt. Here in the north of the city the two gates, **Bâb al-Futûh** and **Bâb an-Nasr**, have been preserved, along with the 600-meter-long city wall between them.

In the south of town, the Bâb Zuweila is the only one of what was once a total of 60 city gates that is still standing. To get there you return to the intersection of the Sh. al-Azhar and Sh. Mu'izz li-Dîn-Illah. The street crossing is flanked by two

93

splendid Mameluke buildings: the **madrasa** on the right and the **Mausoleum of Sultan Al-Ghûrî** (1500-16) on the left.

The distinguishing characteristic of the Madrasa of Al-Ghûrî is its 65-meter-high minaret with its five miniature cupolas. The interior rooms give you some idea of their one time glory: the richly decorated arched construction of the four halls around the inner courtyard, and the fine east wall with its prayer niche, are particularly interesting. The mausoleum opposite nowadays houses an adult education center. Make sure you take a look at the cupola room to the right of the entrance, which has been tastefully renovated and is now used as a library.

If you have a little time to spare, you should squeeze in a visit to the restored **Caravanserai of Sultan Al-Ghûrî**, which is only 100 meters away to the left of the mausoleum. Today, the spacious rooms of the medieval warehouse and traders' hotel are used for exhibitions of contemporary handicrafts.

In earlier times, the road between the madrasa and the mausoleum was covered, and silk merchants spread out their wares between them. Today, too, you can see the colorful bales of cloth piled high, though they are no longer of expensive and luxurious silk, but of cotton or glittering synthetic materials instead. Following the street southwards you will pass by many interesting shops: on the right-hand side one of the now rare fez makers; a little further on a warehouse with sacks of raw cotton. If you dare to walk down the side streets on the left, you will come across numerous little shops, and among them sooty coal workshops, where charcoal for hookahs is made.

The **Bâb Zuweila** at the end of the Sh. Mu'izz li-Dîn-Illah can be seen from quite a distance. It is crowned by the two

Right: Traditional music can often be heard in the Islamic old town.

minarets of the **Al-Mu'ayyad Mosque**. Together they make up an imposing architectural scene, chosen by the Mameluke sultan (1412-21) for his mosque. The portal of the prayer room is decorated with stalactites, arabesques and inscriptions from the Koran, and is sealed off by a solid bronze gate.

The main wing of the great Friday mosque is flanked by the mausoleums of the sultan and his family. Its splendid marble inlays and colorful wooden ceiling are particularly striking. It is well worth climbing up to the minarets and to the city wall just for the view, but you should also be prepared to see some shocking sights from such a vantage point: for nowhere else is the progressive decay of the old town more obvious, despite all the renovation work.

On the other side of the Bâb Zuweila, the Sh. Mu'izz li-Dîn-Illah continues as the medieval **Lane of the Tent Makers**. Colorful festival tents are still manufactured here today. If you turn right after passing through the city gate, you will only be a short way from the **Mîdân Ahmad Mâhir**, with the Museum of Islamic Art.

Museum of Islamic Art

Generousy laid out in the museum's rooms, a wide selection from an enormous fund of more than 80,000 objects, mostly from Egypt, but also from Turkey and Persia, can be seen here.

Islamic art can only be understood when seen against the background of the hostility toward pictures which is rooted in religious rules which forbid the portrayal of people and animals. However, the creative powers of Islamic artists were by no means stifled by this dictate; they were simply concentrated in specific thematic areas. Although, with few exceptions, there is no figured sculpture or painting, the mastering of stonemasonry and calligraphy enabled artists to

create pictorial worlds of quite different dimensions.

The decorative form which has been developed from geometric patterns or plant images is the dominion of Islamic artists. A literally inexhaustable source of this is the Arabic script, with its decorative, curved forms. The art of calligraphy takes on a special significance through the religious content of the basic texts – usually verses from the Koran or short blessings.

One of the most fascinating characteristics of Islamic art is the perfection with which complicated curved forms are combined with empty spaces – a canon of composition which was carried out with a great sense of perfection, and which pervades everything from the slightest detail to the mightiest architecture.

Where there is neither painting nor sculpture, the reigning queen of the fine arts is undoubtedly architecture. But what would architecture be without ornamental stucco reliefs, inlays, and stone and wood carvings?

Together, the mosques and the marvellous exhibits in the museum show the artistic furnishings of Islamic buildings. Alongside many beautiful architectural exhibits, the museum contains wonderful mosque lamps and Koran stands, furniture with valuable inlays, brass works, a lovely and admirable polychromatic marble well, mashrabîya works, ceramics, and a rich collection of carpets on the upper floor.

Around the Citadel

The **Mîdân Salâh ad-Dîn** is an excellent starting point for a visit to the Citadel and the surrounding mosques. Looking around the square you will see some wonderful sights: rising high above the mighty round towers of the **Bâb al-'Azab** and the fortress walls of the Citadel is the cupola of the **Muhammad 'Alî Mosque**; on the other side of the square two monumental structures face each other – on the left the **Madrasa of Sultan Hasan** (1363), on the right the **Ar-Rifâ'î**

95

Mosque which echoes its style (1905). To the right you will see the **Mahmûd Pasha Mosque** of red and white stone (1568). A little further back you will find the rather similar looking **Amîr Akhûr Mosque** (1503).

Your sightseeing trip is best begun with the **Madrasa of Sultan Hasan**, considered to be a masterpiece of Mameluke architecture. The monumental portal is decorated with a cascade of stone stalactites. It leads into a high anteroom, the beautiful interior of which might easily be overlooked in the dim light. On the other side of a dark corridor a splendid inner courtyard opens out. Its square is surrounded by four vaulted halls, the *îwâns*.

Each of the îwâns was reserved for one of the four orthodox law schools of Sunni Islam, and in each of these halls the law scholars taught their students according

Above: A view inside the Muhammad-'Âli Mosque at the Citadel. Right: At the Mîdân Salâh ad-Dîn.

to their tradition. Behind them are several stories of living and studying rooms for the teachers and students. Mosque schools like this one, known as a *madrasa* (Koranic school), were introduced in the 12th century by Sultan Saladin as theological study centers in order to combat and to stamp out the Shiite heresies of the Fatimids.

The cross-shaped ground plan of the complex, to which much of the tomb of the founder is joined, is determined by the four schools of law. The extravagant splendor of this mosque has always been and will always remain tasteful – whether it be the polychrome marble inlay of the floor or the îwâns; or the shining gold mosaic of the prayer niche; or the massive gold- and silver-covered bronze portals which lead to the mausoleum of the sultan. Particularly impressive is the decorative molding with its Kufic inscription from the Koran. The domed burial chamber contains the sarcophagus – albeit unused – of the sultan, as well as a beautiful Koran stand.

The impressive dimensions and luxurious furnishings of the **Ar-Rifâ'î Mosque** make it, too, worth a visit. Here you will find the tombs of the family of the khedive Ismâ'îl and of King Fu'âd, as well as that of the shah of Iran, Reza Pahlevi, who died in exile.

Before climbing to the Citadel, though, you should visit the **Ibn Tûlûn Mosque** (876-79) located nearby, which the Turkish governor Ahmad Ibn Tûlûn had built as the centerpiece of his residence. Although it may not be obvious at first glance, the grandiose simplicity of the mosque complex and the clarity of its decoration makes it one of the finest in Cairo. At the same time, the Ibn Tûlûn Mosque is a good example of the classical conception of a mosque which was not a shrine, but was more of a meeting place for believers. Its characteristic ground plan, with a large courtyard with a walkway shaded from the sun, dates back to the house of the Prophet to which Islamic believers were invited for communal prayer.

The center of the spacious courtyard of the Ibn Tûlûn Mosque is the well house, which when being restored in 1296 was completely rebuilt. Around the courtyard is a colonnade with three aisles, and five aisles in the main wing. The most splendid of the six prayer niches is shaped like an apse, and is adorned with marble inlays and gold mosaics. The twining filigree ornamentation of the pointed-arch arcades and the 128 different carved windows represent an impressive display of the stonemason's skill. Of particular interest is the spiral minaret: it is 40 meters high and reminiscent of the minaret of the great mosque in Samarra, the architecture of which Ibn Tûlûn emulated for his own structure. A fine view of the mosque's crenellated outer walls and of the town can be seen from the minaret.

Next to the entrance, a sign points the way to the **Gayer Anderson Museum**. The two beautifully restored private houses (16th and 17th century) give an idea of the elegant and comfortable life once lived in Cairo.

97

Above: An encounter between old and new on the edge of Cairo.

If you want to go from the Mîdân Salâh ad-Dîn to the **Citadel** on foot, you should go up the easterly street to the New Gate, the **Bâb al-Gadîd**, which was built under Muhammad 'Alî, and there turn right into the fortress. Sultan Saladin began the construction of the Citadel in the year 1176, but it was not completed until 45 years later by his nephew Al-Kâmil. Troops were still stationed here as recently as 1984. Today, a **Police and Military Museum** is housed on the premises of the old state prison, which was closed down in 1985.

The **Muhammad 'Alî Mosque** is the landmark of the Citadel as well as of Cairo. This was built by the sultan in 1830 in the Turkish style. It takes its second name, the "Alabaster Mosque," from its rich covering of this valuable stone. The domed main building with the sultan's mausoleum is joined to the inner courtyard, which is surrounded by col-umned arcades. Despite the effusively-luxurious decor, reflecting the prevailing tastes of the time, and despite its having long been reviled by modern art historians, the building actually does have its charm. One curiosity here is the clock tower on the west front of the courtyard; a gift given by the French king Louis Philippe in return for the obelisk of the Place de la Concorde.

Until the Ottoman victory of 1517, Egypt's sultans made their home in the Citadel. But of all their palaces and mosques, only the **Muhammad an-Nâsir Mosque**, built in 1334, still stands. Its shimmering green cupola and faience-adorned minaret reflect an obvious Persian influence. Going back to time of Saladin, the legendary 90-meter-deep **Well of Joseph** at the back of the mosque supplied the Citadel with water.

At the south façade of the Muhammad 'Alî Mosque is a wide square bordered by the **Gôhara Palace**, built under Muhammed 'Alî in 1814. The west wing is open to visitors and contains paintings, furniture and porcellain dating to the days of the sultan. The lookout terrace in front of the entrance provides a wonderful panoramic view of the city below. On a clear day you can even see the pyramids of Gîza.

The Necropolis

At the foot of the Muqattam mountain range to the south and west of the Citadel, you will find one of the largest cemeteries in the Islamic world. Stretching out for six kilometers, hundreds of cupolas and minarets rise up over the splendid tombs of sultans and high officials. Flat buildings or rows of simple brick sarcophagi characterize the more simple plots in the cemetery. Driving past the necropolis along the great north-south tangent of the **Sh. Salâh Salim**, you will be amazed to see that this necropolis is actually very much alive.

Buses and cars travel through its streets, alongside the donkey carts of the garbage collectors. Power lines and television aerials bring home the fact that the 20th century has arrived in the necropolis. For the tombs here are inhabited by the living – and have been for a long time. As early as in the Middle Ages pilgrims found accomodation here, as did the guards and administrators of the great mausoleums. Scarce housing and immigration from the countryside have turned the necroplis into a densely populated slum quarter since the 1920s. There are now some 300,000 people living here, and you will find small shops and workshops throughout the area. Wide sections of the necropolis are also supplied with electricity and water.

The best way to visit the most interesting parts of the necropolis is to hire a taxi for half a day. To the south of the Citadel is the older, more run down part of the necropolis, where you will find the so-called **Tombs of the Mamelukes**. The **Mausoleum of Imam ash-Shâfi'î**

(1211) is well preserved and decorated, and has been restored many times throughout the centuries. The beautiful cupola is even today an important place of pilgrimage, for the founder of one of the four orthodox schools of law is worshiped as an Islamic saint.

In the immediate vicinity is the **Mausoleum of Muhammed 'Alî**, whose family was laid to rest here, along with their dependants, in ornately decorated marble sarcophagi.

A few kilometers further to the north (about level with the Al-Azhar-Mosque) you will find the **Tombs of the Caliphs**, as Oriental travelers of the 18th century called these splendid Mameluke burial mosques in the northern necropolis. The **Mosque of Sultan Barqûq**, built in 1411, is one of the most important sights in this part of the Islamic cemetery. The best view of this massive mosque, with its columned courtyard, and of all the wonderful cupolas in this part of the cemetery, is from the roof and the minarets above the west wing. The east wing of the mosque contains the prayer niche and a lovely stone pulpit which flank the mausoleum of the sultan and his family. The exteriors of the stone cupolas are decorated with zigzag ribbing, while the interiors are ornately painted with geometrical designs.

The most beautiful building in the necropolis, indeed, a prime example of Islamic architecture in Cairo, is the **Qâ'it Bey Mosque** nearby. It was part of an enormous complex which also included a dervish monastery, hostels and staff accommodations. Behind the splendid, richly-ornamented façade is the madrasa with the mausoleum of the sultan (1468-96). This is luxuriously decorated with marble floors, inlays, colored glass windows and gold mosaics in the prayer niche. The ornamental artwork of the stone tomb cupola – a network of floral arabesques and geometric forms – is best admired from the roof.

THE PYRAMIDS OF GÎZA

To the west of Cairo, where the Sahara borders the Nile Valley, is the plateau of Gîza. Here you will find some of the most famous constructions in human history: the Pyramids of Gîza, built by kings Cheops, Khafre and Mycerinus in the middle of the third millenium B.C.

If you want to have the pyramids all to yourself, you will have to get up very early in the morning, or else go on a long walk into the desert. And even there it won't be long before Muhammad, Alî or Abdu appear and try to persuade you to hire a ride on their animal, which – depending on where you come from – will answer to the proud name of Bismarck, Napoleon or Nelson. But they may also sell postcards, souvenir papyri or offer themselves as a picturesque foreground for a photo of the pyramids.

At seven o'clock in the morning the world is still "at peace": the caravanserei at the foot of the pyramids is still dozing quietly, and the pyramids and the Great Sphinx lie peacefully before you. As the day goes on the scene gets busier. But even the hustle and bustle, the school groups, tourists, traders and camel drivers have their own charm – albeit a very different one.

Even in ancient times the pyramids were regarded as one of the Seven Wonders of the World, and still today their perfection of form and outstanding engineering arouse astonishment and admiration. This aura of wonder was nourished not least by the countless stories and rumors which surrounded them, and which still exist in modern times.

But the Pyramids of Gîza are not the only ones in Egypt, nor are they the oldest. The history of pyramid building

Left: The massive blocks of the Khafre Pyramid were hauled by human strength alone.

started long before the reign of Cheops. More than 30 pyramids from the Ancient and Middle Kingdoms line the edge of the desert between Gîza and Maîdûm, which lies some 80 kilometers further south. And though many of them are in an advanced state of ruin, on a clear day a spectacular pyramid panorama can still be seen at the outskirts of Cairo.

What began as a sand or brick hill over a burial shaft, during the First Dynasty was gradually enlarged to an immense solid cut-stone mass, the façade of which was decorated with splendid niche architecture. Such cut-stone constructions as these, although with a smooth façade, became the tomb form typical of the high officials of the Old Kingdom. Because they resemble the benches in front of Arabic houses they are called *mastabas* (benches). But the builders of the king's tomb strove to achieve monumental proportions. The 60-meter-high Step Pyramid of Saqqâra, with six levels of mastabas one on top of the other, is a fine example of this striving.

The breakthrough to the classical pyramid came during the reign of King Snefru, founder of the Fourth Dynasty. The struggle to achieve this is reflected in the fact that no less than three pyramids were built: the Pyramid of Maidûm, originally conceived as a step building; the so-called Bent Pyramid of Dahshûr, whose steep angle of incline had to be flattened at the top because of the danger of collapse; and, finally, the first true pyramid, the Red Pyramid of Dahshûr.

Snefru's son Cheops had the last word with his pyramid in Gîza. With this masterpiece he had reached the zenith of Egyptian pyramid construction. Even the pyramid of Khafre is not as large, and after Mycerinus the dimensions became ever more modest. During the Middle Kingdom, pyramids were no longer built of stone: a core construction of a stone skeleton filled with mud bricks was surrounded by polished limestone.

101

Above: The Great Sphinx of Gîza has kept its secret for millenia.

The methods and techniques used in the building of the pyramids still puzzle scientists today. Because the written sources of the ancient Egyptians reveal nothing on this matter, one has to resort to theories, and there are many of those. Recent research has come up with the following likely picture of the building of the two great pyramids in Gîza.

The building site was levelled around an outcropping rock core, and a flat plateau was thus created upon which the ground plan of the pyramid was marked out. After the underground burial chambers had been dug, horizontal stone layers were built up to form the solid core. The shining white limestone covering was put in place at the same time.

The stones for the core came from the immediate surroundings, while the coverings of white limestone were brought from Tura on the eastern bank of the Nile; those of Cheops' pyramid came from almost all the limestone quarries in the country. With the aid of rollers and sleds the huge blocks, which had an average weight of two to three tons, were transported on ramps. There is quite a bit of debate today as to what these ramps would have looked like. Most recently, scholars have tended to favor the opinion that a ramp was leaned against one side of the pyramid which could be extended as progress was made. But it must have given way to steps for the last third of the construction. There the architects must have employed the lifting devices of which Herodotus speaks. He also speaks of up to 100,000 people having worked on the pyramid, although modern scholars have figured out that around 20,000 Egyptians more probably worked on it for about 20 years. Of these, 5,000 were specialists, the rest simple laborers.

The pyramids stand tall on the plateau of Gîza, surrounded by the tombs of the royal family and high officials. The largest of all is the **Pyramid of Cheops**. Originally, it had side lengths of 230.38

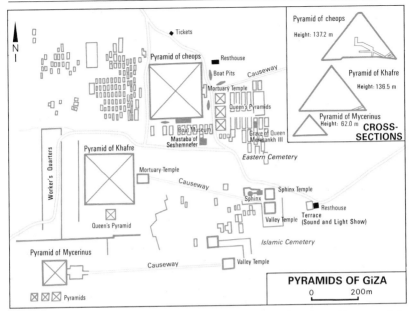

PYRAMIDS OF GiZA
0   200m

meters and a height of 146.59 meters. But because, like all pyramids, it has been used as a stone quarry since the Middle Ages, the Pyramid of Cheops today only has a base length of 227.5 meters, and at its angle of incline of 51°50'40" it is about 137 meters high. The layout of the pyramid's ground plan was aligned to the four points of the compass, so that the diagonal is precisely northeast-southwest. The average deviation is only 3'40". More than two million cut stone blocks make up the enormous Pyramid of Cheops, which is almost 2.6 million cubic meters in volume. The original 210 stone layers, of which 201 remain today, were covered with fine white limestone and granite at the bottom.

The entrance on the north side of the pyramid is covered with huge gabled blocks. It remained hidden beneath the stone covering until the Middle Ages. Today, you enter the monument through a hole made by grave robbers some meters deeper. It almost seems as though the robbers knew their way around the pyramid. For after about 40 meters their tunnel exactly meets the original entrance shaft, still blocked by massive stones, where the diagonal ascent to the Great Gallery starts.

The passageway to the 35-meter-deep underground **Rock Chamber** is closed to visitors, as is the so-called **Queen's Chamber** which adjoins the end of the Great Gallery. For a long time it was thought that in different building phases each of these two chambers had been planned as a burial chamber. However, it is now almost certain that the old architects did not keep changing the plans for the Great Pyramid, but that the complex system of corridors has its roots in religious beliefs.

The monumental architecture of the **Great Gallery** (47 x 1-2 x 8.5 meters) is overwhelming. The walls of polished limestone are covered by a grandiose ceiling in the form of a corbeled vault. The niches above the banquettes on both sides served as anchors for granite blocks which were set free after burial in order to seal the system of corridors. At the end of the gallery you come to a low passageway which was once closed by four stones, only one of which can still be seen today. Behind this is the impressive **King's Chamber** (10.45 x 5.20 x 5.8 meters) at a height of nearly 43 meters. It is covered by red granite and contains the empty shell of the granite sarcophagus. The mummy of Cheops has never been found.

Above the burial chamber there are five chambers for reasons of statics, the uppermost of which has a gabled roof. The air shafts which branch off from the burial chamber were regarded as the dead ruler's corridors to heaven.

To the east of the pyramids once stood the great **Mortuary Temple**, of which only some of the black basalt paving stones have been preserved. Here, on the other side of the modern asphalt road, you will find the beginning of the causeway which was used for burial processions from the Valley Temple (houses have been built over it). The grounds of the Mortuary Temple were flanked by two 50-meter-long pits for the barques in which the Sun God made his journey to heaven according to ancient Egyptian belief. On the south side of the Pyramid of Cheops are two more from the total of five boat pits.

In one of them, in 1954, a fully preserved cedar boat was found in 1,224 separate pieces. Directly above the site of the find a **Boat Museum** was built to house the 43-meter-long and almost five-meter-wide boat, in which it is presumed the grave furnishings, or perhaps even the king himself, were probably brought to the pyramid. The second boat pit beside it is closed, and will remain so for the foreseeable future.

Opposite stand the three small **Queens' Pyramids**, intended for the

Right: Camel riders out for a jaunt in the landscape of Gîza.

tombs of Cheops' mother and two of his wives. Behind them is the **East Cemetery** with the mastaba graves of the royal family and the pyramid temple priests. Only three tombs here are open to the public. The **Tomb of Queen Meresankh III**, Khafre's wife, which is decorated with beautiful reliefs, should be seen (in the fifth street of tombs behind the Queens' Pyramids).

On the way to the Pyramid of Khafre you pass by the **Mastaba of Seshemnefer**, a prince and vizier of the Fifth Dynasty. The tomb itself is closed to the public, but it has an interesting façade with a portico supported by two columns, and life-sized seated figures of the tomb owner, and is certainly worth having a look at.

The **Pyramid of Khafre** is recognizable by the well-preserved limestone covering at its tip. This and the somewhat steeper angle of incline of 53°10' gives you the impression that Khafre's pyramid is larger than that of his father Cheops. In truth, though, it is a little smaller, with a base length of 215.25 meters and an original height of 143.5 meters (today 136.5 meters). The covering of the two bottom layers was of granite, as in the Pyramid of Cheops, and over that came a coating of gleaming white limestone.

At no other pyramid has the funeral complex been so well-preserved. On the east side of the pyramid, which in ancient times was surrounded by a 10-meter-wide covered walkway, are the mighty blocks of the **Mortuary Temple**. An almost 500-meter-long **causeway**, in the form of a limestone-walled corridor, once joined it to the **Valley Temple** on the border of the fertile lands.

At one time, one pair of sphinxes guarded each of the entrance gates to the Valley Temple. The unadorned, solid architecture of this structure makes it particularly impressive. The famous seated figure of the king with the falcon of Horus (which is now in the Egyptian Mu-

seum) was discovered in the open shaft of the anteroom. It was almost certainly one of the 23 statues of the Hall of Pillars, of which today only the rectangular indentations in the alabaster floor remain. Sixteen granite pillars supported the ceiling of the T-shaped hall which is lined with granite slabs.

The corridor to the pyramid causeway leads off to the right. From there you get a good view of the **Great Sphinx** and of the ruins of its temple. For a long time it was thought that this monumental stone creature, with the body of a lion and the face of a man, was a representation of King Khafre. Now it is thought that it was the guardian of a sun temple which stood at the eastern corner of the immense complex of the great Pyramid of Cheops.

Between the paws of the 57-meter-long, 20-meter-high figure, chiseled out of a limestone outcropping, stands the **Dream Stela of Thutmose IV**. On it the Eighteenth Dynasty king tells of a dream he had as a prince in the shadow of the Sphinx. The sun god Harmachis, "Horus on the Horizon," was at that time thought to be personified by the Sphinx. He promised him that he would become king if he freed his image from the sand.

It was probably due to the rise of the cult of the sun during the Fourth Dynasty that Khafre's son and heir erected a considerably more modest tomb for himself. The **Pyramid of Mycerinus**, with side lengths of 102.2 x 104.6 meters and an angle of incline of around 51°, is "only" about 66 meters high. The granite covering of the lower third of the pyramid can still be seen. Over that the pyramid was covered with fine white limestone.

In 1837, the remains of a mummy (probably that of King Mycerinus) were found when the burial chamber was opened. A basalt sarcophagus was also found, but it was lost when the ship transporting it to England sank. On the south side of the pyramid are three smaller secondary pyramids; on the east side the remains of a mortuary temple and of the causeway can be made out.

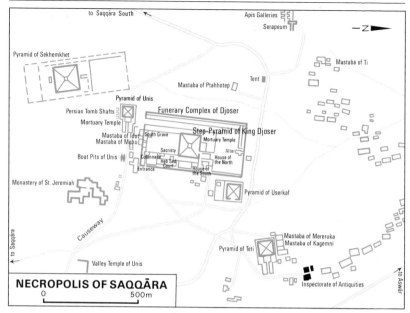

NECROPOLIS OF SAQQĀRA
0   500m

THE NECROPOLIS OF SAQQÂRA

A field of pyramids stretches for several kilometers along the edge of the desert to the south of Gîza. The largest and most important necropolis is **Saqqâra**, 15 kilometers away, and the road leading to it does offer several interesting sights. If you prefer a car journey to a ride across the desert, take Pyramids Road and turn left on the road to Saqqâra about 1.5 kilometers before the Pyramids of Gîza. The road leads along a canal to the countryside environs of Cairo. Small villages line the way, and between the newer concrete buildings many traditional houses made of mud bricks can still be seen. Behind these villages are little palm groves and green fields touching the desert to the west.

During the journey you will come across carpet shops everywhere, the façades of which are covered with layer

Right: The limestone wall enclosing the site of the Step Pyramid of Saqqâra.

upon layer of colorfully decorated carpets. The most famous weaving mill in the village of **Harranîya** was founded in 1952 by Ramses Wissa-Wassef, with the intention of carrying on the tradition of Coptic tapestries.

Four kilometers before Saqqâra the road forks to Abûsîr, the royal necropolis of the Fifth Dynasty. The **Pyramids of Abûsîr** are very badly preserved, with the exception of an outstanding group of three; from north to south these are the tombs of kings Sahure, Niuserre, and the largest of all, Neferirkare.

The huge area of the **Necropolis of Saqqâra** stretches for a length of some seven kilometers. From the beginning of the First Dynasty onwards it served as a cemetery for nearby Memphis. Fifteen kings of the Old Kingdom, countless princes and princesses, and high officials and priests from all other epochs of Egyptian history had their tombs erected here. The importance of this necropolis was so great that a busy pilgrim tourism started as early as during the Eighteenth

Dynasty, for those who wanted to vist the venerable monuments of their ancestors. The Serapeum, the tombs of the sacred Apis bulls, and the burial places of other sacred animals such as the falcon, ibis, baboon and cow, made the necropolis a very important place of pilgrimage in Ptolemaic times.

Even from a distance, the **Step Pyramid of King Djoser** dominates the necropolis. The tomb of this Third Dynasty king (circa 2700 B.C.) is one of the oldest monumental stone constructions in the history of the world, and at the same time marks a very important stage in the development of the classical pyramid. The fascination with stone not only resulted in the tomb being built in dimensions never before seen, but also led to a "petrification" of all known building materials. Numerous buildings in the area around the pyramid were intended to be available to the Pharaoh for eternity, and so wood, reeds and other plants, wickerwork and tiles were reproduced in the eternal material of stone.

The king's tomb stands at the center of an architectural complex which was once surrounded by a 544 x 277-meter-long wall. Fourteen portals are integrated in the niches of this imposing limestone wall, but only the one in the southeast corner really opens into an entrance passage. A small vestibule, closed off by a pair of false stone door leaves, leads to the **Colonnade**. Forty-two recesses are formed by the tongue-walls of the fluted columns, which were carved to look like bundels of reeds. It has been speculated that statues of gods or kings once stood there. Before you enter the broad courtyard in front of the pyramid, take a look at the open doorway to the right, also reproduced in stone.

The Step Pyramid rises to a height of 60 meters, over a ground base of 121 x 109 meters, in six sloping steps. But it was not planned to be a construction of such massive proportions from the beginning: at first a simple single-stepped mastaba was erected over the underground burial chamber, upon which, after several

extensions were made, a four-stepped pyramid was to be built. The building phases of the mastaba can be clearly deduced from the layering of the core stonework. The monumental six-stepped construction, the stone "ladder to the heavens" by which the Pharaoh would climb to the realms of the gods, is the result of a final change in plans.

The true (but not accessible to the public) king's tomb is a chamber, walled in by huge granite blocks, at the bottom of a 28-meter-deep vertical shaft. Forty thousand valuable stone vessels were discovered in the subterranean galleries.

In front of the pyramid to the right is a building with three fluted columns. The actual significance of this "little temple" is unclear, although it may have been a sacristy for the ritual instruments and clothing which the king needed for the celebration of his accession to the throne,

Above: The Step Pyramid of King Djoser in Saqqâra. Right: A papyrus column in the courtyard of the North Palace.

the *Heb Sed*. Behind this sacristy is a chapel courtyard, the **Heb Sed Court**, believed to have been the "petrified" site of the king's jubilee and rejuvenation festival. The mock buildings on either side of the court represent the chapels of Upper and Lower Egypt. Figures of gods representing the provinces of ancient Egypt once stood in their niches.

North of the Heb Sed Court are two courtyards with another pair of mock buildings: the **Palace of the South** and the **Palace of the North**, which may have been the throne rooms of the king, and which symbolized his right to rule over both parts of the country. If you look at the pyramid from here you will see the remains of the polished limestone blocks which once covered all six steps. Inside the Palace of the South there is an interesting stone ceiling simulating wood. Hieratic inscriptions of visitors from the New Kingdom are displayed under plexiglass, visitors who described the "Temple of Djoser" as if "the sky was within and Ra was rising in it."

The papyrus columns on the eastern court wall of the Palace of the North are especially beautiful. They represent the earliest examples of this kind of plant column. Opposite the Palace of the North lie the few remains of the **Mortuary Temple**, and in front of it you find the **Statue Chamber** with the famous seated figure of Djoser (the original of which is in the Egyptian Museum).

If you climb up the sandy terrace on the other side of the Mortuary Temple and walk round the Djoser area you will come to the **South Tomb**. The significance of this long construction, with its underground galleries similar to those of the pyramid, is still a puzzle. The same applies to the neighboring façade with its beautiful frieze of uraeuses, the sacred asp of the Pharoas.

The **Pyramid of Unas** is in the southwestern corner of the Djoser complex. Unas was the last king of the Fifth Dynasty. The monument, which once stood 44 meters tall, now seems more like a heap of rubble. But a visit to its burial chamber is a must. The walls of the anteroom and of the burial chamber itself are decorated over and over with vertical rows of hieroglyphs; each symbol was engraved and painted over in blue. Unas was the first king to have these pyramid texts inscribed in his tomb: they are a collection of ritual phrases, magical formulas and prayers which were intended to safeguard the continued existence of the dead ruler and guarantee his acceptance into the circle of gods. The walls around the solid basalt sarcophagus are decorated with woven reed patterns, and the gabled ceilings with patterns of stars.

The ruins of the **Mortuary Temple** on the east side of the pyramid are strikingly bizarre. The granite pillars of the old portal are the only objects still standing and mark the end of the almost 700-meter-long causeway from the Valley Temple to the Mortuary Temple. About half way up, part of the ascent has been

reconstructed with its original relief decorations. Not far away are two 45-meter-long walled boat pits for the king's solar barque.

At the foot of the steps leading from Djoser's South Tomb to the pyramid of Unas you will notice a 22-meter-deep shaft with the vaulted ceiling of a granite shrine at the bottom. The Tomb of Amentefnacht is one of the **Persian Shaft Tombs**, a group of tombs dating back to the time of the Twenty-sixth Dynasty and the Persian occupation, regarded as the Twenty-seventh Dynasty.

Three of these tombs on the south side of the Pyramid of Unas have been connected by a corridor to facilitate viewing. In the middle is the **Tomb of the Chief Physician Psamtik**, on the right that of his son **Peden-Isis** and to the left that of the royal admiral **Tja-en-nehebu**, whose richly decorated mummy was also discovered. The chambers are decorated with beautiful inscriptions, copies of the Pyramid Texts of Unas. The remarkable burial treasures of Hekaemsaf in the

Egyptian Museum (Upper Floor, Room 3) have left posterity with some idea of the richness of the furnishings of these shaft tombs.

The Mastabas of the Old Kingdom

Here in Saqqâra, too, the mastabas of the nobility are grouped like settlements around the royal pyramids. This type of tomb is rectangular with slightly sloping walls. The burial chamber with the stone sarcophagus is located at the bottom of a vertical subterranean shaft which was filled with stone and earth after the burial ceremony, and was then sealed forever. The altar, on which offerings to the dead were left, looks like a niched doorway, although it was closed – at least to the living, at any rate. The dead, however, could come through this false door at any time to satisfy their appetites with the offerings that had been left for them.

What initially started out as a small chapel on the east side of the mastaba gradually developed, over the course of time, into a devotional palace in the mastaba's interior. The walls were now richly decorated with scenes depicting earthly life, such as working in the fields, fishing and hunting, dancing and playing, artisans busy in their workshops, and many other things.

Of the many mastabas in Saqqâra, only a few are open to the public. While they are certainly all worth seeing, the most beautiful one should not be missed. The **Mastaba of Idut**, a princess of the Sixth Dynasty, lies to the south of the Djoser area. Five of the total of 10 chambers of her tomb are decorated with colorful relief cycles, the other rooms were built as storerooms. In the neighboring **Mastaba of Mehu**, a vizier of the Sixth Dynasty, the wonderful wall paintings have been just as well preserved.

Right: A coach driver patiently waiting for customers in Saqqâra.

About 500 meters northeast of the Step Pyramid you come to a stone hill which was once the **Pyramid of Teti** (Sixth Dynasty). The tombs of his notables are opposite the king's grave. The most famous of these is the **Mastaba of Mereruka**, which the vizier was allowed to erect for himself and his family. The quality of the reliefs is not consistent in all 32 rooms, but the main chambers have been decorated with great care. The offering hall is especially interesting, with its six supporting pillars and its life-sized Ka statue of Mereruka in front of the false door and the offering altar.

It is joined to the east by the **Mastaba of Kagemni**, who, like Mereruka, was a vizier under King Teti. The tremendous dimensions of this complex take in 10 rooms, five of which are decorated with interesting scenes.

To the northwest of the Step Pyramid of Djoser is a large tent offering a pleasant opportunity to stop for refreshments. And for those who do not want to carry on walking through the desert sand, you don't have to: here you can hire horses, donkeys, camels and, for those who feel somewhat insecure in the saddle, even little carriages, all at prices which are open to negotiation.

From here it is not far to the **Mastaba of Ptahhotep** (Fifth Dynasty). The small cultic chapel here is a high point in any visit to Saqqâra. Furthermore, the unfinished reliefs decorating the entrance corridor give you a good idea of the stonemasons' technique.

In the **Mastaba of Ti** (Fifth Dynasty) – which lies hidden to the north of the tent in a sand basin – you will find some of the finest examples of ancient Egyptian reliefs. On the walls of the offering hall is a complete agricultural cycle, from sowing to harvesting (over the entrance and the east wall, left). Scenes such as boat building, statue sculpting and carpentry stretch from the east wall to the south wall. You can see the Ka statue of Ti

through slits in the wall (the original is in the Egyptian Museum). The scenes showing the slaughter of animals on this wall were intended to provide the tomb owner with nourishment. He is also depicted here eating a meal.

Two false doors in the west wall mark the offering place. The procession of offering bearers on the north wall is moving towards this point. Above the graceful female figures is the most famous scene of this tomb: Ti on a boat journey in a thicket of papyrus.

The Tombs of the Sacred Bulls of Apis

On the way to the Mastaba of Ti you pass a concrete semicircle, built to protect the statues of Greek poets and philosophers from the sand and the wind. This was the end of the long Sphinx avenue, which led from the fertile lands through the necropolis. A paved street leading to the **Serapeum** began here.

When the god Serapis was introduced into Egypt at the beginning of the Ptole-maic era, the cult of the Apis bulls had already existed for thousands of years. In Memphis, where a living bull was always kept in the temple as an incarnation of Apis, he was worshiped as the "soul of the god Ptah" and as a god of fertility. After its death, the temple bull became Osiris-Apis and was buried in Saqqâra with great ceremony. The similarity of the names made it easy to fuse the human Serapis into one divinity with Osiris-Apis. His center of worship, and a popular place of pilgrimage, became the Funerary Temple in Saqqâra with its bull crypts, yet today it is almost completely destroyed. The first burial chambers were built under King Amenhotep III in the Eighteenth Dynasty; Prince Khaemwase, one of Ramses II's sons and High Priest of Memphis, built the first gallery. The catacombs which are open to the public were built in the Twenty-sixth Dynasty. The burial chambers are on both sides of the 340-meter-long corridor. Here 29 plundered stone sarcophagi, weighing about 69 tons, were discovered.

MEMPHIS:
The Sunken Royal City

It is highly recommendable to combine a journey to Saqqâra with a visit to **Memphis**, 1.5 kilometers further south in a grove of palm trees near the village of Mîtrahîna.

For more than 3,000 years, Memphis was regarded as one of the most important cities in Egypt. This was the "Scales of the Two Lands" on the border between Upper and Lower Egypt. Founded around 3000 B.C. by Menes, the legendary first king of the First Dynasty, again and again throughout the course of history it became the royal residence and center of administration.

Memphis's golden age was that of the Old Kingdom, despite the fact that the kings of the Fourth and Fifth Dynasties resided in their palaces in the pyramid

Above: The fallen Colossus of Ramses II. Right: The Alabaster Sphinx. Far Right: Another view of Ramses II, in granite.

cities of Gîza and Abûsîr. The confusions of the First Intermediate Period depleted Memphis of its capital status. But tradition and its convenient location meant that the old royal city was never forgotten, and it developed into a lively metropolis equalled in the whole of the Orient only by Babylon.

Only when Alexandria was founded did Memphis's star begin to fade, although it long remained esteemed and important as the place where kings were crowned. The strengthening of Christianity finally resulted in this heathen metropolis fading into complete obscurity. The founding of Fustât brought about the wholesale pillage of stones from the existing buildings to supply the new construction work. Centuries of continued destruction coupled with annual flooding of the Nile virtually flattened the once flowering city. It was first rediscovered in the 19th century.

Little more than a broad expanse covered in piles of rubble remains of the splendor of ancient Memphis. And even

this area has not been thoroughly researched. A few finds from the ancient metropolis are, however, exhibited in a small **Open-air Museum**.

To the right of the entrance to this outdoor museum, in the shadow of a protective concrete construction, lies the toppled **Colossus of Ramses II**. The limestone statue, originally 13.5 meters in height (today 10.5 meters), shows the Pharaoh dressed in royal clothing, with a pleated apron and the classical striped head covering, from the headband of which a solid stone uraeus rises whose "fiery breath shall destroy the enemies of the king." Around the chin the ceremonial royal beard is bound – an artificial beard; this was part of the royal apparel of the otherwise clean-shaven king. The statue's crown is weather-worn. The royal cartouches are engraved in the breast plate, the arms and the belt. Two of the five names of a Pharaoh are always surrounded by the oval of the cartouche, whose form goes back to a protective knotted amulette.

A second **Colossus of Ramses** of red granite found nearby was set up in front of the train station in Cairo in 1954. A third granite colossus has recently been erected again and impressively dominates the entire area.

The center of the complex is a beautiful **Alabaster Sphinx**. The 4.25-meter-long and eight-meter-high statue has no inscription, but its style suggests the Eighteenth Dynasty. Perhaps is was King Amenhotep II who had this sphinx erected to be the guardian of the temple of the god Ptah, for it must have been very near this location that a temple to Ptah, who was the principal god of Memphis, once stood, and to which the Colossus of Ramses belonged.

On the other side of the road you can see the walls of the **Embalming Site of Apis**, with its beautiful alabaster embalming tables (Twenty-sixth Dynasty). This is where the sacred animal of Ptah, the Apis bull, was mummified before it was buried in the tombs of the necropolis of Memphis in Saqqâra.

CAIRO

The area code for this region is 02

Arrival

Most visitors to Cairo arrive by plane. The international airport is situated at the northern outskirts of the city in the suburb of Heliopolis. On departure from **Cairo Airport** please remember that it consists of two separate terminals next to each other: Terminal 1 – for international flights except Egypt Air; Terminal 2 – all Egypt Air flights.

Accommodation

Hotels are concentrated around the pyramids in Gîza, in the city center and near the airport in Heliopolis. The comfortable hotels in Gîza guarantee a relaxed stay, and the enterprising tourist is best served with a hotel in the city center.

LUXURY: Pyramids: **Mena House Oberoi**, Pyramids Rd., tel. 3833222, fax. 3837777; **Pyramids Park**, Cairo-Alex Desert Rd., tel. 3838666, fax. 3839000; **Jolie Ville Mövenpick**, Cairo-Alex Desert Rd., tel. 3852555, 3835006; **Forte Grand Pyramids**, Giza, Alexandria Desert Rd., tel. 3830383, fax. 3830023; **Oasis Hotel**, Alexandria Desert Rd., tel. 3831777, fax. 3830916; **Sofitel Le Sphinx**, Alexandria Desert Rd., tel. 3837444, fax. 3834930. *City Center:* **Cairo Marriott**, Gazîra Island, tel. 3408888, fax. 3406667; **Le Meridien Le Caire**, Rôda Island, tel. 2905055, fax. 2918591; **Nile Hilton**, Corniche an-Nîl, tel. 5780444, 5780666, fax. 5780475; **Ramses Hilton**, Corniche an-Nîl, tel. 5754999, fax. 5757152; **Semiramis**, Corniche an-Nîl, tel. 3557171, fax. 3563020; **Helnan Shepherd**, Corniche an-Nîl, tel. 3553900, fax. 3557284; **El-Gezîrah Sheraton**, Gazîra Island, tel. 3411333, fax. 3405056. *Heliopolis:* **Heliopolis Mövenpick**, Cairo Int'l Airport Rd., tel. 2470077, 4180761; **Swisshotel El Salam**, Sh. 'Abd al-Hamîd Badâwî, tel. 2974000, fax. 2976037; **Le Meridien Heliopolis**, Sh. 'Urûba, tel. 2905055, fax. 2918591.

MODERATE: Pyramids: **Pyramids Hotel**, 198 Pyramids Rd., tel. 38735900, fax. 3834974. *City Center:* **Arc en Ciel El-Borg**, Gazîra Island, tel. 3400978, fax. 3403401; **El-Nil**, Garden City, tel. 3542800, fax. 3552878; **President**, 22 Sh. Taha Husein, tel. 3400652, fax. 3411752; **Victoria**, 66 Sh. al-Gumhûrîya, tel. 5892290, fax. 5913008; **Windsor**, 19 Sh. al-Alfi, tel. 5915277, fax. 5921621.

BUDGET: Pyramids: **Lido Hotel**, 465 Pyramids Rd., tel. 5730272, fax. 5750292. *City Center:* **El Husein**, Mîdân Husein, near the Khân al-Khalîlî, tel. 5918664, 5918089; **Green Valley**, 33 Sh. 'Abd al-Khalik Sarwat, tel. 3936317; **New Hotel**, 21 Sh. Adlî, tel. 3927033, fax. 3929555.

YOUTH HOSTEL: **El-Manial**, 135 Sh. 'Abd al-'Azîz as-Sa'ûd, tel. 840729.

Restaurants

All luxury hotels have one or more excellent restaurants serving international and Egyptian specialities. In addition, we can recommend the following restaurants:

ORIENTAL: City Center: **Abu Shakra**, 69 Sh. al Qasr al-'Einî; **Arabesque**, 6 Sh. Qasr an-Nîl; **Felfela**, 15, Hôda Sha'arawî (street branching off Sh. Tal'at Harb); **Hagg Muhammad as-Samak**, Sh. 'Abd al-'Azîz (opposite the Omar Effendi department store); **Sofar**, Sh. Adlî; **Al-Hati**, Md. Halîm. *Pyramids:* **Christo's**, Pyramids Rd. (opposite the Mena House Hotel), outstanding fish specialties; **Garden Felfela**, Cairo-Alex Desert Rd.; **Sakkara Nest** and **El-Dâr**, both on the road to Saqqâra.

INTERNATIONAL: City Center: **Carroll**, 12 Sh. Qasr an-Nîl; **Estoril**, 12 Sh. Tal'at Harb, (entrance in the small passage to Sh. Qasr an-Nîl); **Paprika**, Corniche an-Nîl (next to Broadcasting House); **Rex**, Sh. 'Abd al-Khâliq Sarwat.

CAFÉS: **Groppi**, Md. Tal'at Harb; **Groppi's Garden**, Sh. 'Abd al-Khâliq Sarwat; **Indian Tea House**, Sh. Tal'at Harb (in the passage); **Lappas**, Sh. Qasr an-Nîl.

Museums / Galleries

Egyptian Museum, Md. at-Tahrîr, open daily 9 am to 4 pm (on religious holidays to 3 pm).

Akhnaton Gallery, Sh. 26th July (opposite Hotel Marriott Omar Khayyam) – This is a state-operated art center with three galleries for contemporary art, a library and a small cinema. Open daily except Friday 10 am to 1:30 pm and 5:30 to 9:30 pm.

Coptic Museum, Old Cairo, open daily 9 am to 5 pm.

Railway Museum, Md. Ramsîs. Open daily except Monday 9 am to 1 pm.

Agricultural Museum / Cotton Museum, Sh. ad-Dokkî, open daily except Friday 9 am to 4 pm.

Islamic Museum, Md. Ahmad Mâhir, open daily 9 am to 5 pm, closed Fridays 11:15 am to 1:15 pm.

Museum of Royal Carriages, 82 Sh. 26th July – unique collection of royal carriages.

Mahmûd Khalîl Museum, 1 Sh. Kafur, Cûza – excellent collection of Impressionist art, including works by Renoir, Degas, Manet, Monet, Gauguin, Toulouse-Lautrec and Van Gogh. Open daily except Mondays 10 am to 6 pm.

Manial Palace Museum, 1 Sarây Manial, Rôda Island (next to Club Mediterranée) – The interior of the palace, built in 1901, houses a collection of manuscripts, embroidery, ceramics, carpets and paintings; the small **Hunting Museum** in the garden can be visited daily from 9 am to 2 pm.

Visiting Mosques

In Egypt almost all mosques may be visited by non-Muslims. Remember that clothing should be respectful and not revealing. Women must cover their heads with a scarf in the Al-Azhar Mosque. Before entering a mosque, shoes must be taken off. Some mosques supply felt covers for shoes; it is customary to leave a small tip for this service. Many mosques are closed Fridays between 11:30 am and 1:30 pm.

Cairo by Night

Two daily sound-and-light shows in several languages take place at the Pyramids of Gîza, at 6 pm (in summer at 6:30 pm), 7 pm (in summer at 7:30 pm)and 8 pm (in summer at 8:30 pm): Mondays in English, French and Spanish; Tuesdays in French and Italian; Wednesdays in English, French and German; Thursdays in Japanese, English and Arabic; Fridays in English and French; Saturdays in English, Spanish and Italian; Sundays in Japanese, French and German.

An additional show is planned for the Citadel. For further information, inquire at your hotel.

All luxury hotels run discotheques and nightclubs with live music and Oriental shows featuring belly dancing, dervish dancing and Oriental folklore. The majority of nightclubs are clustered around Pyramids Road. Native flavor and reasonable prices can be found at the **Granada** at the Mîdân Opera, with belly dancing, Oriental shows and the occasional magician showing a few conjuring tricks.

The State Travel Agency, Misr Travel, will arrange *Cairo by Night* tours: **Misr Travel**, 7 Sh. Tal'at Harb, tel. 3930010.

Tourist Information

The brochure *Cairo by Night and Day*, published by the Ministry of Tourism, lists the most important addresses in the city. This brochure is obtainable at all hotels and branches of the **State Tourist Agencies**: Main Office, 5 Sh. Adlî, tel. 3913454; at the airport, tel. 667475 and at the pyramids, tel. 3850259.

Cairoscope is a monthly publication listing the town's complete cultural and entertainment events day by day. An additional useful source of information is the monthly *Egypt Today*, with numerous addresses, a calendar of events and interesting features.

Hospitals / Pharmacies

Al-Salâm Hospital, 3 Sh. Syria, Mohandisîn, tel. 3029131, 3029091-95; **Al-Salâm International Hospital**, Corniche an-Nîl, Ma'âdî, tel. 3638050; **Anglo-American Hospital**, Al-Gazîra (next to Cairo Tower), tel. 3418630.

PHARMACIES with 24-hour service in the city center: **Ataba-Pharmacy**, Md. al-'Ataba, tel. 5910831; **Esaaf Pharmacy**, 37 Sh. 26th July, tel. 743369.

Transportation

Buses constitute the main form of public transportation in the inner city of Cairo. The red-and-white or blue-and-white city buses cover quite a widespread network of scheduled routes. The main bus terminal is at Mîdân at-Tahrîr (temporarily moved to the square between the Ramses Hilton and the Egyptian Museum due to construction work), further major bus links are Mîdân Ramsîs (train station), Mîdân al-'Ataba (near the Khân al-Khalîlî) and Mîdân Roxy in Heliopolis. As most buses are packed to the bursting point it is advisable to catch at one of the terminals, if possible.

From Mîdân at-Tahrîr, bus No. 900 runs to the pyramids, No. 400 to airport Terminal 2, No. 422 to airport Terminal 1. The Citadel is served by buses No. 72 and 609, the Khân al-Khalîlî by bus No. 66. The small white Mercedes buses, which only sell seat space but at fairly affordable rates, make an excellent alternative form of public transportation.

From the Mîdân at-Tahrîr (in front of Mugamma') bus No. 82 takes you to the pyramids, No. 27 to the train station and to the airport, and No. 75 takes you to the Citadel.

The first underground service in the whole of Africa opened in Cairo in 1987. When looking for an underground station, watch for a red M – for Metro – in an octagonal star. City maps with clearly marked stations are on display at all underground entrances.

There is, in addition, a small but adequate network of trams known as the Heliopolis Metro. Three trams, starting behind the Egyptian Museum at Mîdân 'Abd al Mun'im Riyâd, run to Heliopolis via the train station.

Excursions

Organized city tours and tours to the pyramids, to Memphis and Saqqâra can be booked through all travel agents. For individual tours it is recommended to hire a taxi.

The Pyramids of Gîza can be easily reached by public transportation (see above); Saqqâra and Memphis, however, are not on the regular public transportation routes.

The carpet weavers in Harranîya and Kirdâsa, on the road to Saqqâra, are worth a separate excursion by themselves.

For those firm in the saddle a desert ride from Gîza to Saqqâra is an unforgettable experience. Comfort-lovers may content themselves with a short ride around the pyramids. Horses and grooms can be hired in the caravanserai at the foot of the pyramids, opposite the Mena House Hotel.

Here are a few destinations for recommended daytours:

The Oasis of Fayyûm and the Pyramids of Maidûm (for route, see page 138); the monasteries in the Wâdî an-Natrûn (for route, see page 71); Alexandria; the canal towns of Suez and Ismailia (for route, see page 215; check current security regulations first!).

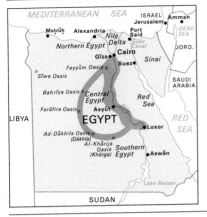

CENTRAL EGYPT AND THE OASES

GÎZA AND BENI SUEF
FAYYÛM OASIS
THE PROVINCE OF MINYÂ
ASYÛT AND THE OASES
THE PROVINCE OF SOHÂG
THE PROVINCE OF QENA

GÎZA AND BENI SUEF

The Nile Valley begins to the south of Cairo with fertile green fields and palm groves, the shining ribbon of the wide river and a beautiful network of irrigation canals. Whereas the desert often comes right up to the banks of the river on the eastern side, the fertile lands on the west bank going upstream are always wider. For this reason most of the settlements are here, and there are numerous villages and towns along the western road. The capitals of the provinces of the same names – Gîza, Beni Suef (Arabic: *Banî Suwaif*), Minyâ, Asyût and Sohâg (Arabic: *Suhâj*) – line the west bank, until at Qena (Arabic: *Qinâ*) the east bank becomes more populated again.

This section of the Nile Valley has become a problem zone for tourism, as has the Fayyûm Oasis southwest of Cairo. The provinces of Minyâ and Asyût especially have attained tragic notoriety as a result of terrorist attacks by Islamic fanatics and bloody police operations. Official agencies therefore advise against traveling to central Egypt at the present time. It should be taken into consider-

Preceding pages: A view over the Islamic cemetery of Minyâ. Left: A proud fellah, one of many who till the Egyptian soil.

ation that certain (varying) routes or places could be closed off to foreigners. Depending on current conditions, though, the situation could change on short notice.

Driving on the road from Gîza going south, just past Saqqâra the **Pyramids of Dahshûr** come into view. The field of pyramids at Dahshûr has only been open to the public since 1996. After the dark brick pyramid of Sesostris III (originally 78 meters high, today only 27) in the north, the first real pyramid of ancient Egypt can be seen, the so-called "Red Pyramid" (101 meters high), built by King Snefru, the father of Cheops. The ruined "White Pyramid" of Amenemhet II follows, and in the extreme south is the 97-meter-high "Bent Pyramid" of Snefru, which has two different angles of inclination. Beside this is the "Black Pyramid" of Amenemhet III (about 30 meters high), who had a second pyramid built in Fayyûm near Hawwâra.

About 30 kilometers further on, just before Al-Maharraqa, is the turnoff for the **Pyramids of Lisht**, which the founder of the Twelfth Dynasty, Amenemhet I and his son, Sesostris I, had built near their new residence. It is hardly worth visiting these pyramids, both of which have disintegrated into nothing more than stone hills.

119

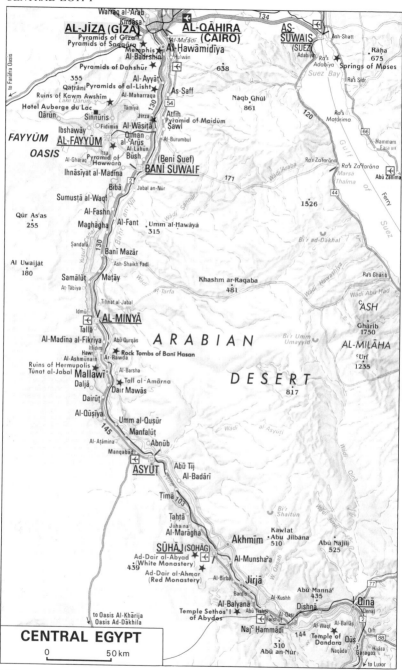

Warrāq al-ʿArab
Kirdāsa
AL-JĪZA (GIZA)
Pyramids of Giza
Pyramids of Saqqāra
Memphis
Al-Badrshīn
Pyramids of Dahshūr
355
Qatrāni
Pyramids of al-Lisht
Ruins of Kawm Awshīm
Al-Maharraqa
Hotel Auberge du Lac
Qārūn   Tāmiya
Sinnūris
Ibshawāy   Fidimīn
FAYYŪM   **AL-FAYYŪM**   Qīmān
    al-ʿArūs
OASIS   Al-Gharaq   Pyramid of   Al-Lāhūn
    Hawwāra
    Itsa   Būsh
Ihnāsiyat al-Madīna
    Birba
Sumustā al-Waqf   Jabal an-Nūr
Al-Fashn
Maghāgha   Al-Fant
    Umm al-Hawāya
    315
    Sandafā
    Banī Mazār
Qūr Asʿas   Ash-Shaikh Fadl
255
    Samālūt   Matāy
Al Uwaijāt   At-Tābiya
180   Tihnat al-Jabal

AL-QĀHIRA (CAIRO)
Al-Maʿādī
Al-Hawāmidīya
    Hulwān
    638
Al-Ayyāt
Aṣ-Ṣaff
Naqb Ghūl
861
Atfīh
Pyramid of Maidūm
Al-Wāsitā
Al-Burumbul
(Beni Suef)
BANĪ SUWAIF
171   Wādī ʿAraba

AS-SUWAIS (SUEZ)
    Ash-Shatt
Adabīya   Rāha
Raʿs   675
Adabīya   Springs of Moses
Raʿs Sidr
Raʿs Matārima
66
Hammam
Faraun
Raʿs Zaʿfarāna
Marsa
Thalma
Abū Zanima
1526
44

Wādī Sannūr
Bahr an-Nīl
130
Yūsuf
Wādī   Wādī
    At-Tarfa
Khashm ar-Raqaba
481
Bahr   Bi'r ad-Dākhal

A R A B I A N
Idmū
AL-MINYĀ
Tallā
Al-Madīna al-Fikrīya   Abū Qurqās
Itlīdim
Al-Ashmūnain   Ar-Rāwda
Hawr   Rock Tombs of Banī Hasan
Ruins of Hermupolis   Al-Barsha
Tūnat al-Jabal   **Mallawī**
Daljā   Tall al-ʿAmārna
    Dair Mawās
Dairūt
Al-Qūsiya
    Umm al-Qusūr
    Manfalūt
Al-Atāmina
Manqabad
ASYŪT   Abū Tīj
    Al-Badārī

Bi'r Umm
Umayyid

D E S E R T
817

Ra's Ghārib
Wādī Abū Had
°**ASH**
Ghārib
1750
AL-MILĀHA
°Urf
1235

Tīma   103
Tahtā
Juhaina
Al-Marāgha   Akhmīm
SŪHĀJ (SOHĀG)
Ad-Dair al-Abyad
(White Monastery)   Al-Munshaʾa
459   Ad-Dair al-Ahmar
(Red Monastery)   Al-Birbā   Jirjā
    Bardīs   Al-Kushh
Al-Balyanā
Temple Sethos I   Abū Tisht
of Abydos   Al-Qasr
Najʿ Hammādī   144
    310
Abū an-Nūr

Kawlat
Abu Jilbāna
510
Abū Najīli
525
Bi'r
Shaitūn
Abū Mannāʿ
435

Wādī Qinā
Wādī al-Asyūtī
Wādī Qinā

Dishnā
77
Abū   V **Qinā**
al-Waqt   (Qena)
Al-Ballās
Temple of   Qūs
Dandara   Hijāza
Naqāda   Baragus
to Luxor
88

to Farāfra Oasis
Lake Qārūn
54
130
2
Bahr an-Nīl
145

to Oasis Al-Khārija
Oasis Ad-Dākhila

Suez Bay
Gulf of Suez
Ferry
120

The **Pyramid of Maidûm**, on the other hand, is very impressive indeed. Its unique shining white step tower can be seen from a great distance on a clear day. There are two turnoffs to Fayyûm near Gerza (Arabic: *Jirza*); both roads are passable, but are full of potholes. The southernmost of these roads, a few kilometers beyond Gerza, leads straight to the pyramid.

The Pyramid of Maidûm is in many respects an oddity. It actually consists of three polished limestone-covered pyramids. The innermost pyramid was a seven-stepped, 72-meter-high construction. This was covered soon afterwards by a second, eight-stepped, and therefore higher (by 10 meters) and wider covering. But then the architects of King Snefru, the first king of the Fourth Dynasty who built two further pyramids in Dahshûr, discovered the pure form. And so they turned the step pyramid of Maidûm into a true pyramid, which rose over a square, with a side length of 144.32 meters, to a height of 92 meters.

Today, as a result of the effects of the elements and thousands of years of plundering, it almost looks like a Babylonian temple tower. A 25-meter-high cone of debris surrounds the lower third of the true pyramid, while above it only the third to the seventh steps can still be seen. The transition between the two is visible in an area of roughly hewn blocks, used as fillers when the first extension was made to the pyramid.

The **Burial Chamber** was not changed during alterations. A diagonal passageway leads down from the entrance in the north of the pyramid to a depth of 58 meters. It joins with a vertical shaft underneath the limestone chamber. The small **Mortuary Temple** on the east side was never decorated. It used to lie within a two-meter-high wall which surrounded the pyramid. A few hieratic inscriptions in ink by pilgrims from the New Kingdom can just be made out at the entrance. The causeway, which used to be flanked by walls, ended at a valley temple which today has sunk below the ground water level.

Although it was far away from the royal residence, the Pyramid of Maidûm was not as isolated in ancient times as it is today. As the center of a large necropolis, it was at the same time the center of worship of a pyramid city. The most famous finds from the tombs of two of Snefru's sons are considered to be among the masterpieces of ancient Egyptian art: the statues of Rahotep and his wife Nefertiti, and, of course, the naturalistically painted Maidûm geese from the tomb of Prince Nefermaat (in the Egyptian Museum in Cairo; Ground Floor, Room 32).

An unknown prince was buried in the great **Brick Mastaba No. 17** on the northeast corner. The descent to the undecorated burial chamber is difficult, but an impressive granite sarcophagus awaits those brave enough to try.

Back on the main road you continue past Al-Wasta (Arabic: *Al-Wâsitâ*), where the railroad tracks fork to Fayyûm, and on to **Beni Suef**. Here the Upper Egyptian Nile Valley is at its widest. The provinical capital, with its 220,000 inhabitants, is a prominent center of agriculture. It also became the most important traffic junction to the south of Cairo in 1985, when the Nile bridge was opened.

FAYYÛM OASIS

Near Beni Suef one of the main roads forks into the province of Fayyûm. Fayyûm can also be visited on the desert road from Gîza in a comfortable day trip. The 1,800-square-kilometer oasis lies in a depression of the Sahara. This depression is irrigated not by artesian wells, but by the Bahr Yûsuf, the River of Joseph. The annual floods used to reach Fayyûm via this tributary of the Nile, which forks to the north of Asyût (today

off the Ibrahîmîya Canal), and, during a long geological process, the whole area gradually turned into a swampy lake district. But of the ancient Egyptian *Pa-Yôm*, the sea which gave Fayyûm its name, only Lake Qârûn, now but a sixth of its original size, remains. At one time so many crocodiles lived in this lagoon landscape that throughout the entire Pharaonic epoch the crocodile god Sobek was worshiped as the principal god of the oasis.

The cultivation of this area was one of the greatest achievments of the Pharaohs of the Twelfth Dynasty (1991-1789 B.C.), who even had their royal residence temporarily built at the entrance to the oasis near Al-Lâhûn. A second golden age began with Ptolemy II (third century B.C.), who had the swamp completely drained and who distributed the reclaimed land near the lake amongst Greek veterans. A great number of new towns were built during this period, and even in the time of the Roman emperors the oasis was an important provider of grain.

Of all the ancient places little has been preserved, yet the journey through the Fayyûm is charming for its scenery alone. The intensively farmed land is Cairo's garden, providing the city with grain, fruit, vegetables and flowers. Now and again you can still see the typical dove towers of Fayyûm on the edges of the picturesque villages. These villages, with their houses so close to one another, sometimes look almost like medieval castles rising from the green plain.

In the heart of the oasis is the provincial capital, **Madînat al-Fayyûm**. Despite its population of about 300,000, it lacks many of the common features associated with a large city. The main attractions in the town center are the four loud, creaking **water wheels** which, with their great buckets, transport the waters of the Bahr Yûsuf into higher basins, albeit nowadays only as nostalgic showpieces.

Above: The Pyramid of Maidûm. Right: Working in the fields.

The River of Joseph, which flows through the town in a paved bed, is a good course to follow on a tour of the town. Both banks are lined with shops and stands selling, among other things, pretty items of basketwork.

The ancestral line of Madînat al-Fayyûm goes back to the Middle Kingdom. But the wide expanse of ancient *Shedet*, the *Crocodilopolis* (crocodile town) and later *Arsinoë* of the Greeks, is today no more than a field of rubble and debris near Qimân Fâris, on the northern edge of the town. Today, the buildings of a new high school are gradually obscuring the traces of the past, or at least those that did not come to light during emergency excavations carried out prior to the beginning of construction.

Not far away, at the northern entrance to the provincial capital, the so-called **Obelisk of Sesostris I** has been erected once again: this is an almost 13-meter-high granite pillar, on the rounded tip of which a stone Horus falcon might well once have perched.

A popular day trip is to **Lake Qârûn** in the northwest of the province of Fayyûm. It is 50 kilometers long, 12 kilometers wide, salty and rich in fish life. The country road leads straight through the fruit plantations of the Fayyûm, from the capital to the beautifully renovated **Hotel Auberge du Lac** on the lake. On the way you pass the villages of **'Ain as-Sillîn**, with its small freshwater spring in the middle of a beautiful park, and **Fidîmîn**.

To the east of the lake on the desert road to Cairo are the ruins of **Kôm Au-shîm** (Arabic: *Kawm Awshîm*), the ancient *Karanis*. Two small temples and several mud brick Ptolemaic buildings, some still partly painted, have been well preserved. One of the more interesting finds made at Karanis was a number of papyri which tell us a lot about the life of the Greek settlers.

The road to **Qasr Qârûn** on the westernmost tip of the lake leads almost straight along the south shore of the lake. Only a few traces still remain of the ancient Ptolemaic town of *Dynosias*, but

123

the temple building of the Sobek shrine is in excellent condition. About 200 meters further northwest is the **Qasr**, a huge fortress ruin, built in the time of Emperor Diocletian (third/fourth centuries A.D.) to safeguard the caravan route into the oases of the Libyan desert.

The most important sights of the Fayyûm are to be found in the southeast of the oasis, close to the main road from Madînat al-Fayyûm to Beni Suef. About eight kilometers outside the town, just before Hawwârat al-Maqtâ, you come to the **Pyramid of Hawwâra**, the tomb of King Amenemhet III, who contributed greatly to the development of Fayyûm. A giant temple area, luxuriously furnished with reliefs and statues, once belonged to the mud brick pyramid which was originally covered with limestone (58 meters high; side lengths 106 x 106 meters). This temple area was the *Labyrinth* written of by ancient authors, who called it one of the wonders of the world. Herodotus reported that there were 3,000 rooms, a suite of pillared halls and courtyards "full of countless beautiful things." A few fragments of granite colums are all that remain of this today.

Among the most important finds of Hawwâra are 400 (of 750 known) mummy portraits from the time of the Roman emperors. At that time it was common among the Greco-Roman population of Egypt to wrap a naturalistic image of the deceased, usually a crayon drawing on wood, over the face in the mummy bandages. These pictures are of incalculable importance to researchers studying ancient portrait painting (can be seen in the Egyptian Museum in Cairo, Upper Floor, Room 14).

Ten kilometers further to the southwest, near the little town of **Al-Lâhûn**, the father of Amenemhet III founded a

Right: A view over the Nile from the tomb terrace near the ruins of the village of Banî Hasan.

city. Today, the once-splendid Pharaoh's royal residence, a beautifully decorated 70-room palace and elegant villas, is little more than a pile of debris. But the pyramid of the founder of the town, Sesostris II, is still visible as a mud brick hill without its original covering of white limestone. It was once 48 meters high and rose from a base of 107 square meters over a rocky core and a "skeleton" of limestone filled with mud bricks. To the south of the pyramid excavators found the famous "Treasure of Lâhûn" in the grave of the king's daughter, Sat-Hathor-Junit: the treasure consisted of the princess's jewelry, her mirrors and little pots for creams and ointments (in the Egyptian Museum in Cairo, Upper Floor, Room 3).

THE PROVINCE OF MINYÂ

Because the 120-kilometer-long road between Beni Suef and Minyâ has no historical sights worth visiting along its route, drivers are advised to take the less-traveled new desert road on the east bank of the Nile.

The provincial capital of **Minyâ** stretches along the west bank of the Nile between the Ibrahîmîya Canal and the river, about one kilometer wide at this point. As Minyâ is the only city for miles around with hotels and a tourism infrastructure, it is an ideal base for visits to many archeological sites, including Banî Hasan, Hermopolis, Tûnat al-Gebel (Arabic: *Tûnat al-Jabal*) and Tall al-'Amârna. Minyâ, a university town and center of the Upper Egyptian cotton trade, was joined to the east bank and the roads running to the Red Sea when the Nile bridge opened in 1987. The town itself is well kept and has a wide Nile promenade. On market day, Monday, it becomes a bustling place.

The Islamic cemetery of Minyâ is particularly impressive. It is a huge cupola necropolis on the opposite east bank. **Zâ-**

wiyat al-Amwât, the "Corner of the Dead," begins a few hundred meters south of the Nile bridge at the village of **Zâwiyat an-Nâsir**, and stretches for more than three kilometers on the edge of the desert hills, a dense row of mud brick cupolas.

A path on the south side of the cemetery leads up to a hill where you have a wonderful view over the cupolas and the Nile. A little higher up are the almost unrecognizable ruins of a step pyramid from the Third Dynasty and some (nearly completely destroyed) rock tombs.

The Rock Tombs of Banî Hasan

Twenty-three kilometers south of Minyâ, at Al-Fikrîya, is the turnoff to **Abû Qurqâs**, where a ferry, especially put into service for tourists, embarks for the tombs of Banî Hasan. Even though the tombs will soon be easily accessible on the new road being built on the east bank, you should not miss the opportunity of traveling by boat through the idyllic Nile

scenery, with its long stretching "islands" of rushes. On the other bank a minibus waits to take visitors to the foot of the concrete ascent, although a short walk through the fields is a more pleasant way of getting there.

The gentle ascent leads past the ruins of the old village of Banî Hasan, which is supposed to have been abandoned after a catastrophic flood, to a narrow terrace halfway up the hill. There you will find an incomparable panorama, particularly if you arrive in the late afternoon, when the sun's rays bathe the Nile Valley in a silvery red light.

Regional princes and governors of the Middle Kingdom had their tombs hewn from the rocks of this slope. Some of them built great halls of worship, whose entrances line the sepulchral terrace. The simple tomb shafts of their subordinates and officials are a little further down, "at their feet," so to speak. The wall paintings of the princely tombs, which were cleaned only a few years ago using a special technique, are among the most extra-

ordinary treasures of ancient Egyptian art. Although in the older tombs there are traces of less skilled provincial artists, the paintings in the tombs of Ameny and Khnumhotep can be measured against those of the greatest court artists. Perhaps the most bewitching thing about them is the variety of subjects which enrich the well-known motifs with completely new elements.

In Banî Hasan there is the usual canon of agricultural pictures, intended to ensure survival in the afterlife with the scenes of sacrifice and worship. But alongside these you will see many unusual pictures of mythical creatures, including a snake-necked panther, or griffins surrounded by desert animals. There are also unique portrayals of wrestlers showing up to 130 holds.

Four of the 12 decorated tomb complexes are usually accessible to the public. You would be best off visiting tombs

Above: Typical Nile landscape near Banî Hasan. Right: In a palm grove.

No. 17 and No. 15 from the Eleventh Dynasty first, and then going on to tombs No. 3 and No. 2 from the Twelfth Dynasty at the northern end of the terrace which rise above the cupolas of an Islamic cemetery at this point.

The tombs of **Baqet** (No. 15) and his son **Kheti** (No. 17) are almost identical in architecture and decoration. In each one a square hall is divided by lotus bundle columns, which are partially broken away today. Wrestling scenes dominate the east wall, which probably allude to military confrontations since they are combined with scenes of the siege of a fortress. The picture strips on the north wall (left) show a hunt in the desert at the very top. Below this you will see barbers, weavers and basket weavers; though most striking here are the dancers and ball players.

On the south wall (right) scenes of artisans, farmers and sacrificial worship are shown. The pictures on the entrance walls can only be seen in the tomb of Kheti. On the left they show him on a

hunt in a papyrus thicket, and further to the right there is a mock door, as well as a number of country scenes.

The other two tombs are also almost identical. They each have a small anteroom with two columns and an attractivley painted chamber of worship, whose lightly vaulted ceiling is supported by four 16-sided columns. In the slightly older **Tomb of Amenemhat** (No. 2) – sometimes also known as Ameny – the statues (which are unfortunately rather badly preserved) of the tomb owner, his wife and mother can be found on the back wall in the niche.

The high point of a visit to Banî Hasan is a visit to the fascinating neighboring **Tomb of Khnumhotep** (No. 3). In a long biographical inscription on the pedestals in the chamber of worship, the prince and "Commander of the Eastern Desert" tells the history of his family, and thereby a portion of the history of his province. The larger-than-life-sized portrayals on both sides of the statue niche of the tomb owner, which show Khnumhotep catch-

ing birds and fishing, are also impressive. Directly above this you can see the charming **Bird Tree**, a small tree with the most various types of birds sitting on its branches.

The most famous scene of the tomb, though, is the **Caravan of Semites** in the middle of the north wall: a group of 37 Bedouins, men, women and children, distinguished from the Egyptians by their colorfully-patterned clothes and their hair styles. They are bringing trading goods, in particular much sought after eye make-up.

Although there are no clues in Egyptian sources to the presence of Joseph in Egypt, one can imagine that the trading caravan in which he went to the Nile was very much like this one. The caption names the leader of the Bedouins as *Heka-chasut*, "Ruler of the Foreign Lands," a title which entered Pharaonic history in the Greek form *Hyksos*, and which described the Semitic foreign kings who ruled Egypt for 300 years after the death of Khnumhotep.

127

Hermopolis and Tûnat al-Gebel

At Ar-Rawda, 40 kilometers south of Minyâ, you will come to a well-signposted road leading west to **Al-Ashmunain**. There, nestled in picturesque palm groves, you will find the ruins of **Hermopolis Magna**, the ancient Egyptian *Shmunu*. This was the "City of the Eight Primeval Gods" who symbolized the chaos before the world was created, and was the mythical primeval place of creation, which later became the center of worship of the god Thot, whom the Greeks identified with Hermes.

Throughout Pharaonic times, temples, chapels and splendid buildings were constructed on this site, which was probably already settled in prehistoric times. But apart from the countless blocks, statue remnants and columns scattered throughout the area, nothing has survived. Two restored 4.5-meter-high quartz **baboon statues** give some idea of the past splendor of the area. Originally King Amenhotep III had eight of these erected in the temple. Remains of a **St. Mary's Basilica** have survived from Christian times (fifth century A.D.). Beneath the foundations of the church, archeologists discovered traces of a temple of Ptolemy III – and not just that: it was the first temple to be built in the purely Greek style outside Alexandria.

Ten kilometers away in the western desert is **Tûnat al-Gebel**, the last great necropolis of Hermopolis, which grew up in Greco-Roman times around a temple of Thot and the **catacombs** of his sacred animals, the ibis and the baboon. From the Twenty-sixth Dynasty on, hundreds of thousands of the mummified animals, to which a variety of other species was later added, were buried in clay vessels or limestone coffins in the labyrinthine bu-

Right: One popular form of public transportation – a group taxi in Mallawî filled to the brim.

rial galleries, some of which are open to the public. The **sanctuary** above the entrance to the catacombs, where the god Thot answered oracles on feast days, is also interesting. In the **chapel** at the foot of the entrance steps (right), which was originally equipped as a burial chamber for the mummy of a baboon, the priests of Thot met in nocturnal worship. The catacombs were linked by road to the great temple in the south of the necropolis. A garden area for breeding animals also belonged to this temple. What remains of the complex today are a few pillars and a sâqîya (water wheel) from Ptolemaic times.

The oldest and most beautiful tomb here is the small **Mortuary Temple of Petosiris**, who was Thot's high priest in Hermopolis around the year 300 B.C. The relief decor, which was carved into a thick layer of plaster, is a beautiful example of the Greco-Egyptian mixed style. But only the secular scenes of the anteroom, such as the pictures of the harvest cycle (narrow wall left) and the grape harvest (narrow wall right), show a Greek influence. The religious motifs of the chamber of worship remain inseparable from Egyptian artistic styles. The deep shaft leads to the tomb chamber. This is where the beautifully preserved mummy coffin of wood with colored glass inlay was discovered (now in the Egyptian Museum in Cairo, Ground Floor, Gallery 49).

Behind the tomb of Petosiris is a veritable city of tombs, some of which are constructed like houses, with, in some case, painted interior rooms. In the **Tomb of Isidora** you can still see the mummy of a young woman who drowned in the Nile in 120 B.C.

About 200 meters north of Tûnat al-Gebel you will see a steep slope in the distance. This is where Akhnaton had one of his 14 stelai chiseled, which marked the borders of his new capital city in Tall al-'Amârna.

Tall al-'Amârna:
Akhnaton's City of the Sun

A few kilometers south of the district town of **Mallawî**, a signposted road leads to the ferry that takes you to Tall al-'Amârna on the east bank of the Nile. From At-Till, where you leave the ferry, there is a "tractor connection" to the ruins of the **North Palace** and the **Northern Group of Tombs** on the edge of the mountains two kilometers away.

Tall al-'Amârna (Amerna) is an artificial place name which archeologists gave the ruins of Akhnaton's city of the sun in allusion to the Arabic clan of the Banî 'Amrân who settled here.

Akhet-Aton, "Horizon of Aton," was the name which the king gave it when he moved his royal residence from Thebes to this previously unsettled area around the year 1339 B.C. Here, where no other god had been worshiped before, he was able to develop his monotheistic religion before forcing it on the rest of the country.

The heart of the new capital, which grew from nothing in only a few years, was the Great Temple of Aton, next to the royal residence, with the main palace and a further small Aton temple that once stood on a wide boulevard. Luxurious residential areas with lavish gardens and villas were grouped around this center. Among them was the workshop of the sculptor Thutmose, from which the world-famous bust of Akhnaton's beautiful wife Nefertiti came.

The whole area stretches for kilometers like a ribbon parallel to the Nile, in a semicircular basin cut by a wide Wadi in the middle. This is where the king had his tomb built. Regarded as a work of heresy, like the other buildings in Amarna it was destroyed and forgotten soon after his death.

The rediscovery of the city of the sun began in early 1887 with a sensation: cuneiform tablets from the "archive of the foreign ministry" of Amarna appeared in the antiquities trade. These tablets contained the Babylonian correspondence of

129

the royal house with princes and kings of the Middle East. Excavations were begun, and not only were the buildings of the state archive soon found, but it was also possible to ascertain the basic outline of the entire town. Most of this has been buried again by the sand, but in the **North Palace** you can still make out the ground plan of individual rooms and columned courts which were grouped around the square basin of an artificial pond.

In the Egyptian Museum in Cairo you will find fragments of floor and wall paintings from Amarna, the graceful, stylized landscapes of which give some hint as to the playful elegance of the palace decoration (Amarna Room and Central Hall).

The reliefs of the **Rock Tombs** give a good idea of the life in the palaces and temples of Amarna. They are decorated in what was the new style of those days: that is to say, with soft flowing lines, with greater freedom of movement and with the organization of the mural seen as a unified composition, describing only a single event. The focus of the painting was now no longer of the existence in the afterlife of the deceased, but of the king instead. Revolutionary new motifs were brought into play showing unusually detailed portrayals of the human life of the king: he is shown eating and drinking, and kissing and playing with his children! The picture of his god is shown above everything he is doing. In contrast to all other Egyptian gods, Aton is portrayed abstractly as a sun disc with rays ending in hands: the so-called Radiant-Aton.

The 25 mostly incomplete rock tombs are concentrated on the mountain slope of the valley in two areas about six kilometers apart from one another. Three of the six north tombs in particular are

Right: As it was 2,000 years ago – evening falls on a street in the city of Khârga.

worth a visit, although they suffered under the iconoclasm of the restoration. Tombs No. 1 and No. 2 are separated by a valley cleft from the other four areas and are approached by a separate path. Some parts of the walls are only clearly visible with a flashlight, despite electric lighting.

On both walls of the entrance to the **Tomb of Huya**, the Harem Chief (No. 1), the royal couple can be seen at a banquet: to the left with a goblet of wine with the Queen mother Tiyi; to the right eating roast goose and other kinds of roast meat. On the south wall of the columned hall (right) Akhnaton accompanies his mother into one of the solar temples of Amarna dedicated to her; on the north wall opposite he is carried into the audience hall in a litter to accept the gifts of foreign emissaries. In the central nave of the uncompleted transept is the statue niche with the portrayal of a burial procession, unique to Amarna.

The **Tomb of Merire II** (No. 2), which has a similar ground plan, was only decorated with reliefs in the columned hall, and even there only in part. The large mural to the right, which depicts a ceremonial reception in the twelfth year of his rule, is impressive. Below the baldequin, in front of the royal couple who are shown holding hands, are scenes of military games and foreign delegations bringing gifts.

The most beautiful tomb of all was intended for the high priest **Merire I** (No. 4). To the left of the entrance of the hall of columns are colorful reliefs showing the decoration of the tomb owner with the collars of the gold of honor. On the long wall next to it you can see the royal couple's journey from the palace to the great Temple of Aton, which consists of a series of open courts with countless sacrificial tables beneath the open sky.

To the right of the entrance to the columned hall Akhnaton and Nefertiti can be seen making an offering to Aton; the

small relief of a group of musicians in the pedestal below is especially interesting. The subject of the long wall is once again a great offering celebration. Of particular interest here is the splendid picture of Merire's estate on the narrow wall adjoining it.

ASYÛT AND THE OASES OF THE NEW VALLEY

The provincial capital of **Asyût** has almost 300,000 inhabitants. It is the largest city in Upper Egypt and the seat of the oldest university of the Nile Valley. While it has little to offer in the way of historical sights, the lively bazaar quarter near the station is interesting, as is the **weir** in the north of the city which regulates the waters of the Ibrahîmîya Canal and the Bahr Yûsuf with its 111 gates.

Foreign tourists usually just stop in Asyût on the way to Khârga (Arabic: *Al-Khârija*) and Dâkhla (Arabic: *Ad-Dâkhila*), the "pearl" of the chain of oases parallel to the Nile, to which Farâfra (Arabic: *Al-Farâfira*) and Al-Bahrîya also belong. The main attractions of the oases are not the villages themselves, but rather the magnificent and diversified desert landscapes of the Sahara in which they are embedded.

The turnoff to the oases is eight kilometers north of Asyût at **Manqabâd**. After a journey of 165 kilometers through stony desert you will come to an escarpment, below which a huge depression stretches in a grandiose panorama. This is where **Khârga** begins, the "outermost" of the four oases. The administrative town of the same name, 70 kilometers away, is the capital of the **New Valley**.

The name of the province is the magic formula for a land reclamation project started in 1960. The aim of this project is to create a second Nile Valley in the depression of the oasis belt by opening the rich underground fresh-water reservoir. This aim has only been partly fulfilled, as there were several unexpected results along the way, such as salination of the

131

topsoil, a lowering of the water pressure because of the overloading of the artesian wells, and, despite significant incentives, Nile Valley farmers have shown little interest in resettling the area.

In the town of **Khârga** the little crooked old lanes of the bazaar are ideal for a shopping trip. Khârga's **Archeological Museum**, which opened in 1988, fully documents the rich history of the oases right back to the Paleolithic Age. Before the gates of the town stands the ancient showpiece of the oases set in the middle of a palm grove: a **Temple of Amen**, dedicated in about 500 B.C. by the Persian King Darius I. Next to it stretch the ruins of the Roman town of **Hibis**, with impressive mud brick buildings belonging to the early Christian **Cemetery of Bagawât**.

A number of new settlements line the road from Khârga to **Bârîs**, which follows the course of the *Darb al-'arba'în,* the old "40 Day Track" to the Sudan. In Roman times this important caravan route was guarded by a chain of fortresses, one of which was **Qasr al-Ghuwaida**, which lies 20 kilometers south of Khârga and has a well-preserved Amen temple from Persian times.

The southernmost fortress, the **Qasr Dûsh**, with contains the ruins of a Roman Isis temple, can be reached from Bârîs via a passable desert track.

The 200 kilometer road between Khârga and **Mût**, the main town of the depression of **Dâkhla**, leads through a desert area rich in variety. With 60,000 inhabitants, the so called "inner oasis" is not only the largest, but also the most beautiful of all the oases of the New Valley. The rose-colored rocks of the escarpment, which can always be seen on the horizon, gave rise to its poetic name: "The Rose Oasis." Palm groves and orchards complete the idyllic scenery.

Right: Not all houses in Egypt are equipped with water pipes.

On the northern outskirts of Mût a sign points the way to the **Mût Tourism Wells**, a hot spring, typical of the whole oasis chain. This spring has been channeled into thermal baths, and in contrast to some of the more romantic places, is easily accessible.

The most picturesque place in Dâkhla is **Al-Qasr**. Sadly, its beautiful medieval town center was recently partially destroyed as a result of heavy rainfall. A few kilometers outside Al-Qasr are the **Roman Tombs of Al-Muzawwaka**, with colorful paintings of ancient Egyptian scenes of the mortuary cult.

A little further to the southwest you come to the Roman **Amen Temple of Dair al-Hajar**, which is still half-buried under the desert sand. Not far away are some **thermal springs** in enchanting surroundings. They can only be found, however, with the help of locals.

An asphalt road now joins Dâkhla with the two northern oases of the New Valley. As with most roads in the oasis area, it is often difficult to drive on because of the sand drifts and potholes. It arches into the Libyan Desert, which touches the edge of the **Great Sea of Sand**, with its huge waves of dunes about 100 kilometers west of **Al-Mawhûb**.

About 130 kilometers further on you come to **Qasr al-Farâfra**, the pretty main town of **Farâfra**, of the smallest of the four oases. To the north of here the **White Desert** stretches to the edge of the high escarpment. The landscape of the immense White Desert was formed by erosion, and has bizarre limestone formations which rise from the flats like strange, miraculous animals.

At **Al-Bahrîya**, the "northern" oasis, you will once again find the splendor of lush oasis gardens surrounding the main town here, **Bawîti**. At the foot of the cliffs of Bawîti, and its sister town **Al-Qasr**, is a sea of fruit trees and date palms, on the edges of which there is a series of hot springs.

THE PROVINCE OF SOHÂG

The stretch of approximately 100 kilometers between Asyût and Sohâg has, on both sides of the Nile, charming landscape and offers many lovely views of the river. With only 50,000 inhabitants, **Sohâg** is a comparatively small provincial capital. Since the completion of the 665-meter Nile bridge, it has been joined with the town of **Akhmîm** on the opposite side of the river to form one large community.

On the eastern edge of Akhmîm you will find the few – though spectacular – remains of the once important capital of the ninth Upper Egyptian province. During building work in 1981, the ruins of a temple of the fertility god Min were discovered, along with two 10-meter-tall alabaster statues of King Ramses II and his daughter-wife Merit-Amen, which are considered to be masterpieces of the sculptor's art from the time of Ramses.

Sohâg is above all famous for its Coptic relics of the past. On the edge of the desert, six kilometers west of Sohâg, is one of the oldest monasteries of Egypt: the **White Monastery** (*Ad-Dair al-abyad*), founded by the great Abbot Shenute at the beginning of the fifth century. It takes its name from the surrounding walls of white limestone blocks (which have darkened somewhat over the centuries), most of which were taken from Pharaonic temples in the region. The basilica as it appears in its present form is a Constantine church which was enlarged by Abbot Shenute. The frescos of the apse date back to the 11th century.

Five kilometers further north is the brick building of the **Red Monastery** (*Ad-Dair al-ahmar*), which dates from around the same time. It is dedicated to the Coptic saint Amba Bschoî. Only a section of the fifth-century basilica is now used as a church. The frescos of the apse date from about 1300.

Once again it is an ancient Egyptian building which belongs to the great sights of this province: the Temple of Seti I of Abydos. Fifty kilometers south of Sohâg,

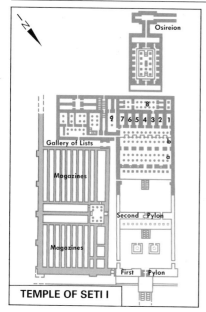

TEMPLE OF SETI I

at **Balyanâ**, a signposted road leads through fields and villages to the temple on the edge of the fertile lands 11 kilometers away.

From the very beginnings of Pharaonic history, **Abydos** was an important religious center. It developed from a royal cemetery in the first two dynasties into one of the most sacred of all places of pilgrimage in ancient Egypt. The focus on death and the afterlife existed since earliest times through the god Khontamenti. But he soon gave way to the great Osiris, the murdered and resurrected god, on whom all men placed their hopes of life after death.

Beginning at the latest from the Middle Kingdom onwards, his resurrection was celebrated at the tomb of Osiris in the Royal Cemetery of Abydos in an annual mystery play, which featured strictly secret rites and a procession in memory of his burial. Thousands upon thousands of

Right: Ramses II in the temple of Abydos, a religious center of ancient Egypt.

pilgrims took part in these celebrations, and whoever among them could afford it dedicated a stele or a statue to Osiris, not least of all so as to be able to remain near the sacred site forever. It was regarded as particularly beneficial to be buried in Abydos, or at least to have a small shrine erected as a cenotaph there. And so today, to the southwest of the almost completely ruined town, with its Temple of Osiris, stretches a huge necropolis, where kings, too, had their splendid chapels and temples built as cenotaphs dedicated to the great god Osiris.

The ancient place of pilgrimage lies in ruins; plundered, destroyed and dilapidated. Yet, by some miracle, one building has survived thousands of years relatively undamaged: the **Temple of Seti I**, built of the finest white limestone. Its elegant classical reliefs reflect a high point in Egyptian art.

Once linked to the Nile by a canal, the unusually ordered complex rises in two terraces, both with open courtyards, to a covered temple building. Here seven parallel processional ways cut through columned halls and lead finally to seven sanctuaries. Ramses II completed the temple after his father's death. He had all seven of the planned entrances, with the exception of the central portal, walled up and decorated with inscriptions and large reliefs.

The murals of the first columned hall, with 24 papyrus-sheaf columns, also come from the time of Ramses II, as even those unschooled in ancient Egyptian history can probably tell. For, in contrast to the slightly raised bas-relief favored by Seti I, Ramses preferred slightly sunken reliefs. There are some lovely examples of this on the north wall (right): (a) shows Ramses being ritually purified by Horus and Thot. Then he is prepared to be accompanied by Horus and the jackal god Wepwawet to Osiris, Isis and Horus, in order to present them with a casket for papyrus scrolls; (b) shows Seti I offering

incense to Osiris and Horus. To the left he is shown with a large incense burner in front of Osiris on the throne in the company of various goddesses.

The partly colored relief cycles of the seven **sanctuaries** are especially interesting. These were dedicated to the gods Horus (1), Isis (2), Osiris (3), Amen-Ra (4), Ra-Harakhti (5) and Ptah (6), and to Seti I himself (7). In almost identical pictures they show the king opening the shrine in the morning, offering incense to the god's image and then anointing it with his little finger, and bringing it jewelry and strips of cloth as garments. At the back of the room he is usually seen making his offerings in front of the god's barque. In reality, this would have stood in front of the shrine.

From the Osiris Sanctuary you move into the transversely-lying **Osiris Hall** (8), a beautiful separate shrine with reliefs and three cult chapels. Directly behind this, outside the temple, is the cenotaph of the king, the so-called **Osireion**: a monumental subterranean hall of pillars, which is entered via a 110-meter-long tunnel and several chambers. Above this was once probably a tree-covered hill, a symbol of the primeval hill of the beginning of the universe. Today you can only see the 10 monolithic granite pillars which are half sunken below the increasing water level.

The Osireion is reached via the side wings where, next to the lovely **Chambers of Worship of Ptah** (9), the famous **Gallery of Lists** is found. Crown Prince Ramses stands with his father Seti I in front of a list with oval rings of names, covering the whole wall surface. The list mentions all of Seti I's ancestors going back to Menes, the founder of the empire. Illegitimate rulers, such as the Hyksos or Amarna kings, were deliberately omitted, for they did not rule in accordance with the official royal dogma.

Some 300 meters away to the northeast, Ramses II had his own temple built. Unfortunately, its colorful and fascinating reliefs have only survived to a height of two meters.

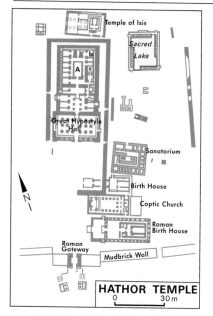

HATHOR TEMPLE
0   30 m

THE PROVINCE OF QENA

The only important town on the way from Abydos to the provincial capital of Qena is **Naj' Hammâdî**. It is at the northern end of the great Nile arch, where the railway track crosses the river to stay on the east bank until Aswan. This up-and-coming town has one of the largest sugar factories in Upper Egypt and the largest aluminum works in Africa. A barrage built in 1930 in the north of the town regulates the water flowing into the province of Sohâg.

In scientific circles Naj' Hammâdî became world-famous in 1946. A few kilometers further east, near the ancient *Chenoboskion*, where St. Pachomius founded the first monastery in Christian times, (third to fifth century A. D.), Coptic manuscripts were discovered. The 13 codices contain religious writings which

Right: The Temple of Dandara, the main center of worship of Hathor, the goddess of love and music.

became invaluable sources for the research into Gnosis – one of the most important religious movements of late antiquity.

Fifty kilometers south of Naj' Hammâdî a turnoff marks the way to the **Temple of Dandara**, the center of worship of the goddess of love and music, Hathor, the great mother and goddess of the sky. Once the center of a capital of the sixth Upper Egyptian province, the temple complex, enclosed by a huge mud brick wall, now lies alone on the edge of the desert. The history of the shrine can be traced to Cheops, but those parts which have been preserved were only built in Ptolemaic-Roman times. In the center is the temple building of Hathor. The pylon was never finished, so as soon as you walk through the Roman gateway you find yourself in front of the **Great Hall of Columns**, whose massive capitals dominate the façade, along with the face of the goddess whose ears are those of a cow. Twenty-four monumental columns support the ceiling of the hall, which represents the sky and is decorated with astronomical pictures, winged suns and flying vultures.

The central procession path rises in the classical Ptolemaic style through another smaller hall with columns and two anterooms for the offering tables and the shrines of the guest gods. You then come to the **Holy of Holies** (A), which is enclosed by a circle of 11 chambers. The mural paintings, some of which were irreverently hacked out during the Christian era, show scenes of offering and worship which the king, who is often not even named, is performing before Hathor and her god-husband Horus of Edfu. The most beautiful reliefs are in the **crypts**, a secret system of passageways where the precious idols depicted on the walls were kept (entrance at b).

From the inner anteroom you come to the **New Year's Chapel** (c), with an interesting ceiling relief of the goddess

Nut, in which the first rays of the morning sun are shown shining down onto the Hathor Temple. On New Year's Day the priests went from there to the temple roof (still accessible today) and placed the statue of the goddess in the small columned chapel with the Hathoric capitals for its "unification with the sun."

The same idea of the renewal of the life force is also portrayed in the pictures of the two **Osiris Chapels** on the north side of the roof. The resurrection is symbolically represented by the god lying on a bier; he is shown touching his forehead as a sign of awakening consciousness. A relief plate from the east chamber is famous all over the world: the *Zodiac of Dandara*. This is a depiction of the celestial disk with the 12 signs of the zodiac, the original of which is now in the Louvre in Paris.

The temple roof offers a fine view of the surroundings, and of the whole temple area, with the two **Birth Houses**, which celebrate the divine origins of the king, the ruins of a Coptic **basilica** (fifth

century A.D.) and the mud brick remains of the **Sanatorium**, a sort of temple clinic. To the south is the **Holy Lake**, surrounded by picturesque palm trees, and a small **Isis Temple** from the time of Augustus.

Eight kilometers south of Dandera the last bridge before Esna crosses the Nile and leads to the provincial capital of **Qena**, which, despite its size (250,000 inhabitants), is only interesting to tourists as a departure point for the main road to the Red Sea which starts here. The well-known Qena potteries, in which the large, light-colored water jugs are made, are on the west bank at **Al-Ballâs**, 16 kilometers south of Dendera.

Another interesting pottery village is on the east bank between Qena and Luxor, which is only 62 kilometers away. About halfway along the road, not far from Qûs, a Coptic initiative has been organized in the village of **Garagos**, whereby beautiful ceramics and hand-woven carpets are sold in a handicraft center to finance a social center.

CENTRAL EGYPT AND THE OASES

Central Egypt and the province of Fayyûm are considered to be strongholds of Muslim fundamentalism. The freedom of movement of tourists is, therefore, generally severely restricted. Depending on the current situation, certain locations can be off-limits to visitors, including, sometimes, entire regions. Individual travelers should, for this reason, inquire about conditions in places on their itinerary before leaving for Egypt (at a tourist agency or an Egyptian travel board). Most archeological sites in this region cannot be reached by public transport-ation, which can make sightseeing here difficult, as taxis, buses and private vehicles are only allowed to travel here when accompanied by military escort.

Transportation

BY BUS: The *Upper Egypt Bus Company* oper-ates buses from Cairo to the Fayyûm and all larger Nile Valley towns between Cairo and Aswan several times a day. Point of departure in Cairo: Md. Ahmad Hilmî bus terminal, behind the train station on Md. Ramsîs. For travel with deluxe buses, buy your ticket one day prior to departure at the bus company's counter in the bus terminal. The same company runs a regular schedule of buses to the oases of the Libyan desert, but from a different bus terminal! Departure point in Cairo: The bus terminal at the intersection of Sh. Al-Azhar and Sh., Port Said. These buses run daily on the desert route between Cairo and the oases of Al-Bahrîya and Dâkhla. The Khârga oasis can only be reached from Cairo with the bus via Asyût. One of the four daily buses to Khârga continues on to Dâkhla. Buses to the oasis of Farâfa run Satur-days, Mondays and Thursdays.

BY GROUP TAXI (at present not possible for foreigners!): Group taxis to Madînat al-Fayyûm leave Cairo (or more precisely Gîza) from Mîdân Gîza. Group taxis to Beni Suef, Minyâ and Asyût leave from the group taxi stand for Upper Egypt on Md. Ahmad Hilmî (next to the main Cairo train sta-tion). Passengers who want to continue on to the oases or further south will have to change at Asyût.

BY TRAIN: There are several southbound trains daily from Cairo which stop in Beni Suef, Minyâ, Asyût, Sohâg and Qena. Passengers who want to continue on to Madînat al-Fayyûm will have to change trains at Al-Wasta.

BY AIR: There are two regularly-scheduled Egypt Air flights weekly to Khârga.

NOTE: If you want to visit central Egypt, the Fayyûm or the oases in the New Valley using a private car, check for restricted areas or for the need for special permits beforehand! Information can be obtained from the *Automobile Club of Egypt*, 10 Sh. Qasr an-Nîl, tel. 02/5743355.

THE PROVINCES OF GÎZA AND BENI SUEF

Accommodation

MODERATE: **Semiramis**, Beni Suef, Sh. Safîya Zaghlûl (opposite the train station), tel. (082) 322092, fax. 316017. Al-Lisht can only be reached by private vehicle. The Pyramid of Maidûm is ac-cessible by public transportation to Al-Wasta, and then by taxi from there. Travelers with private trans-portation can combine visiting the pyramid with a day-trip across the Fayyûm.

FAYYÛM OASIS

Area Code 084

Accommodation

LUXURY: **Auberge du Lac**, Lake Qârûn, tel. 700002, 700730, fax. 700730.

MODERATE: **Panorama Shakshuk**, Shakshûk, Lake Qârûn, tel. 701314, fax. 701757.

BUDGET: **Ain el-Sillin**, 'Ain as-Sillîn (near San-hûr), tel. 327471; **Geziret el Bat Hotel**, tel. 749288, 756702; **Oasis Tourist Village**, Shak-shûk, Lake Qârûn, tel. 701565, 987652.

YOUTH HOSTEL: **Youth Hostel**, Madînat al-Fayyûm, Al-Hadîqa No. 7.

Restaurants

The fish restaurants at Lake Qârûn are a popular ex-cursion spot for the people of Cairo, and tend to be packed to the point of bursting, especially on Fridays. The **Auberge Fayoum Oberoi** in the lakeside hotel Auberge du Lac is very elegant. Also recommended are the restaurants of the hotels **Pan-orama** and **Oasis** in Shakshûk. The **Caféteria Jabal az-Zêna**, a few kilometers west of the hotel Auberge du Lac, also serves tasty fish dishes.

Tourist Information

Governorate Building, tel. 322586, 322370.

Routes / Excursions

Most travelers visit the Fayyûm as part of a day tour from Cairo. Travelers going by private car/taxi (don't forget your passport!) might find the follow-ing route suggestions useful, which can also serve as a guideline for a longer stay:

1. Cairo – Gîza (Hotel Mena House) – Fayyûm des-ert road – Kôm Aushîm (60 km) – Lake Qârûn – Auberge du Lac (75 km) – continue either to: Shak-shûk (80 km) – Qasr Qârûn (123 km) – or directly back to the road to Sanhûr (1 km east of hotel Auberge du Lac) – Sanhûr (82 km) – Fidimîn (84 km) – 'Ain as-Sillîn (86 km) – Madînat al-Fayyûm (91 km) – Maidûm (125 km) – Gerza (133 km) – Gîza (203 km) – Cairo.

2. Those who wish to include a visit to the pyramids of Hawwâra and Al-Lâhûn in this tour should get an early start. A pleasant alternative is the approach via the western Nile Valley main road: Gîza – Gerza (70

km) – Maidûm (78 km) – Al-Wasta (88 km) – Beni Suef (115 km) – Al-Lâhûn (137 km) – Hawwâra (147 km) – Madînat al-Fayyûm (155 km) – from here return to Cairo in reverse order via the stations mentioned in the first route.

MINYÂ PROVINCE
Accommodation
MINYÂ (area code 086): *MODERATE:* **Mercure Nefertiti**, Corniche an-Nîl, tel. 341515/16, fax. 326467. *BUDGET:* **El-Shatek**, 31 Sh. al-Gumhû-rîya, tel. 322307; **Lotus**, 1 Sh. Port Said, tel. 324500, fax. 324541; **Ibn Khassib**, 5 Sh. Ragib, tel. 324535.
Restaurants
The **Restaurant of the Mercure Nefertiti** is highly recommended. Simple dishes are available around the train station and in the **Lotus Hotel**.
Tourist Information
State Tourist Office, Governorate Building, Corniche an-Nîl, tel. 320150, 372215.
Routes / Excursions
The most important sights can be visited by car/taxi on a (long) day-tour starting out from Minyâ. It is best to start in Tall al-'Amârna, which is furthest away, and to return to Minyâ via Hermopolis and Banî Hasan. Route suggestions: Minyâ – Mallawî (48 km) – by ferry to At-Till – by tractor to the northern tombs and northern palace – back to Mallawî – Ar-Rawda (60 km) – Al-Ashmunain – Hermopolis (66 km) – Tûnat al-Gebel (76 km) – Abû Qurqâs (96 km) – boat landing – Banî Hasan – Abû Qurqâs – Minyâ (120 km). With the completion of the planned road between Minyâ and Asyût, the last stage of the eastern route from Cairo to Aswan will be finished, and Banî Hasan and Tall al-'Amârna can be reached overland.

ASYÛT AND THE OASES OF THE NEW VALLEY
Accommodation
ASYÛT (area code 088): *MODERATE:* **Badr Touristic**, Sh. at-Tallâga, tel. 329811/12, fax. 322820. *BUDGET:* **Reem Touristic**, Sh. an-Nahda, tel. 311421/22, fax. 311424; Akhnaton Touristic, Sh. Muhammad Tawfîq Khashaba, tel. 327723, fax. 331600. *YOUTH HOSTEL:* **Youth Hostel**, Sh. An-Nimais, Walîdîya Nr. 503.
KHÂRGA OASIS (area code 0092): *MODERATE:* **El-Kharga Oasis**, Khârga, tel. 901500, 904940. *BUDGET:* **El-Wadi el-Gedîd Tourist Chalets**, Khârga (next to the State Tourist Office), tel. 900728; **Hamadalla**, Khârga, tel. 900638, fax. 905017. *South of Khârga:* **Resthouse Al-Nasr Tourism Wells**, An-Nasr Tourism Wells (17 km); **Bulaq Resthouse**, Bulaq (30 km); **Resthouse Baris**, Bârîs (80 km).

DÂHLA OASIS: *BASIC:* **Dar al-Wafdên**, Mût; **Mut Bungalows**, Mût, tel. 941593; **Tourism Wells Resthouse**, on western outskirts of Mût; **Government Tourist Chalets**, at the hot springs of Mût and Al-Qasr (reservations through the Tourist Office in Khârga.)
FARÂFRA OASIS: *BASIC:* **New Resthouse**, Qasr al-Farâfra (at the bus station).
AL-BAHRÎYA OASIS: *BASIC:* **Alpenblick**, Bawîtî, tel. (018) 200790; **Oasis**, Bawîtî; **Resthouse Al-Menagem**, Al-Menagem-Mine, 42 km east of Bawîtî, tel. 981237/38.
Tourist Information
New Valley Tourist Information, Khârga (opposite Hotel Oasis), tel. 901205/206, has information about all the oases.
Routes / Excursions
Route for a round-trip tour of the oases: Cairo – Gîza – Al-Bahrîya Oasis (315 km) – Bawîtî (337 km) – Farâfra Oasis/White Desert (455 km) – Qasr al-Farâfra (512 km) – Al-Mawhûb/Dâkhla Oasis (737 km) – Al-Qasr (776 km) – Mût (804 km) – Khârga (999 km) – Manqabâd/Asyût (1,234 km) – Cairo (1,600 km) – or the other way around.
Khârga is an ideal base for a round-trip tour via Bârîs: Khârga – Qasr al-Ghuwaida (20 km) – Bulaq (30 km) – Bârîs (90 km) – Qasr Dûsh (113 km) – Khârga (226 km).
In Qasr al-Farâfra and Bawîtî/Al-Bahrîya organized jeep tours are available to take you to the White Desert, and also from Bawîtî to the hot springs.

SOHÂG AND QENA PROVINCES
Accommodation
SOHÂG (area code 093): *BASIC:* **Andalus**, Sh. al-Mahatta (at train staion); **El-Salam**, Sh. al-Mahatta (at train staion). *YOUTH HOSTEL:* **Youth Hostel**, 5 Sh. Port Said, tel 24395.
ABYDOS: Very simple rooms in a small hotel at the temple in Abydos. The next good accommodation is 50 km further on in **NAJ' HAMMÂDÎ** (area code 096): *MODERATE:* **Aluminium Hotel**, on the grounds of the Aluminium Company, 6 km south of Naj' Hammâdî, tel./fax. 581320.
QENA (area code 096): *BUDGET:* **New Palace**, al-Mahatta (train station), tel. 322509.
Routes / Excursions
The drive from Minyâ to Luxor takes approximately 12 hours: Minyâ – Asyût (120 km) – Sohâg (220 km) – Balyanâ (273 km) – Abydos (282 km) – Naj' Hammâdî (326 km) – Dandara (382 km) – Qena (390 km) – Luxor (450 km).
NOTE: Inquire about the present safety reequirements before departure. Even if the roads are open, that does not necessarily mean that the temples of Abydos and Dandara will be open to visitors.

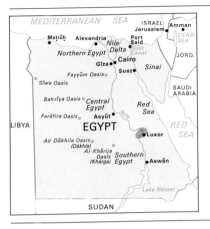

THEBES: CITY OF A HUNDRED GATES

LUXOR

KARNAK

THEBES WEST

LUXOR

Seven hundred kilometers south of Cairo is Luxor (Arabic: *Al-Uqsur*), a town with around 40,000 inhabitants in the province of Qena. For more than 2,000 years the little town on the east bank of the Nile has been a popular place for tourists from all over the world to visit. Today, with its elegant luxury hotels and its international airport, it is a fully developed center of Egyptian tourism. Hundreds of thousands of people come every year to admire Thebes, the "City of the Hundred Gates," as Homer called this shining metropolis of the ancient Orient. He was referring to the huge gates of the Pharaonic temples to which even the Arabic name of the town, *Al-Uqsur*, "The Castles," alludes. The Egyptians usually called the capital of their fourth Upper Egyptian province *Niut*, which became *No* in the Bible.

The landscape of the Nile Valley always has a magical beauty about it, but in Luxor it takes on a very special quality. An aura of eternity surrounds the bare, plantless western hills, which rise like a majestic stage on the edge of the green

Preceding pages: Colossus and obelisk of Ramses II in front of the Temple of Luxor. Left: In the Great Hypostyle Hall of Karnak.

fields. The wide, ponderous river completes the picture. And suddenly you understand exactly why the ancient Egyptians chose this place as the site of their holy city.

The Nile divided ancient Thebes into two worlds: into the city of the living on one bank, and the realm of the dead on the other. On the east bank were most of the splendid palaces and villas, the residential houses, the markets and warehouses. During the course of history Thebes developed from an unremarkable provincial capital into a lively metropolis: the royal residence of the Pharaohs of the New Kingdom and the center of worship of the King of the Gods Amen-Ra.

Traces of settlements from the distant past have been found. Yet it was the Theban Prince Mentuhotep II, who united the land of the Nile after the horrors of the First Intermediate Period and who established Thebes' fame. In about 2037 B.C., it became the capital of the empire for the first time. But this was just an episode, for the kings of the Twelfth Dynasty moved back to the strategically more important north.

Thebes' finest hour came at the onset of the Eighteenth Dynasty, half a millenium later, when its rise to becoming the shining center of the Egyptian Empire began. Once again Theban princes had

143

fought for the unity of the land, this time against the Hyksos, the Asiatic foreign rulers who had settled in the Nile Delta. For a period of 200 years Thebes retained its status as the capital – until King Amenhotep IV, the first great prophet of monotheism who is better known to history under the name Akhnaton, left the residence of his ancestors and moved his court to Amarna.

His descendants ultimately returned to the north, but Thebes remained the religious center of the country. The temple of Amen-Ra in Karnak became the heart of a kingdom of god on earth, and played a significant political role until the town was destroyed by the Assyrians in the seventh century B.C. The holy city never recovered from this blow, even though new buildings were constructed under the Ptolemies and the Romans.

Today, the once splendid metropolis of Thebes has long since disappeared into the ground. Whatever remnants of the city might have remained lie buried beneath the houses of modern Luxor and the surrounding villages. Only the mighty temple complexes in the heart of Luxor and in nearby Karnak have survived the passing millenia. But even they had to be painstakingly dug out of hills of sand and rubble.

On the west side of the Nile is the "Realm of the Dead" – a range of mountains whose highest peak rises above the fertile plain like a natural pyramid. In the shadow of these desert mountains lies the Valley of the Kings, the mysterious burial grounds of the Pharaohs of the New Kingdom. Their mortuary temples line the edge of the strip of fertile land. But only a few of the more than 20 of these *Houses of Millions of Years* reflect the splendor of the necropolis which was then, as it is today, actually very much alive. The priests and the officials of the necropolis administration lived there – indeed, the west bank of Thebes even had its own mayor. The artists and craftsmen

of the kings' tombs lived near their places of work in a walled-in settlement. Their rock tombs in Dair al-Madîna are famous for the wonderful paintings they contain. As a matter of fact, in the heights of the western mountains there are more than 450 beautifully ornamented private tombs all together.

Old Thebes today is a tourist stronghold, and this, of course, has taken its toll: in some places Luxor's streets seem like one great noisy tourist bazaar where just about everything is on offer – from small souvenir camels to the shopping bags in which your newly-acquired treasures can be carried home. At certain times even the temples and tombs are transformed into noisy fairgrounds. And

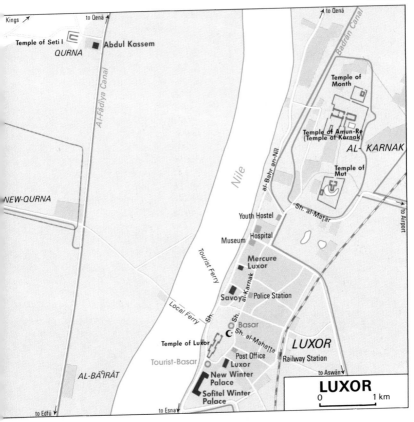

the sacred places, which have survived so many thousands of years, seem as if they will burst under the sheer numbers of so many tourist groups.

But this should not put you off! There are still corners of Luxor where the authentic character of a small, lively Oriental city can be found – for example, in the mornings in the the old bazaar street behind the Temple of Luxor.

Very early in the morning, or at noon, when everyone is having lunch, you can even walk through the Great Hypostyle Hall of Karnak alone and absorb the solemnity of this gigantic shrine. For those with romantic leanings the sound and light show in the Karnak Temple every evening is highly recommended.

But if you cannot bear the (not at all exaggerated) sentimentality of the texts, at least visit the Temple of Luxor in the evening, for there, at sunset, the spotlights are turned on and the reliefs and columns are illuminated in a mysterious light – without the slightest distraction of sound effects.

Luxor is a small town, ideal for walks – whether along the Nile promenade or through the innumberable little streets with their countless souvenir stands. The old bazaar quarter, with its fruit and vegetable market, lies directly behind the Temple of Luxor. The terrace café of the Mercure Luxor Hotel, located directly on the banks of the Nile, is a popular meeting place.

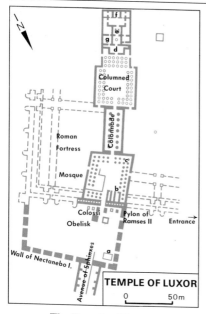

The Temple of Luxor

Only a few paces away from the Winter Palace Hotel, you will find one of the best-preserved temple complexes in Egypt towering up on the bank of the Nile. This is the Temple of Luxor, dedicated to the Theban trinity of gods, Amen, Mut and Khonsu. An inscription tells how King Amenhotep III had the holy shrine built of "fine sandstone," with "a bed of frankincense on a floor of silver," and with a wide courtyard "the columns of which are lotus buds." But this only refers to the temple tract at the back with the various chambers of worship, the great columned court and the monumental colonnade.

The temple was completed in its present form only 100 years afterwards, when Ramses II had another columned courtyard and a huge pylon built in front of the colonnade.

Right: A "street sweeper" at the First Pylon of the Temple of Luxor.

A visit to the temple starts at these gate towers. You will find the best view from the **Sphinx Avenue**, which leads to the temple from the north. It is the last part of a three-kilometer processional path which led to the temple city of Karnak. Hundreds of sphinxes, between which flowers and trees were planted, once lined the avenue, which until now has only been partly excavated. In the New Kingdom it consisted of ram sphinxes, but these were replaced by the classical type of sphinx, with a king's head, during restorations carried out under Nektanebo I (Thirtieth Dynasty).

The wall with the sandstone gate, which was built under the same ruler, can hardly be seen today. Even the **Roman Fortress**, as with most of the other Roman buildings around the temple, can only be recognized by a few individual parts. The small **Chapel of Hadrian** (a), however, has recently been restored. The Roman emperor dedicated it to the god Serapis on January 24, in the year A.D. 126; his 50th birthday.

The reliefs of the great **Pylon of Ramses II** (24 meters high, 65 meters total width) are best seen – and photographed – in the early morning light. The reliefs and texts portray the Battle of Qadesh which Ramses II glorified in all his temple buildings as a victory over the Hittites.

The west tower, on the right, shows the Egyptian army encampment and the king meeting his generals. The king is portrayed larger than life, as befitted his rank. On the east tower he can be seen on his chariot, resolutely storming into battle. On the far left is the fortress of Qadesh (in Syria), to which the fleeing Hittites have retreated.

Four baboons decorate the pedestals of the 25-meter-high red granite **obelisk** in front of the east tower. Only the pedestal remains of its ancient original, which Muhammad 'Alî sent to Paris as a gift to France. Since 1836 it has stood at the

center of the Place de la Concorde in Paris.

The grandiose stone monuments which became famous under the irreverent appelation of "small skewer" (Greek: *obeliskós*) have captured the imagination of travelers in Egypt since time immemorial. But there are still many questions to be answered. The significance of the stone pillars, erected as giant monoliths in pairs in front of the temples of the gods during the New Kingdom, is still being puzzled over. The form of the obelisk has existed since ancient times, but the pillars of the sun temples of the Fifth Dynasty were made from single stones and stood alone. Perhaps such an obelisk was seen by the Egyptians as a giant petrified ray of sunshine; the mythical site which was first touched by the rays of the morning sun. This would be borne out by the fact that the pyramid-shaped obelisk tips, and sometimes the shaft, too, were covered with gold.

The actual manner in which these obelisks were erected is not entirely clear to modern researchers. An elaborate ramp construction was very probably necessary, with the help of which the obelisk could have been tipped slowly onto its base, which was covered by a mass of sand to slow down the sinking of the blocks, some of which weighed more than a thousand tons.

Of the six **Colossi of Ramses II** which once stood before the pylon, only the two seated figures of grey granite (15.6 meters high) and a heavily restored statue (right) remain today. A relief on the south wall (c) of the adjacent **Columned Courtyard of Ramses II** shows how the pylon looked in ancient times. It depicts a festive procession, marking the occasion of the dedication ceremonies, led by 17 princes moving towards the pylon with its two obelisks, six colossi and four poles with flags flying.

The **Courtyard** (50 x 57 meters) itself is enclosed by a double row of 74 smooth columns with closed papyrus capitals. The same type of column appears in front of the granite **Chapel of Queen Hat-**

shepsut (b). But these older papyrus-shaped columns from the Eighteenth Dynasty are much more delicate, and the plants they portray also look far more realistic.

The **Mosque of Abû al-Haggâg** in the northeast corner of the courtyard is impressive not only because of its beautiful walls, but also because of the lofty heights to which it rises. This shows how deeply the temple was once buried under the sand.

Eleven huge statues, nearly all of which are made of granite, and two seated colossi dominate the southern half of the courtyard. They all carry the name of the great Ramses, but six of them were already built under Amenhotep III.

The Temple of Amenhotep III starts with the **Colonnade** (52 x 20 meters). Its 14 papyrus-shaped columns rise to a height of 16 meters and have open capi-

tals. The fine reliefs on the side walls (from the time of Tutankhamen and Horemheb) show the *Opet Festival*, the greatest state festival of the New Kingdom: Amen and his wife Mut and their son Khonsu visited Amen's "Southern Sanctuary" in Luxor every year at the time of the flooding of the Nile. The statues of the gods traveled the short journey from Karnak to Luxor in a magnificent ship which was pulled upstream along the bank of the Nile. A colorful crowd of people, musicians and dancers accompanied the procession, at the end of which were sacrificial ceremonies (the journey there is shown on the right, the return journey on the left).

An extensive **Columned Courtyard** (52 x 46 meters) opens out behind the colonnade. This is surrounded by a double row of ribbed papyrus-bundle columns. Pictures of this court of the Temple of Luxor were sent around the world in 1989, for during work on the foundations, Egyptian archeologists stumbled upon a sensational find: an

Above: Exterior wall of the Mosque of Abû al-Haggâg in the Temple of Luxor. Right: At the livestock market of Luxor.

ancient statue depot containing more than 20 mostly well-preserved statues. The statues of gods and kings are all of stone; the oldest ones come from the time of Amenhotep III. They have been on display in the **Luxor Museum** since 1992.

The covered temple building begins on the south face of the courtyard with a small hall of 32 columns, which is like a stone thicket of papyrus. The adjoining room (d) was also once a columned hall, but was rebuilt by Roman soldiers in the third century B.C. as a **chapel** for the worship of their emperor. They covered the Pharaonic reliefs with plaster and painted figures of court officials on it.

The complex of the cult chambers begins with the **Hall of Four Pillars**, where the sacrificial altar once stood. Directly beyond is the **Sanctuary** (e) for the god's barque. The large granite shrine was built in the name of Alexander the Great. It shows the conquerer, dressed as a Pharaoh, performing sacrifices to the gods. Behind it is another ritual chamber and the room where the god's statue was

kept (f). In front of the barque sanctuary a door to the left leads to one of the most famous rooms of the temple. Unfortunately, the reliefs of the **Birth Room** (g) have not been well preserved, due to the iconoclastic destruction of Akhnaton. With the help of the morning sun (or a flashlight) you can make out some of the pictures on a relief cycle portraying the divine birth of King Amenhotep III.

The most interesting scene is immediately to the left in the central strip of pictures on the long wall: here the ibis-headed god Thot, a messenger of Amen-Ra, tells the Queen Mother that she is to bear a holy child. One is, of course, reminded of the Christian story of Christmas here.

On the Nile Promenade, across from the Luxor Temple, a small **Museum of the Mummification Process** recently opened its doors. Animal mummies, coffins, implements used in mummification, and many other things help illustrate this aspect of the ancient Egyptians' provisions for life after death.

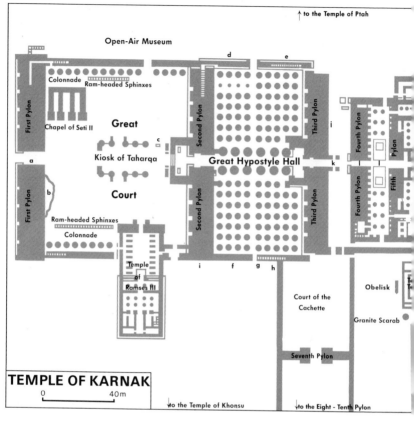

TEMPLE OF KARNAK

0   40m

↓to the Temple of Khonsu   ↓to the Eight - Tenth Pylon

KARNAK:
Temple City of Amen-Ra

Ancient Egypt's greatest holy place, the temple city of the King of the Gods Amen-Ra, lies near the present-day village of Karnak, two kilometers north of Luxor. The way there leads along the wonderful new Nile Promenade. On foot it takes a good half hour. A coach ride is perhaps a more inviting way of getting there, especially on hot days.

After a short distance, the modern edifice of the **Luxor Museum** can be seen on the Corniche to the right. The museum, which opened in 1976, offers an outstanding look into the art and history of old Thebes. The items on exibit are clearly displayed, well illuminated and have descriptions in several languages.

About one kilometer further on, the street branches off to the **Temple of Karnak**. Once the religious center of an empire, Karnak is today a gigantic archeological site with an overwhelming number of individual buildings. For 2,000 years – from the Middle Kingdom to Ptolemaic times – the great Pharaohs of Egyptian history built their temples, chapels and monuments here, and undertook restorations, extensions and renovations. Separated from each other by powerful brick walls, there are three main groups of buildings. The dominating center of these is the large **Temple Complex of Amen-Ra**. Sightseeing tours concen-

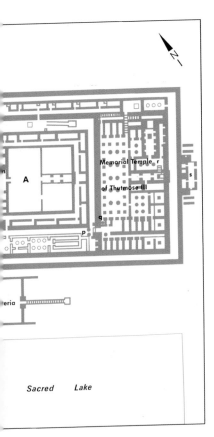

Memorial Temple of Thutmose III

Sacred Lake

The rule of thumb to understanding the complex is as follows: an Egyptian temple grows from the inside to the outside, from the holy of holies to the courtyards and gate buildings. The historical nucleus of the Amen Temple was therefore the point where the empty **Courtyard of the Middle Kingdom** (A) today extends. A few granite thresholds mark the point where the sanctuary used to be. That is all. According to the inscriptions, the kings of the Eighteenth Dynasty had the shrines of their ancestors removed, and replaced the older brick buildings with nicer ones of stone. But they also used the bricks of the older buildings as building material. And so in the Third Pylon, archeologists discovered the blocks of no fewer than 14 chapels. Among them were those of the oldest shrines of Karnak: the **White Chapel of Sesostris I** (1975-29 B.C.), famous for its fine reliefs, and the **Alabaster Chapel of Amenhotep I** (1525-04 B.C.).

The core of the present-day temple was built under Thutmose I (1504-1492 B.C.), and was protected from the outside world by two great gate buildings, the **Fourth** and **Fifth Pylons**. His daughter Hatshepsut (1479-57 B.C.) and her most bitter rival, Thutmose III (1479-25 B.C.), changed and extended this place of residence of the gods considerably: inside the temple countless chambers and chapels were built around the barque shrine (m), as well as a further gate construction, the **Sixth Pylon**. Several obelisks were erected, as well as the **Festival Temple of Thutmose III**, to the east. But this was not enough. The main temple, the axis of which runs parallel to the course of the sun from east to west, now also received a north-south axis: the **Seventh** and **Eighth Pylons** became the beginning of an imposing processional road to Luxor, leading to the "Southern Temple" of Amen-Ra.

Amenhotep III (1392-53 B.C.) was the next great builder in Karnak. He not only

trate on this, for the **Temple Complex of the Theban God Montu**, which borders it to the north, is closed to visitors. The **Temple of the Goddess Mut** – the wife of Amen-Ra – to the south lies almost completely in ruins, with little more than its foundations intact.

An aerial photograph and a layout plan in the First Pylon of the Amen Temple (a) illustrate the immense size of the area. But by this point, at the latest, you will begin to realize that trying to work out the history of the building can easiliy become confusing – even for experts on Egyptian dynasties! It is well worth having a look at the layout plan before you enter this fascinating labyrinth of wonders.

built the **Temple of Montu** and the **Temple of Mut**, but also built a further great gate, the **Third Pylon** of the central shrine of Amen-Ra. His son Akhnaton (1353-37 B.C.) also endowed Karnak with a temple, an open court enclosed by pillars to the east of the Temple of Amen. But the king's temple was destroyed not long after by Horemheb (1320-1297 B.C.), who used it as filling material in the construction of the **Ninth Pylon**. There it was later discovered: thousands of individual blocks, from which a 17-meter-long relief wall has been reconstructed in the Luxor Museum.

It was Horemheb, too, who built the last great gate construction of the north-south axis: the **Tenth Pylon**, with a sphinx avenue leading to the Temple of Mut. The **Second Pylon** of the central axis was also his work, and this gateway was to remain the majestic main portal for 1,000 years. However, the square in front of it was often rebuilt before it became the present-day **Great Court**: first Ramses II (1279-13 B.C.) decorated it with an avenue of ram-headed sphinxes; his grandson Seti II (1202-1197 B.C.) added a chapel to it and Ramses III (1191-89 B.C.) even added an entire temple.

King Taharqa (690-64 B.C.) had some of the ram-headed sphinxes removed to make way for a monumental columned baldaquin in front of the gate. They were moved in front of the colonnade built 300 years before by the kings of the Twenty-second Dynasty, the so-called Bubastid Kings. The most famous among them, Shoshenq I (945-24 B.C.) had planned to rebuild the square as a giant temple court. But the project was only carried out as far as the colonnade. It was much later when King Nektanebo I (380-62 B.C.) completed the project with the **First Pylon** after all.

Right: Ram-headed sphinxes in the Great Court of the Karnak Temple.

The Labyrinth of Wonders

Coming from the road you first cross a small, almost inconspicuous wooden bridge. The ditch beneath it was once part of a harbor basin into which a branch canal flowed from the Nile. Heavily-laden barges traveled along this canal to the temple, carrying the most varied assortment of wares, and the building materials which were always in demand.

This is where Amen-Ra's magnificent river barge headed when it set of on festival processions to Luxor or the western necropolis. Two **Obeslisks of Seti II** once ornamented the well-preserved **wharves**; today only one of them still stands. An avenue of 40 **ram-headed sphinxes** leads directly to the temple. The sacred animals of Amen are on high pedestals, and between their forelegs in the protection of their heads, each one has a small statue of Ramses II.

The eight-meter-thick surrounding wall is built of bricks of Nile mud. Integrated within it, the largest gate of Pharaonic Egypt forms the entrance to the temple city of Amen-Ra. This **First Pylon** (113 x 43.5 x 15 meters) was never completed. The blocks remained unpolished and have neither reliefs nor inscriptions on them. An exact dating of the building has only been possible since 1985, when the remains of a brick ramp on the back of the southern pylon were found containing bricks stamped with the name of Nektanebo I. This ramp (b) gives evidence of the building methods of the ancient Egyptians.

The **Great Court** has a surface area of 8,000 square meters, making it the largest temple court in the country. Dominating the court is a 21-meter-high column, the only one of 10 papyrus bundle columns of the **Kiosk of Taharqa** that remains standing. Stone barriers once connected the individual columns with one another, which were once roofed in by light wood or other material.

When Amen-Ra embarked on a procession there were many ceremonial stops made along the way. Two of the shrine stations, which only came alive on feast days, are found in the area of the Great Court: the **Chapel of Seti II** (left) and the **Temple of Ramses III**, a fine example of the synthesis of all the typical elements of an Egyptian temple. The temple façade takes the form of a gate tower, the pylon, its reliefs showing the king in the triumphal pose before Amen-Ra: with his arm raised, he is slaying the enemies of Egypt – on the one hand a symbol of the Pharaoh's claim to world power, on the other hand a magic gesture to ward off evil.

Two statues of the king flank the entrance to the colonnaded courtyard whose sides are lined not with columns, but with the so called *Osirian Pillars* – large pillars carved into mummiform statues of the king representing the god Osiris. A ramp brings you to the columned anteroom and the adjacent Hall of Columns. The inner sanctum consists of devotional chambers to the gods Amen-Ra, Mut (left) and Khonsu (right).

To the north of the great court is the **Open-air Museum**. There you can see fragments of the oldest shrines in Karnak. Two chapels have even been entirely reconstructed.

To the left of the entrance are several rows of granite and quartzite blocks with fine reliefs. They come from the **Red Chapel**, a barque sanctuary which stood in the center of the temple at the time of Hatshepsut. Her great adversary Thutmose III may have been responsible for tearing it down; at any rate the individual blocks were later used as fillers for the Third Pylon.

The undisputed masterpiece of the Open-air Museum is the **White Chapel**. Sesostris I had this chapel built for the celebrations marking his government's 30th year. The charming building with 16 pillars of white limestone is the oldest chapel in Karnak. Its wonderfully detailed reliefs show the king making offerings to the god Amen-Min, a syncretistic

an area of 5,406 square meters. The columns of the central nave are 24 meters high and have a circumference of 10 meters, which increases to 15 meters at their open capitals. The 122 columns of the side aisles have a circumference of "only" 6.4 meters and are 14 meters high. Originally the whole hall was covered by a roof.

The difference in height from the central nave to the side aisles was bridged by giant barred windows, some of which have been well preserved. Light fell through them onto the processional path of the divine barque, yet the side aisles were always in semi-darkness.

For more than half a century the Great Hypostyle Hall was a construction site: Amenhotep III built the central colonnade with 12 columns, Horemheb laid the foundations of the side aisles with the Second Pylon. And Seti I and his son Ramses II decorated the Great Hypostyle Hall with scenes of sacrificial offerings and processions: the father in a fine high relief (left), the son in a sunk relief (right).

fusion of Amen with Min, the god of fertility. Its fine reliefs make the **Alabaster Chapel of Amenhotep I** opposite well worth a visit. They also show the king making offerings to Amen-Min.

Back again in the Great Court, turn to face the **Second Pylon** of Horemheb. Two red granite **Colossi of Ramses II** flank the entrance of the dilapidated gateway. The left one is a 15-meter-high statue (c) of the king, with a smaller statue of his daughter and wife Merit-Amen. It was usurped by Pinedjem (c. 1065-45 B.C.), one of the priest-kings of the Theban Divine State in the Twenty-first Dynasty.

Passing through a small anteroom and the 29.5-meter-high portal you come to the architectural masterpiece of Karnak: the **Great Hypostyle Hall**. A hundred and thirty-four papyrus-bundle columns rise like a monumental petrified forest on

The most interesting pictures are found on the outer walls. They show the military campaigns of Seti I (d-e) and Ramses II (f-g) to Syria and Palestine. Ramses also celebrated his favorite subject in Karnak, the Battle of Qadesh, but here he included a copy of the famous Egyptian-Hittite peace treaty (h).

The reliefs and inscriptions of Shoshenq I (i) are of great interest to Bible scholars. He was the biblical Sisak who conquered Rehoboam of Judah, the successor of Solomon, in 927 B.C. Jerusalem is also mentioned among the conquered cities. Each of the towns is represented as a wall ring with the upper body of a chained opponent.

On the back (j) of the almost completely destroyed **Third Pylon** of Amenhotep III you will find the depiction of the more than 30-meter-long Nile ship of Amen-Ra, in which the King of the Gods

Above: Gigantic statue of Ramses II and his wife. Right: Hathor leading the king to Amen (relief in the Great Hypostyle Hall).

sailed on the Nile to his festival processions. Of the original four obelisks (near k) which once stood before the **Fourth Pylon** of Thutmose I, only one can be seen today: a monolith of red granite, 23 meters high and weighing 143 tons, with a dedication inscription of the same Thutmose I who also built the **Fifth Pylon**. Hatshepsut had two almost 30-meter-high obelisks erected (l) in front of this Fifth Pylon. Today, the tip of the southernmost one lies on the Holy Lake, the **Northern Obelisk** still stands in its original position. The clear shading of color on the granite shows how high the stone covering of Thutmose III once was. For here, too, he tried to extinguish at least the memory of the name of his hated predecessor, even though the golden tips of her obelisks continued to shine over Karnak.

Through the small, badly preserved **Sixth Pylon** of Thutmose III you reach the barque sanctuary (m). The two **Heraldic Pillars** of Thutmose III rise before it. The plants on the pillars are sculpted from the granite in the most classical severity of form: in the south (right) the lotus of Upper Egypt, in the north (left) the papyrus of Lower Egypt. To the left of the pillars two masterpieces from the time of Tutankhamen have been put on display again: the partly restored **Quartzite Statues of Amen and Amaunet**, Amen's companion in the myth of the creation of Hermopolis.

The **Granite Barque Shrine** was built on the site of an older chapel in the name of Philip Arrhidaeus, the half brother of Alexander the Great. It housed the sacred barque of Amen-Ra in which the god's statue was carried in ceremonial barque processions. The chambers of worship with the shrine of the god were behind the barque sanctuary. There are some lovely colored reliefs on the southern exterior wall which can be seen from the walkway. On the walls of this walkway Thutmose III had the annals of his 18 military campaigns and his gratitude to Amen-Ra inscribed. On the north wall (n) you can see two obelisks depicted

155

next to many valuable metal vessels and jewelry. Directly behind this is a room (o) with Hatsheput's beautiful colored reliefs. But the figure of the queen was completely hacked out – another of Thutmose III's acts of revenge.

On the other side of the Court of the Middle Kingdom (A) is the **Festival Temple of Thutmose III**. One enters the shrine, laid out at right angles to the main axis, through the central columned hall. Two statues mark the real entrance (p) a little further to the south. Immediately to the left of this is the chamber (q) containing a copy of the famous **Karnak Tablet of the Kings**, which shows Thutmose III making an offering in front of 62 statues of his named ancestors (original in the Louvre).

The unusual ground plan of this temple is dominated by a three-aisled hall of columns: 32 columns flank the slightly raised central aisle, which is supported by

20 columns looking like tent poles – a stone ceremonial tent unique to this temple. To the east of the hall of pillars is the **Botanical Garden** (r). Here you will see some fine high reliefs (only preserved in the lower section) in which Thutmose III had the flora and fauna immortalized, in almost school-book fashion, which he had seen during his military campaigns in the Middle East.

A modern wooden stairway leads to the temple's exit. Behind it, a small hill offers a good view of the whole area, and of the building ruins to the east of the Festival Temple. Along the rear of the building is a second **sanctuary** (s), another of Thutmose III's small temples. Unlike the great Amen Temple, this one faces the rising sun in the east and – in former times – an almost 31-meter-high obelisk (which today stands in front of the Lateran Palace in Rome). This was not only the tallest obelisk in ancient Egypt, it was also the only one which was erected to stand on its own (and not as one of a pair). Ramses II enlarged the

Above: Coachmen in Karnak holding a conversation. Right: Quartzite statue of Amen.

shrine to the east of the obelisk with a small temple, to which 600 years later King Taharqa added a hall with 20 columns, similar to the one in front of the Second Pylon. The 19-meter-high **East Gate** of Nektanebo I encloses the whole Amen Temple area.

The **Holy Lake** (200 x 117 meters) provided water for the priests' purification rites and served as the scene for ceremonial boat processions; or, unique to Karnak, as a pool for the sacred geese of Amen. Around the pool were the residences of the priests, storerooms, stables and rooms in which offerings were prepared. The produce needed in the temple and the food for the temple staff came from estates belonging to the temple. These were free of taxes because they belonged to the gods. This practice applied to all temples, but in the case of the Karnak state temple it led to enormous economic power.

Next to the mostly subterranean temple complex of King Taharqa, seen as the mythical tomb of Osiris, is now a small incongruously profane café. Tourist guides fondly call it the Coca-Cola Temple, a pleasant spot for a break. Only a few steps further on you come to the monumental **Granite Scarab of Amenhotep III** and the tip of the **Obelisk of Hatshepsut**.

A passageway leads to the neighboring **Courtyard of the Seventh Pylon**. This is the beginning of a succession of courtyards and gateways, aligned on a north-south axis all the way to the Tenth Pylon. At the beginning of the 20th century a spectacular discovery was made in the courtyard of the Seventh Pylon: more than 800 large stone figures and more than 17,000 bronze statuettes were excavated from the so-called *Cachette* – an ancient storeroom which was constructed during a "clearing up operation" in Ptolemaic times.

Of the many chapels and complexes of the temple city of Amen-Ra, there are

two which are especially worth visiting. The first is the small **Temple of Khonsu** in the extreme southwest. Construction of the temple began under Ramses III, but the relief decoration was only added under the priest-kings Herihor and Pinedjem. In front of this is the mighty **Southern Gate**, built by Ptolemy III, where the sphinx-lined boulevard to Luxor had existed since the New Kingdom.

Almost diagonally opposite is the small **Temple of Ptah** next to the **Northern Gate**. The temple was built by Thutmose III as a chapel, and Ptolemaic kings erected six delicate pylons in front of it. The headless stone statue of the god Ptah in the central sanctuary is impressive, as is the statue of his divine wife Sekhmet, on the right.

It is a special experience when the guard closes the gate: you will see the statues of the gods lit up by a single beam of light falling through a narrow shaft in the ceiling, illuminating them with a mystical luster while the rest of the room lies in semi-darkness.

THEBES WEST:
The Realm of the Dead

Since the mid-1990s there has been a bridge over the Nile south of Luxor, but a river crossing by ferry is still a more romantic way to get from one bank to the other. For the ancient Egyptians the west was synonymous with the Realm of the Dead. This is where everyone wanted to be buried, where the sun sinks over the horizon: in the "Beautiful West," as it is referred to in countless writings.

Beautiful did not necessarily refer to a paradise, but rather to the hope of a life after death; of resurrection and a new existence. For every evening the sun god went down in the west, into the depths of the beyond. And every morning he rose rejuvenated and shone again in the eastern sky. "You die in order that you might live" is one of the basic truths of ancient Egyptian belief, recorded in the oldest collections of religious aphorisms: the *Pyramid Texts.*

From the boat moorings the road leads through the fertile green fields and past idyllic hamlets. After a few kilometers you come to the edge of the desert and the heights of the western mountain range. Here you will find one of the largest cemeteries in Egypt. It stretches for almost eight kilometers and its temples and tombs run on three levels, parallel to the edge of the fertile lands. The royal mortuary temples are on the plains, the private tombs on the mountain slopes, and finally, in the innermost and most secret zone, in the ravines and valleys of the rocky massif, are the burial grounds of the kings and queens, princes and princesses.

But, at the same time, there are also some refreshing examples of the life of the living to be found in this realm of the dead. Many little villages are scattered over the intensively farmed fertile plains. Many families even live on the slopes of the western mountains – next to, above, and sometimes even inside the tombs of their ancestors of Pharaonic times. Their bright, cheerfully-painted mud brick houses have now become a tourist attraction in themselves.

It is customary all over Egypt – despite the Islamic disapproval of pictures – for a Mecca pilgrim to paint his house with motifs from his pilgrimage. But in Thebes West especially, a bubbling enthusiasm for painting seems to have found a new release – perhaps as a positive peripheral result of tourism. You will see not only the black cube of the Ka'aba of Mecca, or the pious pilgrim and his various means of transport – from the somewhat nostalgic camels to airplanes – but also the colorful palette of scenes of the everyday life of the villagers.

There are plenty of opportunities to look at these houses from close up; even to look inside them. Often you will find alabaster workshops behind the painted walls. Their hand-crafted products range from Pharaonic paraphernalia, cheap mass productions of every shape, size and color, to beautiful high-quality alabaster bowls.

The Valley of the Kings

When Thebes became the capital of the newly united empire of the Pharaohs at the beginning of the Eighteenth Dynasty, the kings also had their tombs erected here. But suddenly pyramids were no longer built, as had been the custom for more than a thousand years. Rock tombs were built instead in a hidden valley of the western mountains, far away from the royal mortuary temples on the fertile lands. Scholars have long puzzled over the reasons for these innovations, which were probably the result of several different factors. But the pyramids, which were also the symbol of the immortality of the

Left: Souvenirs are sold everywhere – even at the entrance to the Valley of the Kings.

god-king, were not given up altogether: the almost 500-meter-high mountain summit of **Al-Qurn** ("The Horn") dominates the Valley of the Kings like a natural pyramid.

The isolation of the valley may have influenced the choice of this new type of burial ground. It appeared easy to guard and seemed therefore safe from grave robbers. For the past had shown on more than one occassion that grave robbers did not stop even at the tombs of the kings. Perhaps the separation of tombs and places of worship had something to do with such safety considerations, too. But in the main they reflect a new religious perception of the world. For now Amen became the focus of the royal mortuary temples, and the worship of the dead ruler was only carried out in the side chambers.

The oldest tomb in the Valley of the Kings comes from the time of Thutmose I, whose architect Inene stated proudly that he was one of the few people who knew of the secret place where the Pharaoh was buried: "I oversaw the digging of the rock tomb of His Majesty, all alone, without being seen or heard."

As with all royal tombs of the early Eighteenth Dynasty, this one, too, consists of a steep, graded stairwell, an anteroom and a burial chamber leading off into a side room reserved for offerings. As time went on the complexes became larger, but only after Pharaoh Akhnaton's monotheistic interlude did the ground plan change: along a straight axis, long corridors flanked by niches and chambers guided the light of the sun deep into the interior of the mountain to the burial chamber.

Even today an aura of mystery seems to surround the Valley of the Kings: "... the silence of the world of the dead, as oppressive as the midday heat. A land from which no one can return, which

Right: Sunset over the Nile near Luxor.

everyone carries within him, now made visible before your eyes: the afterlife" (from Erik Hornung's *The Valley of the Kings*).

The walls of the tombs of the kings lavishly illustrate the ancient Egyptians' idea of the afterlife with an abundance of texts and pictures. These are the *Books of the Underworld*, and their symbolic language is often incomprehensible, even to scholars.

Visions of the afterlife, sometimes given in "geographical" details, had been the subject of a rich literature surrounding death since the time of the pyramids. But in the *Books of the Underworld* of the New Kingdom it was transformed into a veritable "science of the afterlife." At the center of these writings is the nocturnal journey of the sun through the so-called "Hidden Realm" and its triumphal rebirth in the morning. Because the dead king wanted to take part in this miracle himself, he had the nocturnal path of the sun portrayed in his tomb chamber.

The oldest book, called the *Amduat,* describes "that which is in the underworld" as being divided into 12 separate chambers. These chambers corresponded to the 12 night hours of the ancient Egyptian measurement of time. The ram-headed sun god travels through this dark realm in a golden barque and awakens the blessed dead to a new life, giving them light and food. But he also sits in judgement of the damned, and has them burned in the fires of hell or has their heads cut off.

Again and again the texts emphasize the importance of the dead knowing all the names of the places of the underworld, and all the creatures and demons that populate them. For only through this knowledge does he have power over the dangers of the threatening underworld. The last night hour shows the rebirth of the sun god transformed into a scarab, symbol of the morning sun.

The *Amduat* remained the most important wall decoration in burial chambers until the end of the New Kingdom. Only under Horemheb did priests begin to conceive new books of the underworld. First came the *Book of Gates*, which portrays the nocturnal journey of the sun in similar terms to that of the *Amduat*. But here the 12 hours are separated by portals or gates protected by daggers and fire-breathing serpents.

The somewhat more recent *Book of Caverns* divides the afterworld into caverns, not hours, which the sun god lights up, usually in the form of the disk of the sun. Ovals portraying the tombs of the blessed dead are characteristic of this book. The *Book of the Earth* is another of these "great books." But it consists mainly of a group of individual scenes celebrating the resurrection of the sun from the shadowy depths of the afterlife in impressive pictures.

The most famous book of ancient Egyptian afterlife literature is without a doubt the *Book of the Dead*, a loose collection of verses illustrated with vignettes. A total of 190 chapters of this book are now known. A selection of these was placed in the tomb with the deceased, but never all the chapters together. This was a magical instrument for a safe continued existence after death. In contrast to the royal *Books of the Underworld*, these writings were available to ordinary mortals, too.

But all these texts and pictures were not intended for the eye of the observer. After the burial ceremony the tombs were closed forever and the entrances filled in. The immense riches which the kings took with them to the afterlife soon tempted grave robbers. Investigative committees and trials yielded little, for even the priests apparently took part in the robberies. Because the robbers usually burned the mummies, out of fear of the curse of the Pharaohs, the priest-kings of the Twenty-first Dynasty tried at least to save the corpses of their honored ancestors. They hid them so well that they were only rediscovered at the end of the 19th

century, when they were brought by boat to Cairo.

For almost 500 years, from the Eighteenth to the Twentieth Dynasty, the Pharaohs were buried in the Valley of the Kings. Of a total of 62 tombs, 25 of them are royal burial places. The others, relatively simple shaft or chamber tombs, either belonged to high officials or have not yet been identified.

If you take into consideration the fact that one or another of the tombs is always temporarily closed for restoration work, you will find that, as a rule, only around 10 of the tombs will be open to the public at any one time.

The most important of the tombs are described in chronological order here. If you have a lot of time, you should also try to visit them in this order. This will aid your understanding of the increasingly complicated picture sequences some-

what. The tombs are all well marked (see map page 144). Tables with ground plans can be found in front of the entrances.

Tomb of Thutmose III (No. 34): The entrance to the tomb is in a narrow crevice in the extreme south of the valley and is reached today by way of a steep iron staircase. Steps and railings lead through a roughly-hewn, sloping passageway to an anteroom, the ceiling of which was made into a star-covered night sky. There are no fewer than 741 divinities and demons of the underworld listed on the walls.

Stairs lead from there into the oblong burial chamber, which is decorated with a star ceiling and an imitation of an oversized papyrus. All 12 hours of the *Amduat* are represented here in line drawings and cursive hieroglyphics on the walls. To the right, behind the quartzite sarcophagus of the Pharaoh, decorated with fine reliefs, is the resurrection scene: the barque of the ram-headed sun god passes through the body of a snake. The rejuvenated morning sun floats as a large

Above: A painting in the tomb of Seti I.
Right: Heads from Tutankhamen's entrails shrine (Egyptian Museum, Cairo).

162

scarab in front of the oval end of the underworld.

Tomb of Amenhotep II (No. 35): Like his father Thutmose III, Amenhotep II also had his burial chamber decorated with a star ceiling and the *Amduat*. But the strict right angle ground plan, with its straight lines, is different here, as is the decoration of the pillars. While the king and the gods of the dead are portrayed here only in outline, they are also depicted with unbelievable perfection of detail.

In the deeper-lying area of the room is the quartzite sarcophagus in which the king's mummy was found undamaged, decorated with flowers. In the side chambers, 11 other royal mummies were discovered by archeologists. They had been brought here to safety by the priest-kings of the Twenty-first Dynasty.

Tomb of Tutankhamen (No. 62): If you have already seen the wealth of treasures from Tutankhamen's tomb in the Egyptian Museum in Cairo, you will probably be amazed at how small the most famous of all the tombs of the Valley of the Kings is. A corridor leads down into the antechamber, which in turn leads to a small side chamber and to the burial chamber, which has another side room. In the center of the burial chamber stands the open quartzite sarcophagus, with its three richly-ornamented coffins. In the largest of these lie the mortal remains of the Boy King. This makes Tutankhamen the only Pharaoh of the New Kingdom who has been returned to his original tomb in the Valley of the Kings.

The pictures of the burial chamber show, on the east wall (right), the royal funeral procession. On the north wall, his successor Ay, dressed in the leopard skin of a priest, carries out the Mouth Opening Ceremony in order to bring his predecessor back to life; in the middle, Tutankhamen can be seen being greeted by the sky goddess Nut, and beside this, Osiris is shown embracing the king. On the west wall, the first hour of the royal guide to the underworld, the *Amduat*, is sketched; on the south wall, Tutankhamen stands between Anubis, the god of enbalming, and Hathor, ruler of the Theban Realm of the Dead.

Tomb of Horemheb (No. 57): The tomb of the last king of the Eighteenth Dynasty is entered through a corridor running 105 meters deep into the mountain. The colored reliefs of the two antechambers are among the finest in the whole valley. They show the king being accompanied by the gods into the interior of the tomb and bringing them offerings. The decoration of the burial chamber is incomplete, but it is for this very reason that it is so interesting: for the working methods of the artists can be clearly seen. They sketched texts and pictures in red coloring, and then made their corrections in black while others began the reliefs next to them.

For the first time, the *Book of Gates* is used as the subject of a series of pictures. An oversized *Osiris' Hall of Judgement* is shown, where the ruler of the underworld judges the fates of the dead. The red granite sarcophagus here is also quite impressive. To the left of it, a small side chamber opens out with a beautiful picture of Osiris.

Tomb of Seti I (No. 17): The 100-meter-long tomb of the first important king of the Nineteenth Dynasty is famous for the unrivalled elegance of its fine reliefs. The first two corridors are decorated with the *Litany of Ra*, a hymn to the sun god, and with pictures from the *Amduat*. The end of the steps in front of the third corridor are flanked by two pictures of the goddesses Isis and Nephthys. The walls of the third corridor show more scenes from the *Amduat*. The neighboring room, with the so-called "Tomb Robbers' Shaft," nowadays explained in mythological terms, leads to a four-pillared hall with further pictures of the nocturnal journey of the sun god. The

Right: Entrance to the tomb of Ramses VI in the Valley of the Kings.

portrayal here of the four known human races is particularly interesting: Egyptians, Asians with pointed beards, Libyans and Blacks are shown (on the left wall, lower register).

Straight ahead you will find the two-pillared hall with incomplete reliefs from the *Amduat*. To the left are two corridors leading deeper into the tomb, with scenes from the Mouth Opening Ceremony. First of all you come to the antechamber, a room with wonderful reliefs of the king before the gods, and then to the burial chamber, which is divided into a higher room of pillars and an arched crypt. This is where the discoverer of the tomb, Giovanni Belzoni, found the wonderful alabaster sarcophagus which today is to be seen in the Soane Museum in London. The ceiling is decorated with astronomic motifs and the stars from the northern constellation, which can no longer be identified today. The small chamber with the *Book of the Heavenly Cow* is the most interesting of the side rooms (next to the first pillar on the right): the goddess of the sky, Nut, is portrayed here as a cow. The barques of the sun god glide along her body.

Tomb of Merenptah (No. 8): The tomb complex of the son of Ramses II (whose own tomb is closed to the public) lies 110 meters underground. The relief cycles (which are badly preserved in part) show scenes from the *Book of Gates,* gods and hymns to the sun god. The burial chamber is very impressive with its splendid sarcophagus lid of red granite showing the dead king as Osiris in high relief.

Tomb of Ramses III (No. 11): With a length of 125 meters, this tomb is one of the largest in the Valley of the Kings. The reliefs have been well preserved in the upper chambers and the corridors, the first two of which are decorated with the *Litany of Ra* and with extracts from the *Amduat*. A total of 10 side chambers with rare and beautiful pictures lead from

these corridors. The chambers on the right hand side mainly show tomb offerings; on the left, offering scenes and scenes of worship are portrayed.

In the last chamber on the left is the famous (though damaged) picture of the two harp players, from which the tomb takes its nickname, the "Tomb of the Harpers." The neighboring hall bridges the deflection of the axis which was necessary when workers digging the corridors came across another tomb. On the walls are large paintings of gods and kings. The connecting series of rooms show mainly pictures of the nocturnal journey of the sun god through the underworld. The lower rooms have been badly damaged.

Tomb of Ramses VI (No. 9): The wonderful state of preservation of the colored reliefs and paintings make this tomb one of the climaxes of a visit to the Valley of the Kings. A flight of corridors and small rooms leads in a straight line into the interior of the mountain to the burial chamber. The side walls are dec-

orated with scenes from the *Amduat*, the *Book of Gates* and the *Book of Caverns*; the ceiling paintings symbolize astronomical constellations. Countless inscriptions in Greek script show that even in ancient times visitors came here.

As in no other tomb the pictures of the burial chamber seem to be a single celebration of resurrection and the rebirth of the sun in endless variations. On both of the narrow walls the *Book of the Earth* is portrayed: countless gods and goddesses raise the rejuvenated morning sun like a ball from the depths of the earth. A deep niche appears behind the great remains of the granite sarcophagus in the center of the crypt. There, the final picture from the *Book of Gates* shows the god Nun lifting the sun barque from the dark primeval waters to the light of day.

Perhaps the finest portrayals of this tomb are to be found on the arched ceiling of the crypt: the long-limbed body of the goddess of the sky, Nut, is to be seen twice – once in the form of the sky during the day, characterized by a single row of

stars, and once as the night sky, through which the sun is traveling until it is reborn from the womb of the goddess in the morning.

Tomb of Ramses IX (No. 6): A series of corridors leads to the burial chamber 82 meters deep inside the mountain. The murals once again depict the nightly travels of the sun god through the underworld, and show the king bringing offering for various gods. In the third corridor to the right is an unusual scene: the resurrection of the deceased Pharaoh. In the symbolic language of the ancient Egyptians, allegoric pictures express this important event. The mummy of the king can be seen, but the body is inclined and the arms stretched over the head, meaning that the king has just awoken from death. The completion of the act of resurrection is suggested by the scarab over the king's head, the most important

Above: Queen Nefertari bringing offerings to the goddess Isis. Right: Relief from the tomb of Prince Amen-her-khepeshef.

symbol of resurrection of the sun god, who renews himself daily. The side walls of the burial chamber are decorated with gods and demons. Here, too, the vaulted ceiling is ornamented with a picture of the goddess of the sky, Nut, whose slim body appears twice, as the symbol of both the skies of morning and of night.

The Valley of the Queens

In a picturesque side valley in the extreme south of the Theban western mountains is the *Place of Beauty*: the tombs of the queens, princes and princesses of the New Kingdom. Eighty tombs were found here, more modest constructions than those of the kings, and sometimes even without wall decorations. The most beautiful date from the time of Ramses II and Ramses III.

Tomb of Nefertari (No. 66): The tomb of Queen Nefertari, wife of Ramses II, is famous for the beauty and artistic perfection of its colorful reliefs. Six years of restoration work were completed in

1992. Since 1995, 150 visitors a day have been allowed in for 10 minutes (tickets available at the ticket office at the ferry landing, Thebes West).

A staircase leads down into the anteroom. As everywhere in the Valley of the Queens, the reliefs are cut into a layer of stucco which covers the somewhat crumbling limestone. On the left they illustrate the wishes of the dead, as described in the 17th chapter in the *Book of the Dead:* "To play board games, to become a living Ba, the soul of a bird, and during the day to pray to the sun" – who appears between the two lions on the horizon or as a sacred phoenix. Next to this you see the queen's mummy with Isis and Nephthys as female falcons weeping over it. There is also the heavenly cow and six demons of the afterlife armed with knives. Offerings were left on the ledge below.

To the right in the neighboring chamber are wonderful representations of the queen and various gods. At the end of the corridor, under a picture of the winged goddess Maat, you will find the opening to the burial chamber with three side rooms. The wall decoration, which, unfortunately, has been badly damaged by salt deposits, shows the beautiful queen before the gods.

Tomb of Titi (No. 52): Titi was the wife of one of the Ramses, but it is still not known which of the 11 kings of this name she married. Pictures of the winged Maat, the personification of the eternal world law, decorate the entrance to the long corridor, which describes the path of the queen to the gods in the interior of the tomb. The main chamber contains depictions of gods and demons, and is surrounded by three small side rooms: to the left is the tomb shaft, to the right, a beautiful picture of the Hathor cow in the western mountains, and in the center, the ruler of the afterlife, Osiris, on the throne.

Tomb of Amen-her-khepeshef (No. 55): This prince's tomb, with its beautifully-preserved stucco reliefs, is one of

the main attractions in the Valley of the Queens. A small anteroom is reached by a staircase. Here the prince, always as a youth with a child's curls, is shown with his father Ramses III making offerings to the gods who accompany them further into the underworld. The individual portals are only opened to those who know the names of the terrible guards. So extracts from the 144th chapter of the *Book of the Dead* are painted on the walls as a magical aid to the little prince. In the unadorned burial chamber lies the granite sarcophagus which was almost certainly not intended for the mummified fetus (in the glass case).

Tomb of Kha-em-Waset (No. 44): This somewhat larger tomb belongs to another of Ramses III's sons, and is decorated with a similar series of pictures. But here the burial chamber is decorated, too: a lion and a jackal guard the tomb (at the entrance); Ramses III offers sacrifices and is led to Osiris (back wall) by Isis and Neith (left) and Nephthys and Selkis (right).

167

The Private Tombs

On the other side of the fertile lands, on the bare hills of the western mountains, a huge necropolis grew up in which the aristocrats, the kings' loyal advisors and high state officials, but also lower Theban priests, artists and artisans, could build their tombs with royal approval. Together with countless undecorated shafts, some 450 private tombs have now been found. They are decorated with paintings, and occasionally with reliefs. Many of them are badly damaged, but the **Tombs of Sheikh 'Abd al-Qurna** are among the shining highlights of any visit to Egypt.

Situated in the middle of the village is a group of rock tombs from the Eighteenth Dynasty. Their colorful series of pictures are much easier to read than the mythological underworld pictures of the

Above: Modern house murals in Sheikh 'Abd al-Qurna. Right: Musicians from the tomb of Rekhmire.

kings' tombs. The catalogue of subjects depicted in these tombs includes agricultural scenes, splendid banquets, pleasant boat journeys, but also touching burial processions. As always, of course, these pictures had a magical reality for the dead. But here, it seems, a world view more inclined to this life could be traced in pictures aimed at the observer. And, indeed, visitors did come to the tombs: every year, at the *Beautiful Feast of the Desert Valley*, relatives – after they had performed certain rituals – held a banquet at the place where the dead were buried.

A private Theban tomb was comprised of four principal elements: the open forecourt, in which people gathered for festivals; the transept, representing the symbolic border between this world and the next, decorated with worldly scenes; the long hall, which represented the dead person's way to the netherworld and which was devoted primarily to religious pictures; and, finally, the burial chamber, usually undecorated, which was inaccessible to the living.

After the chambers had been hewn from the rather soft limestone rocks, the walls were smoothed with mud plaster and finally covered with a thin stucco layer. They were then painted over with calcimine *al secco*.

Tomb of Rekhmire (No. 100): The Tomb of Rekhmire, a vizier under Thutmose III, is an impressive complex high above the plain. The paintings in the transept illustrate his official duties as vizier. Of particular interest in the left wing are the portrayals of Asians, Nubians, inhabitants of Punt and Cretans. They are shown bringing their tributes, which include elephant tusks, ostrich eggs and feathers, beautiful vessels, incense trees and exotic animals, including giraffes, baboons, elephants, and even a brown bear.

On the entrance wall of the right wing you will see a painting of a royal statue workshop, and opposite that a hunt in the desert. The long hall has an imposing sloped ceiling. The murals on the right show a banquet with many guests, beautiful servant girls and musicians. Opposite, various period workshops producing bricks, stone vessels, jewelry, statues and furniture have been depicted with careful attention to detail.

The funeral procession (left) is next, then acts of worship before the statue of the dead (right). A barque journey of the statue on a pool in a palm grove can also be seen. On both sides of the prayer niche, high up in front, the tomb owner is shown sitting in front of a richly covered offering table.

Tomb of Sennefer (No. 96): A few steps above the tomb of Rekhmire is the tomb of Sennefer, who was mayor of Thebes at the time of Amenhotep II. The chambers of worship located above ground are not accessible, but Sennefer had his burial chamber designed in an unusually luxurious way.

Visitors climb down 44 steps through a tunnel to the antechamber. Here the unique creeping vine motifs which gave the tomb its nickname, the "Vine Arbor Tomb," can be seen. On vines which

thor, the pictures of his burial procession (left) and the texts and scenes of the 151st chapter of the *Book of the Dead* (right). These place the mummification of the corpse under the protection of the divine embalmer Anubis.

Tomb of Nakht (No. 52): The small tomb of Nakht, temple astronomer and scribe during the reign of Thutmose IV, is perhaps one of the most beautiful rock tombs of Egypt. The entrance is via a modern anteroom where photographs are displayed of the scenes from the transept, which is the only part of the tomb with mural paintings. This gives you an opportunity to study the paintings before you are allowed to see the originals, as part of a small group, inside the tomb.

The pictures on the left show the entire agricultural cycle in great detail, from sowing to harvesting. The pink speckled effect of the false door was intended to magically transform it into permanent pink granite. But it is the scenes of the banquet next to it that bewitch the visitor, with its beautiful female musicians and graceful women, whose finely pleated dresses are colored gold by the melting cones of ointment they carry on their heads. In the right wing, Nakht and his wife can be seen sitting at an offering table, hunting in a papyrus thicket and on a bird hunt. The picture of the grape harvest (on the narrow wall) is particularly beautiful.

seem to be rooted in the floor of the chamber, splendid grapevines laden with fruit climb the walls and cover the ceiling, the uneven contours of which also imitate the structure of a vine arbor. The walls show scenes of servants bringing the tomb furnishings: death masks, collars, furniture and vessels. On both sides of the entrance to the burial chamber you can see Sennefer with his wife Sennefret, carrying sacred musical instruments in the form of a rattle (*sistrum*) and a wide chain (*menit*).

The walls and the four pillars of the burial chamber, too, are decorated with wonderful paintings. Most of them show the dead man with his wives, whether at prayer, while making offerings or at the dinner table. Of great significance for the dead were the portrayals of the great gods of the afterlife, Osiris, Anubis and Ha-

Tomb of Menena (No. 69): Menena was a contemporary of Nakht, obvious right away from the similarity of the wall paintings. In the transept you can see the estate administrator supervising field work on the left, and at a banquet on the right. The first part of the long hall immortalizes the burial celebrations. Then, the judgement of the dead is shown (left), whereby the heart of the deceased is weighed against a statuette of Maat, the goddess of truth. Opposite this is a charming portrayal of a hunt in a papyrus thicket.

Above: The tomb owner Nakht and his wife during sacrificial rites. Right: Nubians, Asians and Libyans as portrayed in the tomb of Ramose.

Tomb of Ramose (No. 55): The vizier of Amenhotep III and his son Akhnaton had this true palace of a tomb built at the foot of the western mountains. It has a wide forecourt, a monumental pillared hall and a colonnade with its own chamber of worship in the form of a long hall. But when Ramose died decoration of the walls of the transept had only just begun. Their unusually fine reliefs and paintings are among the masterpieces of ancient Egyptian art. They show Ramose dressed in the high apron of a vizier in various scenes of sacrifice (to the right of the entrance) and in the circle of his loved ones at a festive banquet (to the left of the entrance).

On the long wall the funeral procession moves towards the tomb, before which the mummy of the dead man has been placed for ritual treatment. Directly below this the ramp leads to the underground burial chamber. The (partly incomplete) reliefs on the back wall are a unique example of Akhnaton's revolutionary rejection of the traditional conventions of style. The king appears on both sides of the (blocked) passageway to the long hall. On the left, portrayed in the traditional manner, he is shown sitting under a baldequin accepting Ramose's homage. But on the right the Amarna style has become dominant: under the rays of the sun god Aton, the king, accompanied by Nefertiti, is shown leaning out of the palace window down to Ramose. The vizier, richly bedecked in necklaces of the gold of honor, is being enthusiastically fêted by the courtiers.

Dair al-Madîna:
The Village of Artists

In a valley basin not far from the Valley of the Queens are the stone witnesses to a lucky archeological find: the village of artists and artisans who worked in the tombs of the Valley of Kings and in other important cemeteries in Thebes West. However, the French archeologists did not only stumble upon one of the few known settlements from Pharaonic times:

by chance they also discovered a colorful chronicle of its inhabitants.

In a "rubbish ditch" they discovered around 5,000 *ostraka*, clay and limestone shards used for notes, sketch blocks, letters or reports. With these it became possible to attach names to the otherwise unknown master craftsmen. Indeed, even their families, their moods and dogmatism are now known.

The founder of this artists' village was probably King Amenhotep I, who was revered here as a patron saint after his death. On average, 40 to 60 artists and craftsmen lived in the village with their families. The walls of their small two-storied houses have been well preserved, some, in fact, still show traces of their original paintwork.

The ancient Egyptian week had 10 days, on weekends and feast days no

Above: A galloping group of riders in the Western Mountains. Right: Hathoric capital in the temple of Hatshepsut. Far right: Hard at work in an alabaster factory.

work was done. Once a month (that is to say every three weeks) was payday. Payment took the form of natural produce, i.e., grain, which served as currency in bartering. When payment became even more infrequent, and finally ceased altogether in the Twentieth Dynasty, the artists reacted with the first known strike in the history of the world.

The chapels of the gods are in the north of the settlement, along with a small **temple** from Ptolemaic times which was later transformed into a monastery by Christian monks, and which gave the region its name: *Dair al-Madîna*, "The Town Monastery."

The slope in the west of the village became the artists' tomb hill. At one time places of worship rose above the beautifully painted rock chambers, crowned with small mud brick pyramids. As a rule, two of these tombs are open to the public. These are the tombs of Sennedjem and Inhercha.

Tomb of Sennedjem (No. 1): The tomb of the craftsman Sennedjem was

found unplundered. Sennedjem belonged to the guild of the craftsmen of Dair al-Madîna as "a servant at the place of truth" in the Nineteenth Dynasty. The beautiful tomb furnishings are in the Egyptian Museum in Cairo (Upper Floor, Room 17).

You climb down some a staircase into the vaulted burial chamber, which is painted all around with illustrations and texts from the *Book of the Dead*. The most famous row of scenes is that of the *Realms of the Blessed* on the narrow wall to the right, which shows the deceased and his wife in colorful pictures sowing and harvesting in the afterlife. The portrayal of the tree goddess (above left in the vault of the ceiling), whose body grows from a tree trunk, was also intended to ensure the physical well-being of the dead in the afterlife.

Tomb of Inherkha (No. 359): Almost directly opposite the tomb of Sennedjem is the Tomb of Inherkha, chief overseer of the craftsmen under the kings Ramses III and Ramses IV. The paintings of the lower of the two rock chambers are fantastically preserved. The free brush strokes with which the artist sketched the outlines of the objects and figures of his own tomb can be clearly seen. The pictures show the deceased with his family, scenes of worship, and extracts from the favorite 17th verse of the *Book of the Dead*. Of particular interest is the picture of the Great Tomcat – a symbol of the sun god Ra – destroying evil in the form of a serpent.

The Temples of Dair al-Bahrî

A 300-meter-high, semicircular rock basin surrounds the temples of Dair al-Bahrî; once three huge temple complexes to which three monumental processional paths led from the fertile lands. Three whitewashed parallel causeways – between 37 and 46 meters wide, with limestone wall embankments and sphinxes and statues – ended in the gardens in front of the temple terraces. These oases, created by human hands,

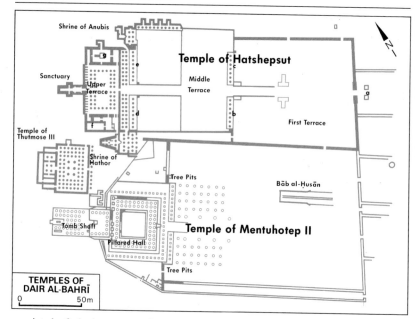

Shrine of Anubis

Temple of Hatshepsut

Sanctuary

Upper Terrace

Middle Terrace

First Terrace

Temple of Thutmose III

Shrine of Hathor

Tree Pits

Bâb al-Husân

Temple of Mentuhotep II

Tomb Shaft

Pillared Hall

Tree Pits

TEMPLES OF DAIR AL-BAHRÎ

0   50m

consisted of shady groves of tamarisks and sycamores, watered by the artificial basins of small temple pools which stood in the midst of flower beds.

Most of this has long since disappeared, and only lives on in the old texts and plans drawn up by archeologists. But the unusual terrace architecture of the temple ruins gives you some idea of the former splendor of the place. The temples, together with the rocky cliff in the background, formed a truly spectacular stage for the celebrations surrounding the annual *Beautiful Feast of the Valley*, during which the divine barque of Amen visited the temple on the west bank of the Nile in a great procession.

The oldest complex in Dair al-Bahrî, the **Mortuary Temple of Mentuhotep II**, has been badly damaged. The founder of the Middle Kingdom had his tomb shaft hewn 150 meters into the inside of the mountain and built a massive terrace

Right: Waiting for tourists at the entrance of the temple of Hatshepsut.

in front of it. This was surrounded by the regular rows of a virtual stone forest of 140 pillars. Even today experts disagree on the structure's architectural and religious concept: Was there a pyramid at one time above the massive terrace, or did it look like a great mastaba, symbolizing the primeval hill of the beginning of creation? In the forecourt a large crater can be seen: the *Bâb al-Husân*. Its name, "Gate of the Horse," comes from one of the most popular anecdotes told by archeologists. Howard Carter's horse stumbled into the "treasure trove" here, which opens out into a burial chamber after a 150-meter corridor. And this is where, among other things, the famous seated statue of the king was found, wrapped in linen bandages like a mummy with its skin painted black – the symbol of fertility and resurrection (Egyptian Museum, Cairo, Ground Floor, Gallery 26).

About 500 years later, to the north of the Temple of Mentuhotep, the **Terrace Temple of Hatshepsut** was built. This is an architectural masterpiece, the only

example of this form of temple in Pharaonic Egypt. The temple rises in the three giant artificially-built plateaux of a huge step construction towards the inner sanctum, which was dug from the mountain as a rock chamber. It is thanks to the work of archeologists and restorers that you can visit the terrace complex today, for when the temple was discovered in the 19th century, it was simply a pile of rubble, the result of a long chain of destruction, ranging from the acts of revenge of Thutmose III and Akhnaton's iconoclasm to natural disasters.

The road which leads from the fertile lands to the temple follows the course of the ancient processional path, once an avenue of more than 100 sandstone sphinxes. The gate, now completely in ruins, was flanked by two persea trees in Hatscheput's time. The stumps of the 3,500 years old trees can still be seen in the hollow (a), where they are protected by fences.

The **Lower Terrace** is, strictly speaking, the forecourt of the temple, but there is little there to remind you of the once blooming garden and papyrus plants. On both sides of the ramp the façade of the **Central Terrace** is formed into a colonnade. The (badly preserved) reliefs show on the left (b) the transportation of a pair of obelisks from Aswan to Thebes, and on the right (c) the queen hunting in a papyrus thicket.

Two shrines flank the pillared walkways on the Central Terrace: on the right stands the **Chapel of Anubis**; on the left the little **Chapel of Hathor**, a rock grotto with a hall of pillars. The Hathoric capitals of the pillars are gracefully carved. They show the goddess' countenance (from the front!) with the ears of a cow. The delicate wall reliefs, by comparison, show Hathor in the form of a cow.

The most famous scenes in the temple show an expedition to the Land of Punt, from where the ancient Egyptians got frankincense and myrrh, and which today is localized in eastern Sudan and northern Eritrea. The narrow wall of the **Punt Hall** (d) shows the Egyptian delegation being

175

greeted by the inhabitants of Punt, who are accompanied by their queen (whose voluptuous figure seems to be less a clinical picture and more an ideal of fertility). They are also shown exchanging Egyptian daggers, chains and gold for frankincense trees and elephant tusks. The lake dwellings of Punt shown in the background are particularly beautiful. On the long wall you can see the Egyptian sailing ships being loaded up, and the return journey across the Red Sea. Back in Egypt, Hatshepsut (chiseled out) dedicates the precious frankincense, which is being measured out in bushels, to Amen.

The relief cycle in the **Birth Hall** (e) shows Hatshepsut's divine origins (this can only be clearly made out in the morning light). From left to right the scenes show: Amen with the queen mother Ahmose holding hands on a bed; Amen in front of the ram-headed Khnum, who is making the queen and her Ka (as a young boy!) on the potter's wheel; Thot telling Ahmose of the birth of her divine child; and finally Ahmose on her way to the Birth Hall.

The splendid, colorful reliefs of the **Anubis Chapel** have been extremely well preserved by comparison. The luxuriantly laid banquet tables in front of the gods on the rear wall of the columned anteroom are particularly beautiful.

The **Upper Terrace** is closed for restoration work. It consists of an open columned court in front of the central Amen sanctuary, side rooms for the worship of the dead queen and her father (f), and a sacrificial courtyard for the worship of the sun (g).

The remains of a third shrine in Dair al-Bahrî were only discovered a few years ago. And, although the **Temple of Thutmose III** was probably destroyed during a landslide in ancient times and later used as a quarry, wonderful reliefs

have been excavated, some of which can be seen in the Luxor Museum.

The Mortuary Temple of Seti I

If you want to have an Egyptian temple all to yourself, this is this is the place you should head. Forgotten by tourist groups, the Temple of Seti I is found near the little village of Qurna. Its relief decorations are, as in all the other buildings of this king, of special elegance and grace.

Hardly anything remains today of either of the **pylons** which once separated two great courtyards in front of the temple. But the sanctum of Amen and the dead king has been to a large extent preserved. A **colonnade** of papyrus-shaped columns forms the façade of the three-membered temple tract. On the walls you can see Seti I making offerings before the ram-headed barque of Amen. The central aisle leads first to a **hall of papyrus-bundle columns** containing beautiful reliefs showing the king making offerings.

The pictures in the six **side chambers** show various acts of devotion before the gods, among which Seti can also be found. The temple rooms proper follow the raised transept: the **Barque Room** with the pedestal for the sacred barque of Amen, and behind it the **Four-pillared Hall** for the statue of the god.

In the left-hand temple tract are chambers of worship for Ramses I, the father of Seti I. The right wing is decorated with Ramses II's reliefs. He had the temple completed after the death his father Seti I. The center of worship in this part of the temple was a long courtyard, once surrounded by columns, with an altar to the sun god.

The Ramesseum: Mortuary Temple of Ramses II

The "Tomb of Osymandias," as the Roman author Diodorus called the

Right: The broken remains of the great colossus in the Ramesseum.

temple complex of Ramses II, is surely one of the most charming temple ruins in West Thebes. Its well-restored state of ruin radiates that romantic magic which makes the discovery of ancient cultures so fascinating. Huge blocks and statue fragments lie spread around the grounds as if scattered by the hand of a Titan. Like giant memorials, a row of enormous Osirian pillars towers above the area. And all this is set against the imposing background of the tomb mountain of Sheikh 'Abd al-Qurna.

On the other hand, the temple architecture – including even sections of the relief decoration – is in such fine condition that you can easily get a good impression of their original splendor. Surrounded by a strong wall made of Nile mud bricks, the temple was comprised of two pylons with large courtyards, a peristyle, and the now almost completely destroyed chambers of worship to Amen and the deceased king. A great number of storerooms built of mud bricks, priest's homes and a temple

school were grouped around three sides of the stone temple building.

Scenes on the great **Entrance Pylon** once again celebrate the Syrian wars of the great Ramses (on the north tower, left), in particular the Battle of Qadesh (on the south tower, right). The steps to the **Second Pylon**, of which today only the north tower still stands, were once flanked by two 17.5-meter-high **granite colossi**. One of these gigantic seated figures is still there, though broken into huge pieces of gargantuan proportions. One index finger alone is a full meter long, and the chest measures seven meters! The Second Pylon, too, shows Ramses on a chariot as the hero of Qadesh, storming the ill-fated fortress surrounded by the river Orontes.

In the west of the Second Courtyard is a **colonnade** made of two rows of Osirian pillars and papyrus-shaped columns. This forms the façade of the once covered temple building, which begins at the peristyle. Beautiful reliefs can be seen on the walls of the small neighboring **Eight-**

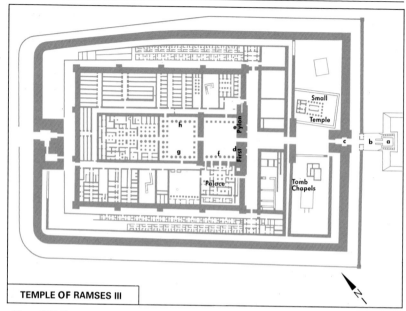

TEMPLE OF RAMSES III

pillared Hall, especially on the back wall to the right. Ramses is sitting in front of the *Ished* tree of the god Atum of Heliopolis who, with the scribe goddess Seshat and Thot, is writing the name of the king on the leaves of the sacred tree, thereby ensuring the ruler a long and happy reign – even in the afterlife. The other temple rooms have been destroyed.

Madînat Hâbû

The southernmost of the "Houses of Millions of Years," as the ancient Egyptians optimistically called the temples of their dead kings, is the Mortuary Temple of Ramses III in Madînat Hâbû. A double ring wall surrounds the huge temple area, which also includes a series of further buildings: the **Lesser Temple** of the Eighteenth Dynasty, whose huge pylon with the winged sun was only erected in Ptolemaic times; the **Tomb Chapels of**

Right: The southern Colossus of Memnon, an attraction even in ancient times.

178

the Divine Adoratrices of Amen, high priestesses of Amen who held political power in Thebes in the Twenty-fifth and Twenty-sixth Dynasties; and countless farm buildings, storerooms and residential areas.

At the end of the New Kingdom, the center of administration of the whole Pharaonic necropolis was located in Madînat Hâbû. In Christian times the Copts settled here and built a church in the middle of the temple. Only in the ninth century A.D. was this millenia-old place of worship finally abandoned.

In the center of this temple city the **Mortuary Temple of Ramses III** rises up, in some ways almost an imitation of the Ramesseum. A unique feature of Egyptian architecture is the **High Gate** (c) which, together with the stone wall, gives the complex the air of an Asian fort. Directly in front of the **East Gate** (b) of the outer brick wall archeologists have been able to find traces of a **quay** (a) built on the basin of a large lake, which today is filled by sand.

On both towers of the First Pylon the king is portrayed in a traditional pose of triumph, slaying his enemies. The great opponents of Ramses III were the Libyans and the sea peoples, an alliance of various tribes of Asia Minor. The victorious Egyptian battles are the subjects of the first courtyard, whose pictures and inscriptions celebrate Ramses as a war hero. On the back of the pylon he is shown on a chariot (d) or consulting with his generals (e), who verify the numbers of killed enemies by their amputated hands and penises.

Behind the **balcony** (f) in the south wall of the courtyard are the remains of a small **palace** where the king and his court lived during festivals – in this life and the next. The reliefs of the Second Courtyard are dedicated to such temple festivals: in the south (g) a feast in honor of Sokar, god of the dead in Memphis, and in the north (h) the feast of the fertility god Min, a harvest festival at whose center is a procession of the idol led by a white bull, Min's sacred animal. Of the con-necting rooms, the columned hall and a succession of chambers of worship, only portions of the lower walls and the stumps of columns remain.

The Colossi of Memnon

In the middle of the fertile lands are two gigantic seated figures of quartzite: the **Colossi of Memnon**, the legendary king whom killed Achilles before Troy – at least that is who the Greeks thought these almost 18-meter-high statues of Amenhotep III were.

At one time these monoliths guarded the gate to his mortuary temple, of which little otherwise remains. The legend of the song of Memnon, with which he greeted his mother Eos – the goddess of the dawn – every morning made the Colossi a much-visited wonder of the world even in ancient times. The mysterious singing was only silenced when the northern statue's upper body was shattered in an earthquake in 27 B.C. It was restored some 200 years later.

LUXOR
Area Code 095

Transportation

BY AIR: Many international airlines and charter companies offer regular and direct flights to Luxor, and Egypt Air offers Cairo – Luxor flights several times a day.

BY TRAIN: Trains also run regularly from all larger Nile Valley towns to Luxor. Several trains daily serve the Cairo – Luxor – Aswan route.

BY BUS / GROUP TAXI: The *Upper Egypt Bus Company* operates a regular bus route four times a day from Cairo (Md. Ahmad Hilmî Bus Station, behind train station) to Luxor, stopping on the way at all larger Nile Valley towns.

Those wanting to travel with deluxe buses should purchase their tickets at least one day prior to departure at the bus company's counter in the bus station. Luxor can also be comfortably reached from the Red Sea, as there are regular buses operating between Luxor and Hurghada. For reasons of security, these trips can currently only be undertaken with a military escort.

Accommodation

Luxor offers a variety of hotels in all categories. During tourist seasons it is advisable to book rooms well in advance.

Almost all hotels are situated on the east bank of the Nile. The luxury hotels with their broad gardens line the river bank from Karnak, 3 km in the east, to the idyllic Crocodile Island peninsula, 8 km west of Luxor.

But even the moderately-priced hotels have charming locations, whether directly on the Corniche an-Nîl, in the city center or in surrounding side streets. Travelers who don't mind simple accommodation can escape mass tourism by choosing one of the hotels in Thebes West. The warm and heartfelt welcome of the locals more than makes up for the lack of certain comforts.

LUXURY: City Center: **Mercure Luxor**, Corniche an-Nîl, tel. 380944, fax. 374912; **Sofitel Winter Palace** and **New Winter Palace**, Corniche an-Nîl, tel. 380422/23, fax. 374087. *Outskirts of Town:* **Luxor Hilton**, New Karnak, tel. 374933, fax. 376571; **Akhenaton Village**, Club Mediterranée, Sh. Khâlid Ibn al-Walîd, tel. 380850, fax. 380879; **Isis**, Sh. Khâlid Ibn al-Walîd, tel. 372750, fax. 372923; **Luxor Sheraton**, Al-'Awamîya, tel. 374544, fax. 374941; **Mövenpick Jolie Ville**, Crocodile Island, tel. 374855, fax. 374936.

MODERATE: City Center: **Luxor Wena Hotel**, at Luxor temple, tel. / fax. 380017; **Novotel Luxor**, Sh. Khâlid Ibn al-Walîd, tel. 380925, fax. 380972; **Mercure Inn Egotel**, 10 Sh. Ma'bad Luxor, tel. 373321, fax. 370051; **Emilio**, Sh. Yûsuf Hasan, tel.

373570, fax. 374884; **New Windsor**, Sh. Nefertiti, tel. 374306, fax. 373447; **Philippe**, Sh. Dr. Labîb Habashî, tel. 372284, fax. 380060.

BUDGET: City Center: **Mina Palace**, Corniche an-Nîl, tel. 372074; **Pyramids**, Sh. Yûsuf Hasan, tel. 373243; **Ramoza**, Sh. Sa'd Zaghlûl, tel. 372270, fax. 381670; **Santa Maria**, Sh. Television, tel. 380430; **Beau Soleil**, Sh. Salâh ad-Dîn, tel. 372671; **Sphinx**, Sh. Yûsuf Hasan, tel. 373243; **Venus**, Sh. Yûsuf Hasan, tel. 372652.

Karnak: **Horus**, Sh. Ma'bad Karnak, tel. 372165; **Nefertiti**, Sh. Ma'bad Karnak, tel. 372386.

Thebes West: **Abdul Kassem**, next to the temple of Seti I; **Pharao Hotel**, behind the offices of the Department of Antiquities at Madînat Hâbû; **Hotel Marsam**, behind the Colossi of Memnon; **Habu Hotel**, opposite the Madînat Hâbû temple.

YOUTH HOSTEL: **Youth Hostel**, 16 Sh. Ma'bad Karnak, tel. 372139.

Restaurants

The **Mercure Luxor**, **Luxor Hilton**, **Luxor Sheraton** and **Mövenpick Jolie Ville** hotels have excellent restaurants serving Oriental and international cuisine. Simple restaurants with Oriental dishes – and with somewhat more accessible prices – can be found behind the Luxor Temple and around the train station. In addition we recommend: the **Restaurant of the Mina Palace Hotel**, Corniche an-Nîl; the **Restaurant Marhaba**, with a lovely terrace overlooking the Nile, Luxor Tourist Bazaar; the terrace café of the **Mercure Luxor Hotel**, Corniche an-Nîl serves snacks and light meals.

Museums

Luxor Museum, Corniche an-Nîl, open daily 9 am to noon and 4 to 9 pm, in summer 10 am to 1 pm and 5 to 10 pm – extra charge for the hall with the statue finds from Luxor Temple; **Museum of Mummification**, Corniche an-Nîl, same hours as Luxor Museum; **Open-air Museum**, Temple of Karnak, open daily 8 am–5 pm.

Luxor by Night

Sound-and-Light shows in various languages are presented twice a day, at 6 pm (in summer at 6:30 pm) and 7:30 pm (in summer at 8 pm), in the **Temple of Karnak**. The languages of the presentations are in the following order:

Monday – English then French; Tuesday – French then English; Wednesday – English then German; Thursday – Arabic then English; Friday – French then English; Saturday – English then French; Sunday – French then German.

Luxor Temple, open to the public every evening from 6:30 to 9 pm, offers visitors an atmospheric illumination.

Western-style **discotheques** can be found in the Luxor Hilton and Mercure Luxor hotels.

The **nightclubs** in the Old Winter Palace and the Isis Hotel offer live music and belly dancing; the Isis Hotel sometimes also offers international folklore shows.

The **Mövenpick Jolie Ville** holds a regular *Oriental Dinner* with belly dancing and Egyptian folklore shows.

The **Fellah's Tent**, a large tent in the hotel garden of the Jolie Ville, is used as a nightclub or as a stylish backdrop for belly-dancing shows. Performances do not take place regularly, so it is advisable to ask for information at the reception desk.

Tourist Information

State Tourist Office, Tourist Bazaar (next to New Winter Palace Hotel), tel. 372215; at the airport, tel. 383294.

Transportation

The best way to get through town is by **taxi** and **horsecart**. To avoid frustrating haggles with the drivers (and drastic overcharges), ask your hotel for the official fares for the routes in question. The horsecart drivers of Luxor have a long-standing reputation for being a pack of robbers!

Bicycles can be hired at the Mercure Luxor and Jolie Ville Mövenpick hotels. Should you decide to take a bicycle to Thebes West, don't forget to consider the temperature: the route to the Valley of the Kings runs several kilometers uphill through a hot valley basin.

Since the Nile bridge was opened south of Luxor, the tourist ferries have stopped running. Individual travelers, however, can make use of the **local ferries** to cross the river. These land across from Mina Palace Hotel. At the landing on the west bank there are regular and group taxi stands, where a car and driver can always be found. Be sure to negotiate the price of a full- or half-day tour in advance!

Sightseeing / Excursions

THEBES WEST: To visit Thebes West you should plan on at least one entire day; or, better yet, on two days. A minimal tour schedule might look something like this: Valley of the Kings, two hours; Valley of the Queens, one hour; Tombs of Sheikh 'Abd al-Qurna, three hours; Dair al-Madîna, one hour; Temple of Dair al-Bahrî, one hour; Temple of Seti I, one hour; Ramesseum, one hour; Madînat Hâbû, one hour.

In the warmer season it is advisable to start out very early in the day. In the cooler seasons, however, it is best to start out around noon, as tourist crowds have generally departed by then. Make sure to take along a flashlight for visits to the tombs.

The approximately one-hour hiking tour through the mountains from the Valley of the Kings to the Temple of Dair al-Bahrî can be a very special experience for visitors. Good shoes are an absolute must!

The path is fairly easy to find, but if you should have any trouble doing so, the hawkers and other locals populating it will be more than eager to show you the way.

For excursions in Thebes West, or for a pleasant ride through the sugar cane plantations, you can hire donkeys, including their experienced local drivers.

NOTE: Many of the entrance tickets for Thebes West can only be purchased at the ticket office at the *Inspectorate of the Department of Antiquities* (at the intersection behind the Colossi of Memnon) – not at the tombs and temples themselves. Only three tombs in the Valley of the Kings may be visited per day at the present time.

Despite the high admission fee of 100 LE, the tomb of Nefertari may only be visited for a maximum of 10 minutes. In addition, only 150 tickets are sold for this tomb each day. It is therefore advisable to get to the ticket office as early in the morning as possible (open from 6 am).

If you want to take photographs or use video cameras inside the tombs, you must first obtain a permit, which is also available from the ticket office. Even with a permit, though, the use of a flash is not allowed.

Attention: It is not allowed to take a video camera or even a normal camera into the Valley of the Kings without a permit. If you cannot show a permit, you will be asked to leave your camera at the entrance for the duration of your visit.

Opening Hours: As a rule, all sights are open to visitors from 6:30 am to 6 pm (in winter until 5 pm). The **Tomb of Nefertit** in the **Valley of the Queens** is is the only exception (open in winter from 8:30 am to 3 pm, and in summer from 7:30 am to 2 pm; closed from noon to 1 pm).

LUXOR: In addition to its ancient monuments, Luxor offers a broad spectrum of leisure activities and excursions:

Horseback Riding on wonderful Arabian horses to the western desert – for information contact the "Discovery Desk" in any large hotel.

Sailing Tours on the Nile and to Banana Island – a peninsula with lush banana plantations.

Balloon Rides over the Nile Valley.

Swimming is possible at the pools of the Mercure Luxor, Winter Palace and Isis hotels. These are also open to non-residents for a fee.

DAY TOURS: Most travel agencies offer bus trips to the temple of Dandara. These buses leave at specific times – in convoys with military escorts. Whether or not trips to the Temple of Abydos, some 180 km to the north, can be made depends on the current security situation in the area.

As a rule, there are also two of bus convoys daily south to the temples of **Edfu** and **Kôm Ombo**.

FROM LUXOR
TO THE
NUBIAN TEMPLES

ESNA / AL-KA'B
EDFU
KÔM OMBO
ASWAN
THE NUBIAN TEMPLES

The most romantic, though somewhat uncomfortable, way to cover the 220 kilometers between Luxor and Aswan has got to be in a *feluka*. These large sailing boats are today, as they have been for thousands of years, the main method of transport on the Nile south of Cairo. A luxurious alternative is a cruise on one of the elegant floating hotels which pass all the great sights – the temples of Esna, Edfu and Kôm Ombo. But even the overland journey down the Nile Valley is charming and interesting. Now that there is a bridge over the Nile at Luxor, travelers can also head south on the west bank of the river; the road on the east bank, though, is in much better shape.

ESNA

Fifty-three kilometers south of Luxor, at Ad-Dair, is the turnoff for **Esna** (Arabic: *Isnâ*). This little town at the end of a caravan route on the west bank of the Nile has always been a busy trading center. It also became an important agricultural center at the beginning of the 20th century when a large **weir** (874 meters long, 9.5 meters high) was built here; its

Preceding pages: The interior of the Great Temple of Abû Simbel. Left: The Granite Falcon of Edfu.

120 locks once regulated the irrigation of the entire province of Qena.

Esna's main attraction, the **Temple of Khnum**, stands in the middle of the picturesque bazaar, nine meters below street level. The ram-headed god of creation was revered here as long ago as the New Kingdom, yet all that remains of all his chapels is a wonderfully preserved hypostyle hall, which once served as the entrance to a covered temple. The temple was built by the Ptolemies in the second century B.C. The Roman emperors Claudius and Vespasian added this hall of columns some two centuries later. The reliefs are of even more recent date, for they show a series of later emperors who are bringing offerings to the gods, and other rituals just like the Pharaohs of old.

The elaborate variety of forms of the floral capitals of its 24 columns, and the almost countless hieroglyphic texts which have still not been studied much, make this small temple somewhat unique. With what secrecy these texts were sometimes written is demonstrated by two inscriptions within the hall of columns that have yet to be deciphered. They consist almost exclusively of either ram hieroglyphs (southern corner, left) or crocodile hieroglyphs (eastern corner, right). Scholars believe it is most probably a set of hymns to the god Khnum.

AL-KA'B

Back again on the east bank, your journey continues southwards past green sugar cane fields, small palm groves, vegetable and banana plantations and the ever-present desert. After 39 kilometers, you will see, on the right next to the railway embankment, the monumental mud brick wall of Al-Ka'b. This 540 x 570 meter wall surrounds the remains of ancient *Nekheb,* the center of worship of Nekhbet, the vulture goddess who was the patron of Upper Egypt. With its sister-city *Nekhen,* the Greek *Hierakonpolis* on the west bank, Nekheb was always an important political center, even before Menes' unification of the empire. But the temples and the chapels of the once blossoming town are now as dilapidated as its houses. Only a few rock tombs to the north of the expansive basin of Al-Ka'b are worth a visit.

Well preserved colorful reliefs are to be found in the **Tomb of Paheri**, a tutor at the court of Thutmose III, in the **Tomb of Reni**, high priest of Nekhbet from the beginning of the Eighteenth Dynasty, and in the **Tomb of Setau**, also a high priest of the vulture goddess, but not until the end of the Twentieth Dynasty. The tombs of **Ahmose Pen-Nekhbet** and of **Ahmose Sa-Ibana** are famous for their biographical inscriptions.

EDFU

It is only a few kilometers from Al-Ka'b to Edfu (Arabic: *Idfû*), a small district town in the southern province of Aswan. From a distance you can already see the huge pylons of the **Horus Temple** towering above the houses on the west bank, to which a wide bridge leads.

The history of Edfu dates back to the Old Kingdom, and perhaps even further back than that. Today the ancient town is in ruins – it is buried under the houses of the modern town and in the piles of rubble to the west of the temple. But the temple itself, which was dedicated to the falcon god Horus, is one of the best preserved temples of Pharaonic Egypt. Work on this structure began in August 237 B.C., under the rule of Ptolemy III, and was finished 180 years later under Ptolemy XII, Cleopatra's father. Older buildings had been torn down, but to the east of the First Pylon you can still see the foundations of a temple gate from the time of Ramses II.

The façade of the immense **First Pylon** (79 meters high, 36 meters wide) shows Ptolemy XII in the tradional pose, slaying the enemies in front of the main temple gods, Horus and Hathor, who was worshiped in Edfu as the consort of the falcon god. Four deep niches in the wall, with two square openings above each one, served as anchors for huge flag poles which protruded from the gate towers. A splendid winged sun, one of the many forms of Horus of Edfu, decorates the groove above the portal; two granite falcons stand on guard in front of it.

The **Great Court** is surrounded on three sides by a colonnade with 32 columns, the plant capitals of which are in a variety of styles. The paintings on the walls show scenes of sacrificial offerings and rituals, and also the coronation of the king: to the left (a) you can see the Pharaoh with the crown of Lower Egypt, on the right (b) with the tiara of Upper Egypt. At the bottom of each one a boat procession is shown which alludes to the *Holy Wedding* of the pair of gods. Every year the statue of Hathor set off in a splendid convoy to travel the 160 kilometers from Dendera to Edfu to visit her divine husband. The ceremonies took 14 days and were celebrated throughout the town with joyous feasts.

A relief cycle in the **Gallery**, which surrounds the covered building like a protective wall, shows a further major temple festival: the annual games of the

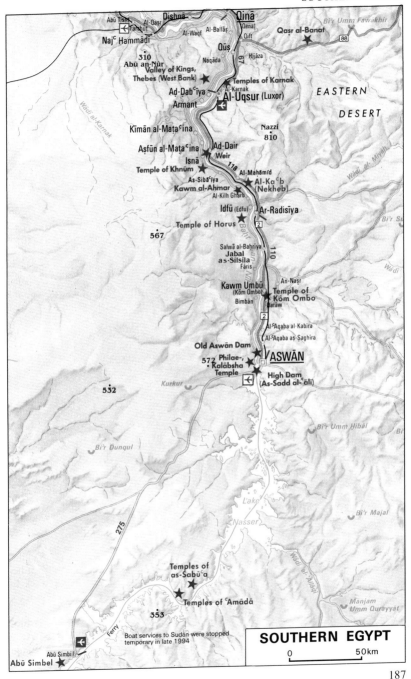

SOUTHERN EGYPT

0   50km

EASTERN

DESERT

Dishnā
Qinā
Abū Tisht
Al-Qasr
Al-Waqf
Al-Ballās
(Qena)
Qasr al-Banat
88
Najᶜ Hammādī
Farshūt
Qift
310
Qūs
Abū an-Nūr
Naqāda
Hijāza
67
Valley of Kings,
Thebes (West Bank)
Temples of Karnak
Ad-Dabᶜīya
Al-Karnak
Al-Uqsur (Luxor)
Armant
Kīmān al-Mataᶜina
Nazzi
810
Aṣfūn al-Mataᶜina
Ad-Dair
Weir
Isnā
118
Temple of Khnūm
Al-Mahāmīd
As-Sibaᶜiya
Al-Kaᶜb
(Nekheb)
Kawm al-Ahmar
Al-Kilh Gharb
Idfū (Edfu)
Ar-Radisīya
Temple of Horus
2
567
Salwā al-Baḥriya
Jabal
as-Silsila
Fāris
110
An-Naṣr
Kawm Umbū
(Kōm Ombo)
Temple of
Kōm Ombo
Bimbān
Daraw
2
Al-ᶜAqaba al-Kabira
Al-ᶜAqaba aṣ-Saghira
Old Aswān Dam
ASWĀN
572
Philae-,
Kalābsha
Temple
High Dam
(As-Sadd al-ᶜālī)
Kurkur
532
Bi'r Umm Hibāl
Bi'r Dunqul
Lake

Nasser
Bi'r Majal
275
Temples of
as-Sabūᶜa
Temples of ᶜAmādā
353
Ferry
Boat services to Sudān were stopped
temporary in late 1994
Abū Simbil
Abū Simbel
Manjam
Umm Qurayyāt

Wādī al-Karnak
Wādī al-Miyāh
Bi'r Su
Wādī
Bi'r Umm Fawākhir
Bahr an-Nīl
Wādī el-ᶜAllāqī

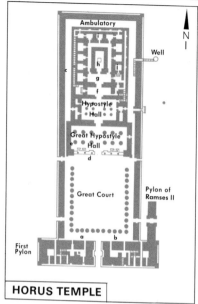

HORUS TEMPLE

Horus legends, which are intended to re-affirm the victory of good over evil. In the metaphorical language of the ancient Egyptians' myths, this is depicted as follows: from his boat the falcon-headed Horus harpoons his opponent Seth, who incarnates evil in the form of a hippopotamus (c).

The inner rooms of the temple are entered via the **Great Hypostyle Hall**, which lies in semi-darkness behind stone curtain walls decorated with reliefs. In front of this is Edfu's emblem – the famous **Granite Falcon** with the double crown (d).

The scenes portraying the foundation of the temple (e) are interesting. Despite some destruction in Christian times they can still be clearly made out. From left to right you can see the king digging the foundation trench, pouring the sacred sand and laying the foundation stone.

Right: Restoration work being performed on the Edfu temple. Far right: A palm-leaf capital in Edfu.

188

You can also see him at the ceremonial purification of the shrine with sodium balls hung around the shrine like a string of pearls, and at the dedication of the temple to Horus.

You reach the center of the house of the gods through a second **Hypostyle Hall** and two **anterooms**, in which the offering table (f) and the shrines of other gods (g) once stood. The **Holy of Holies** (h), with its dark and shimmering shrine, lies on the mythical border between heaven and earth. This idea is also reflected in the architecture: the level of the temple's floor rises continuously toward the sanctuary, while at the same time the ceilings become increasingly low. A granite pedestal for the god's wooden barque stands in front of the monolithic granite shrine. On the walls you can see the king, here Ptolemy IV, in front of the barques of Horus (left) and offering incense to Hathor (right). A copy of a barque was placed in the chamber behind the Holy of Holies (i).

The ceiling decoration of the **New Year's Chapel** (j) is particularly beautiful. It shows the goddess of the sky, Nut, and the 12 phases of the course of the sun in the form of a barque journey. After the first rites of the New Year's Festival had been performed, the priests went from here to the temple roof.

KÔM OMBO

On the way from Edfu to Kôm Ombo (Arabic: *Kawm Umbû*) you cross an important geological border: about 20 kilometers south of Edfu the nummulite stone, which has covered the entire Nile Valley until now, gives way to Nubian sandstone. The strip of fertile land becomes narrower; at **Gebel as-Silsila** (Arabic: *Jabal-as-Silsila*) the cliffs even reach the banks of the river. At the time of the Pharaohs there were great sandstone quarries here, from which the stones for the temples of the whole of

Upper Egypt were hewn. But only little can be seen from the road or train, for you are already crossing the luxuriant garden of the Kôm Ombo basin. It was not until the beginning of the 20th century that this area began to open up, at that time it was little more than a desert. Today agriculture is flourishing, and there is a sugar factory and a food industry. On the edge of the fertile land, in a semicircle around the town of Kôm Ombo, are the settlements of almost 100,000 Egyptian Nubians who have been forced to leave their homes because of the rising waters of the new reservoir.

South of the town is the road to the **Temple of Kôm Ombo**, which is situated on a hill directly on the Nile. Some kind of stone house of worship has probably stood here since the Middle Kingdom, but the construction of the existing shrine was begun under Ptolemy VI (second century B.C.). Part of the wall decoration dates from Roman times.

Because the temple is dedicated to two major deities, the ancient architects simply built two parallel processional paths (instead of the usual one) through the temple halls to two sanctuaries standing side by side. In this way they created a unique double temple: the left side dedicated to the falcon-headed Harwer (Horus the Elder), and the right side to the crocodile god Sobek.

Access to the **Great Court** is through the **First Pylon**, whose foundation walls are all that is left standing. A colonnade of 16 columns with colorful reliefs from the time of Tiberius joins the splendid curtain walls in front of the covered temple building. On the far left is a baptismal scene with the gods pouring holy water in the shape of life characters over Ptolemy XII.

In the **Great Hypostyle Hall** the plant capitals are well worth looking at along with the reliefs. They show the king in the company of various gods. The central wall is decorated with a beautiful picture of Sobek: this time in the form of a crocodile. Through three small anterooms you come to the Holy of Holies, which is

divided into two parts. But apart from the foundation walls it has been completely destroyed. Only the granite barque stands are still there.

The most famous picture in the temple, the *Medical Relief*, is on the back wall of the ambulatory: Trajan (only the lower body still exists) is shown kneeling before the gods, offering them medical instruments, including a forceps, a scalpel and suction pumps, as well as healing amulets. Before leaving the temple, look at the **Chapel of Hathor** next to the entrance gate. This is where some of the many crocodile mummies found in Kôm Ombo are kept.

After a few kilometers the road to Aswan, 40 kilometers away, meets **Daraw**, where every Tuesday a camel market takes place, to which large caravans travel from the Sudan. The closer you get to Aswan, the more African the landscape appears to become.

Above: A happy Nubian girl. Right: Painting on a house in Gharb-Aswân.

ASWAN

For many tourists who travel to Egypt, Aswan is the most beautiful town in the entire Nile Valley. On the west bank its fairy-tale scenery of yellow sand dunes sweeping down to the deep blue waters of the Nile, out of which rise the dark scattered shapes of granite crags, is unforgettable.

These primeval, formless chunks, these massive polished figures, almost look like elephants. And that is why the Pharaohs called their southernmost border fortress on the protracted palm-covered island *Abu*, "Elephant City," today referred to as Elephantine. It is the northernmost of the many islands of the First Cataract, whose rapids were tamed forever when the Sadd al-'âlî, the High Dam, was built.

Opposite Elephantine Island, on the east bank of the Nile, is the modern city of Aswan. The southernmost town in Egypt is the administrative center of the province of the same name, which

stretches from Edfu to the Sudanese border. Ethnically speaking, Aswan belongs to **Nubia**, a cultural area which reaches from Gebel as-Silsila, south of Edfu, to the Sixth Cataract at Khartoum in the Sudan. Even in ancient Egyptian times, though, the First Cataract formed the border to the interior of the African continent – not only for strategic reasons, but also because the mythical sources of the Nile were believed to be the whirls of the rocky barrier.

Despite the fact that the dark skinned Nubians have long been "Arabized," there are families today, indeed even whole villages, where the Nubian languages, Kenuzi and Mahasi, are still spoken. Nubian traditions have also survived in some areas: whether it is in the clothing – white turbans which are otherwise not worn in Egypt, or the colorfully crocheted caps; in music and dance, which contain many African elements; in the handicrafts, with beautifully patterned weaving; or in architecture, for which the spacious inner courtyards are

characteristic, as well as the whitewashed or sky-blue ornamented houses.

Today Aswan has a population of approximately 250,000. The economic rise which the new High Dam brought with it is visible everywhere, but it has by no means reached its planned capacity. Up until now only a few factories have been built in the area; those of the KIMA fertilizer factory and a few small food manufacturers. Iron is mined today, as it always has been, and is brought to the steel works of Heluan near Cairo for smelting.

Aswan's townscape has hardly been touched by industrialization. But there is one black spot which cannot be overlooked: the ugly tower of the Oberoi Hotel on Elephantine Island, which, in addition, has no function. The real "city" consists of only two streets: the approximately two-kilometer-long well-kept Nile promenade, with its string of shops and several Arab coffee houses, and the bazaar street which runs parallel to it. The increase in souvenir shops has so far

191

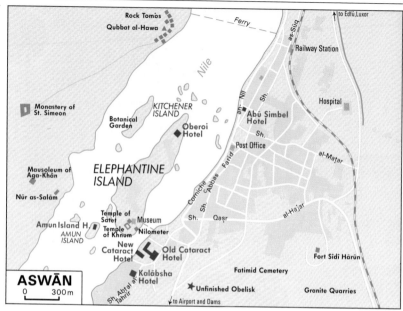

Rock Tombs
Qubbat al-Hawa
Ferry
to Edfü, Luxor
as-Suq
Railway Station
Nile
Monastery of St. Simeon
KITCHENER ISLAND
Abû Simbel Hotel
Hospital
Botanical Garden
Oberoi Hotel
Sh.
Post Office
Sh. Nil
Sh.
al-Maṭar
Mausoleum of Aga-Khan
ELEPHANTINE ISLAND
Corniche
Sh. Abbas Farid
al-Hajar
Nûr as-Salâm
Temple of Satet
Museum
Sh.
Qaṣr
Amun Island H.
AMUN ISLAND
Temple of Khnum
Nilometer
New Cataract Hotel
Old Cataract Hotel
Fort Sidi Hârûn
ASWĀN
0   300m
Kalâbsha Hotel
Sh. Abtal al Tahrir
Fatimid Cemetery
Unfinished Obelisk
Granite Quarries
to Airport and Dams

only added a little more color to the cheerful bustle of the ethnic market, whose wares include a cheerful mixture of everything from shoelaces to videos, and from fruits and vegetables to shaving cream. Up and down the Nile you will not be able to find fresher spices anywhere; even the inhabitants of Cairo order their *fûl sudânî* (peanuts) and *karkade,* the wonderful ruby red hibiscus tea, specially from Aswan.

In addition, Aswan has more than its share of sights, beginning with Elephantine Island, the Botanical Gardens on Kitchener Island, and the west bank with the Mausoleum of the Aga Khan, and on to the picturesque ruins of St. Simeon's Monastery and the Rock Tombs from Pharaonic times.

Sightseeing is always best enjoyed when accompanied by a trip on a feluka, especially since the town area of Aswan has no bridge across the Nile. The feluka

Right: Curiosity and a little baksheesh are good reasons for having your picture taken.

captains are also happy to arrange sailing tours around the cataracts, including a visit to a Nubian village.

But as idyllic as some of these villages may appear to be, they are, of course, no longer untouched by tourism. As a rule you will find howling swarms of children asking for baksheesh, clever mothers who have realized that Nubian caps and chains are a good way of earning some money, and here and there you will unavoidably find a self-proclaimed village tour guide.

The truly spectacular sights, however, lie just outside the city gates on the outskirts of the town: the granite quarries of the Pharaohs, the Aswan High Dam and the Nubian temples, which were saved from the waters of Lake Nasser in an unprecedented international campaign.

The temples of Philae and Kalâbsha have been "resurrected" very close to the High Dam, but you will have to journey another 280 kilometers further south to see the two grandiose rock shrines of Abû Simbel.

Elephantine

Abu, ancient Egypt's southern border town, evolved in Pharaonic times on the southernmost tip of the 1.5-kilometer-long island. Temples, palaces and houses streched in the shadow of a great fortification. Over the centuries these buildings were either replaced by others or, increasingly, incorporated into one another. At the earliest beginnings of Egyptian history, Abu was already well established as an important trading center for the caravans that set off from here to bring back treasures from Nubia: gold, ivory, ebony and spices.

Meanwhile, Aswan (in those days *Sunu,* which the Greeks later called *Syene*) had long been a minor market town. It only became important during Persian times (5th century B.C.). The famous Aramaic *Elephantine Papyri* date from this period. They tell of the bitter feuds between the Jewish military colony and the temple of Khnum: the priests of the ram-headed lord of the cataract area understandably felt provoked when soldiers slaughtered their passover lambs.

Swiss and German experts have been researching Elephantine Island for more than 20 years. Little more than a 30-meter-high pile of rubble remains of its erstwhile splendor. Interesting finds from Aswan and its environs are exhibited near the excavation grounds in the **Archeological Museum**, which was first established in 1912. More than 5,000 exhibits can also be seen at the new **Museum of Nubian Civilization**, which opened in December 1997 on the southern edge of town.

One of the most inconspicuous – but at the same time impressive – relics of Elephantine is the ancient **Nilometer** not far from the museum. It consists of a sloping stair shaft which leads down to the Nile. The height of the water was measured on the scale chiseled into the sides. Using the flood water level the size of the com-

ing harvest, and in particular the amount of taxes which had to be paid, could be calculated. The white marble tablets explain that this Roman Nilometer was restored in the last century. The consistantly low waters of the Nile ever since the construction of the High Dam have made this old instrument obsolete.

The monumental terrace-like arrangement of the **quay**, which was restored in Roman times, can be seen in front of the **Temple of Khnum**. The temple forms the uppermost plateau of a hill of ruins in the middle of decayed mud brick buildings. Only a **granite gate** decorated with reliefs and a huge fallen **granite shrine** further to the west suggest just how imposing the Thirtieth Dynasty temple must once have been.

To the north and a little further down stands – once again – the **Temple of Satet**, Khnum's divine consort. The small peripteros from the time of Hatshepsut has been reconstructed in its original size on a huge reinforced concrete slab. It was rebuilt using single blocks taken from the foundations of a 1,200 year younger Ptolemaic shrine to the same goddess. Apart from the beautiful reliefs, whose missing segments have been tastefully sketched in with delicate outlines, the Satet Temple is an archeological jewel. It is the only Pharaonic temple to have a complete architectural "family tree," which runs from prehistory to Ptolemaic times.

When work on the reconstruction is completed, you will be able to see examples of the individual building phases; but perhaps most fascinating of all is the archaic sacrificial altar which stands in front of two gigantic, polished granite rocks under the sanctuary of the Hatshepsut construction (today under the concrete slab).

A **Ptolemaic chapel** has been reconstructed in the extreme south of Elephantine. Its blocks were discovered in the foundations when the Klâbsha Temple was relocated. The most picturesque view of this edifice appears from the river when you sail past it on the way to the west bank.

The West Bank

Opposite Elephantine the **Mausoleum of the Aga Khân** towers high above the Nile, and above the white villa of the Begûm, which has the rather poetical name of *Nûr as-Salâm* ("Light of Peace"). A wide path leads up to the tomb of the one-time leader of the Ismailite Hodshas, who was revered as a divinely-inspired Imâm by the four million believers of his sect. When he died at the age of 80 in 1957, his son Karîm Aga Khân succeeded him.

The mausoleum was built in the Fatimid style (the Ismailites, who live in India and East Africa, trace their origins to the Fatimids). It has an elegant yet un-

Right: Catching the wind to the Mausoleum of the Aga Khân.

assuming atrium built of sandstone and pink granite, and crowned by merlons and a cupola over the tomb niche. The white marble sarcophagus is adorned with chiseled filigree Koranic inscriptions, and on the wishes of the Begûm it is decorated with a single fresh red rose every day.

From up here there is a fine panoramic view of the whole area of the First Cataract, right up to the High Dam eight kilometers further to the south. On the other side of the Elephantine Island you can see the houses and minarets of Aswan, while directly opposite you will spot the beautifully restored colonial-style palace of the **Old Cataract Hotel**. The hotel's terrace café is no longer an inside tip, but it is nevertheless still a romantic meeting place at sunset. Even the blue-green hue of the New Cataract Hotel ceases being so obvious then.

To the north the red iron mountains of Aswan glow in the distance, and there, where the white sails crowd together, you can make out the harbor of **Kitchener Island**. In the days of the British protectorate this little island belonged to the British General Consul Lord Kitchener who, like many Englishmen, loved tropical gardens. His palm park formed the basis of the wonderful **botanical gardens** which the island was later turned into by the Egyptian government.

In the western desert, not far from the mausoleum, you will find the bizarre ruins of **St. Simeon's Monastery**. However, ever since the wall was built to protect the mausoleum of the Aga Khân from the numerous merchants and camel drivers, it is no longer possible to walk along the paved passageway behind the mausoleum to the monastery. Anyone wanting to hire a camel will have to go down to the bank of the Nile to do so.

The monastery fortress, named after a local saint, Amba Sim'ân (a bishop of Aswan in the fifth century A.D.), was founded around the year 700, restored in

the 10th century, and abandoned altogether in the 13th century because of the constant threat of Bedouin attacks. Surrounded by an almost seven-meter-high wall, the complex stretches across two rock terraces.

The center of the lower level is a three-aisled **basilica** from the ninth century, the nave of which was once covered by a cupola. In the apse you can make out a fresco showing Christ on a throne. Some lovely ceiling paintings in the style of the famous Coptic weavings have been preserved in a grotto on the west side of the church. The upper level is reached by a stone stairway. There you will find the storerooms with a baking room, oil and wine presses, and the originally three-storied living area including a dormitory, a refectory and the baths, including walled in bathtubs.

You can either take a lovely walk through the desert from the monastery to the **Rock Tombs** or, in the style of Lawrence of Arabia, you can go by camel. The road, or rather the trail, arches across

the high plateau towards the central one of three terraces, where the governors of Elephantine and other high officials of the Old and Middle Kingdoms had their tombs built.

Ancient stairs and a wide ramp used for the transport of the sarcophagi lead up from the river bank to the tomb area, which is dominated by the cupola of the **Qubbat al-Hawa**, the tomb of the local holy man Sheikh 'Alî Ibn al-Hawa. The rock chambers, which served as cultic rooms, were dug close to each other into the hill's steep slope. They were then given a smooth layer of stucco and a coat of paint.

In most of the tombs only some individual elements of the wall sections have been preserved, but from them we can see that the pictures contained all the requisite scenes: the false door to the afterlife, the tomb owner at a luxuriously covered offering table or fishing and hunting, harvest pictures and scenes of craftsmen at work. Far from the royal residence the style is a little provincial,

195

and sometimes the proportions are not quite right, which also contributes to the charm of these pictures. The tomb shafts for the coffins were left undecorated and are either sunk into the floor of the interior rooms or of the forecourt.

A path leads along the central terrace, site of the most interesting tombs. The row begins in the south with the **Double Tomb of Mekhu and Sabni** from the Sixth Dynasty (No. 25/26). The immense, unfinished complex seems almost archaic, with its two halls of columns and pillars roughly hewn from the rocks. An inscription in the tomb tells us that Sabni brought the corpse of his father Mekhu, who had died on an expedition to Nubia, home to Elepahtine in order to give him a royal burial.

Beyond the tombs of two governors from the Middle Kingdom (Nos. 28 and 30), both of whom were called Heqa-ib, you come to the **Tomb of Sarenput II** (No. 31), whose strict and imposing architecture is one of the high points on this tomb hill. This is emphasized by the wonderful grain of the unplastered red sandstone in the interior rooms. The tomb of this governor from the Twelfth Dynasty consists of two halls of pillars, connected by a vaulted corridor with six impressive mummy-shaped sculptures of Sarenput. The small offering niche is decorated with enchanting, colorful paintings.

The adjoining **Tomb of Aku** (No. 32) is worth seeing for its beautiful offering niche alone. Some interesting scenes depicting crafts were preserved in the **Tomb of Khunes** (No. 34h), with its intricate nooks and crannies. They were protected for a long time by a layer of plaster that Coptic monks had put there when they converted the tomb into a monastery.

Right: To this day it is still possible to see what methods were used in working the granite quarries of Aswân.

The next group of tombs from the Sixth Dynasty starts with the **Tomb of Horkhuf**, famous for its unique biographical inscriptions. The royal leader of expeditions tells proudly of four successful campaigns to Nubia and also "makes public" King Pepi II's letter of praise, in which the king enthuses over a dancing dwarf whom Horkhuf had brought back from the "land of the inhabitants of the horizon."

The letter from the ruler, who was eight years old at the time, is charmingly childish. He promises Horkhuf a rich reward if the dwarf "makes it to the palace alive, hale and hearty." The tomb owner does not mention whether the outcome of the story was a happy one – but surely he would not have allowed this royal document to be chiseled into the façade of his tomb had the outcome been considered less than good.

The occupant of the neighboring tomb, **Pepinakht** (No. 35), was also famous for his Nubian expeditions, though his were of a military nature. Adjoining this is the **Double Tomb of Heqa-ib and his Son Sabni II** (No. 35d/e). Although the wall decoration seems insignificant today, this tomb was a popular place of pilgrimage in ancient times. Heqa-ib, the governor of Elephantine under Pepi II, was worshiped as a god soon after his death – perhaps because he brought the wars with the Nubians to a peaceful end. In the Middle Kingdom a shrine with exquisite statues was erected to him in the middle of the city of Abu.

On the northern end of the path is the **Tomb of Sarenput I**, (No. 36) the governor of Elephantine at the beginning of the Twelfth Dynasty. The wonderful complex consists of wide steps leading from the Nile to the portal of the forecourt in front of the tomb. The portal is decorated with reliefs. There is a colonnade in front of the façade which was covered at one time. On the façade the tomb owner is portrayed with his family

(right) and his dogs (left). With one exception, the beautiful paintings in the interior rooms have unfortunately all been destroyed.

At the foot of the hill of tombs, along the banks of the river, is a narrow fertile strip which is cultivated by the inhabitants of the village of **Gharb-Aswan** (West Aswan). A pleasant suggestion for the visitor is to take a walk through the pretty village and have a look at the beautiful paintings on the houses. At the entrance to the village you will find the embarcation point for the ferry to Aswan.

Granite Quarries

The granite quarries which supplied the Pharaohs throughout Egyptian history with the valuable material for their vessels, statues, sarcophagi, obelisks, shrines and elements of temples and tombs are to the southeast of Aswan. The journey to the quarries leads past an enormous **Fatimid cemetery**, with its picturesque cupola tombs, most of which are

memorials to local Islamic saints who are still honored today.

The main attraction of the pink granite quarries is the **Unfinished Obelisk**, which dates back to the 15th century B.C., during the time of Queen Hatshepsut. This gigantic monolith, thought to weigh some 1,168 tons, would have become the largest obelisk in Egypt with its height of 42 meters and base area of 4.2 x 4.2 meters, but the ambitious plan was thwarted when the stone developed cracks. Another attempt to carve a smaller obelisk out of the same block also failed for the same reason.

Today the obelisk lies with one shaft surface still embedded in the bedrock. The sides though, provide interesting evidence of the working practices of the Pharaonic quarrymen. With the aid of hammers of dolerite, a much harder material, they carved out a channel around the obelisk, in this way gradually freeing it from the bedrock.

The famous wood source method, whereby the stone was broken with the

197

aid of a dampened wooden wedge, is now thought, according to the most recent research, never to have been used in Egypt – not even in Ptolemaic times, when the notched cuts around the obelisk were made. Iron tools were already known at the time, and axes and wedges were made of metal or hardwoods.

The Dams

To the south of Aswan are the two great dams of the first cataract. The **Old Aswan Dam** was built between 1898 and 1902 by English engineers. The two-kilometer-long granite dam was extended twice and is now 51 meters high, 35 meters along its base, and 12 meters wide at the top. Although the 180 sluice gates were closed only when the Nile floods had started to drain away (so as not to block up the dam with the silt of the first wave of the flood), the reservoir enabled the agricultural areas of the Nile to be increased by 16 percent. Nevertheless, a great deal of the valuable Nile water flowed unused into the sea.

The increasing population made the establishment of new food resources ever more urgent. And so, eight kilometers further south, the **Sadd al-'âlî High Dam** was built with the aid of Soviet credit and Soviet engineers. 33,000 Egyptians and 1,900 Russians worked on this mammoth US$2.5-million project for eleven years, from 1960 until 1971.

The earthquake-proof concrete dam runs along a 111-meter-high arch. It is 3.6 kilometers long, 980 meters wide at the bottom and 40 meters wide at the top. The interior of this giant is made up of 35 percent sand, 55 percent rough rock and 10 percent clay. The center of the dam over the 520-meter-wide river bed is formed by a huge clay core. This spreads

Right: The power and greatness of a Pharoah – the Colossi of Ramses II in Abû Simbel.

further into an injected insulating apron of clay, cement, silicate and aluminate, which reaches 44 meters below the bottom of the dam. The 1.6-kilometer-long water detour runs through a large power station. Each of its 12 Francis turbines has a capacity of 175 megawatts. They are supplied by six water tunnels.

The reservoir, into which the Nile waters are channeled throughout the whole year, is 500 kilometers long and 200 kilometers wide, and reaches far into the Sudan. If the water ever reaches the maximum planned level of 182 meters above sea level (14 meters below the top of the reservoir), it will have reached its maximum water capacity of 164 billion cubic meters. Of these, 30 billion cubic meters would be made up of silt deposits, 90 billion cubic meters would be the normal water storage capacity, and 44 billion cubic meters constitute the flood safety margin.

Anyone interested in knowing more about the dam should visit the little **museum** next to the power plant on the eastern end of the structure. The history of the dam is documented through numerous building plans and photographs. There is also a large model of the dam on display.

The effects of the building of the High Dam have been widely discussed (see page 228), yet few seem to mention the tragic fate which befell the Nubian people. Almost 100,000 Nubians had to be evacuated from their homes when the water level of the Nile began to rise in 1965, eventually covering their houses and fields for all time. The new villages into which they were resettled are still regarded by many of them as temporary housing until they can return to their homes again. But the failure of the Nile floods in the "eight lean years" of the African drought of 1982-89 has meant that so far very little of the fertile silt has been deposited on the shores of the lake – much too little to farm.

THE NUBIAN TEMPLES

The enormous lake which was supposed to flood the whole Nile Valley between the First and Second Cataract threatened not only the present, but the millenia-old cultural heritage of the Nubians as well. All traces of the Nubian kingdoms, from prehistoric to Christian to Islamic times, were to be left to drown in the water. This included more than 20 Pharaonic temples, countless tombs and 13 fortresses from the Middle Kingdom. Without foreign aid it would have been impossible for Egypt and the Sudan to save this priceless archeological inheritance for subsequent generations. So on March 8, 1960, the General Director of UNESCO called for international support for a campaign to save the Nubian treasures and monuments.

A unique project was started, which included the participation of countless scientists and specialists from all over the world. Almost over night, ancient Nubia became the largest archeological excavation site ever known to mankind. Working against – and around – the clock, more than 50 teams of researchers examined and documented the entire area that was to be flooded. Much that would have been irretrievably lost was retained, at least in the plans and sketches of the archeologists. The most spectacular achievement of this campaign was the relocation of 22 monuments. Stone by stone they were taken apart, moved to a safer place and rebuilt exactly as they had been. Some monuments were given as presents to European and American museums, four temples and a tomb are today to be found in Khartoum; but the vast majority were moved to five sites in Egypt. From north to south these are: the temple island of Philae (in the reservoir between the two dams); the temples of New Kalâbsha (one kilometer south of the Sadd al-'âlî); the temples of New Sabû'a (140 kilometers); the tomb and temples of New 'Amâda (180 kilometers); the temples of New Abû Simbel (280 kilometers, near the Sudanese border).

199

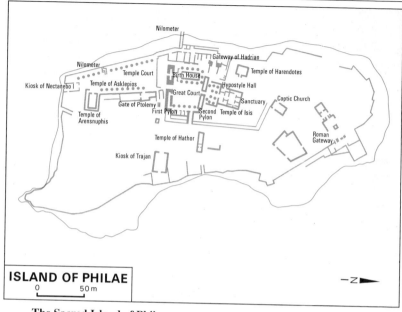

ISLAND OF PHILAE
0   50 m

—z ▶

The Sacred Island of Philae

Philae had already been threatened by the construction of the Old Aswan Dam. Every year, when the sluice gates were closed in autumn, the temples gradually sank under the floods of the reservoir. Over the years the water destroyed the paint on the reliefs, but the sandstone actually hardened because its salts were washed out. However, with the building of the new High Dam, Philae's destruction seemed inevitable.

Since 1964, in the basin between the two dams, the area has been subjected to a daily dousing of water, the variable level of which has reached as high as six meters. Finally, an Egyptian-Italian consortium was formed, and the temple was moved to the neighboring granite island of **Agílkia**. The work was completed in a record 30 months. Total cost of the project: US $30 million.

Right: The Temple of Isis on the island of Philae.

Protected by a cofferdam (which can still be seen today), the buildings were first cleaned, measured and then sawn into 37,363 pieces. In order to reproduce the magical landscape of Philae on Agílkia, 300,000 cubic meters of granite were blasted away, large areas were filled in, and flower beds were planted.

The heart of the holy island is the Ptolemaic **Temple of Isis**, who was still worshipped here when the other temples in Egypt had long been abandoned. When Philae, too, was closed by Emperor Justinian in the sixth century A.D., it meant the end of ancient Egyptian culture. The Christian community, which settled on the island and turned pagan buildings into churches, did not leave until the 13th century A.D.

Beyond the old dam you can get on a boat and sail past the bizarre granite formations to the ancient entrance in the southern part of the island. The small **Columned Hall**, with its delicate Hathoric capitals from the time of Nektanebo I (Thirtieth Dynasty), forms the

south face of the large, asymetrical temple courtyard. The colonnades of the courtyard, with their many different plant capitals, were never completed. To the east of the colonnade are the ruins of a small shrine to the Nubian god Arensnuphis. There you will also find the Asklepios Temple for the worship of Imhotep, the architect of the Step Pyramid of Saqqâra who was revered as a god.

The **First Pylon** of the Isis Temple shows Ptolemy XII conquering his enemies and making sacrifices to the gods. As the last Ptolemaic architect, Cleopatra's father finished the work which had been begun under Ptolemy II a good 200 years before.

There had probably been a shrine to the wife of Osiris on Philae since the seventh century A.D., for close by, on the island of Bigga, the god's tomb was situated in a shady grove, surrounded by 365 altars. Together with the priests, Isis brought milk offerings here every 10 days. Osiris's resurrection was heralded by the floods of the Nile and was celebrated ceremoniously in Philae with annual passion plays.

The **Great Court** is bordered to the east by a colonnade and by chambers for the priests, and in the west by the **Birth House** with its beautiful colonnade. The theme of the murals inside the chapel is the birth of Horus, who was hidden from Seth by his mother Isis in the swamps of the Delta where he was brought up. The back wall of the innermost chamber illustrates this with a picture of the Horus falcon in the center of a fanned out sheaf of papyrus.

The **Second Pylon**, with scenes of Ptolemy XII making offerings, leads to the **Hypostyle Hall**, which served as a church in Christian times. Passing through several small halls you come to the **Sanctuary**. It is in three parts and has some wonderful large reliefs of the king before the gods and the stand for the barque of Isis.

The murals on the **Gateway of Hadrian** to the west of the Isis Temple are dedicated to Osiris. A small scene on the

Thanks to financial assistance from Germany, in 1962-63 this became the first Nubian temple to be moved here from its original position in Kalâbsha, ancient *Talmis*, 50 kilometers further south. Emperor Augustus had it built there on the site of an older shrine. It was a commemoration of the victory on the southern border of the newly won province of Egypt.

The granite plateau of New Kalâbsha lies as a museum island in a reservoir, and can only be reached by boat (landing located below the dam monument). The **Mandulis Temple** is the dominating centerpiece of the island. It has a large terrace and a 32-meter embankment ramp in front of it. A large temple courtyard and the three-roomed covered temple building adjoin the undecorated First Pylon. The main themes of the partly incomplete relief decoration in the interior are offerings to the gods.

From the roof of the temple you will find a wonderful view of the bizarre moonscape of the lake shores and the **Kiosk of Qertassi**, a small columned chapel built in Greco-Roman times next to the sandstone quarries of Qertassi near old Kalâbsha.

On the edge of the town of Old Kalâbsha was also the small **Rock Temple of Bait al-Wâlî**, which has been rebuilt only 100 meters away from the Mandulis Temple. This is the northernmost of a total of seven Nubian temples of Ramses II. Its beautiful, still partly-colored reliefs celebrate the Pharaoh as a victorious military leader.

northern interior wall shows the potbellied Nile god Hapi in a grotto – a symbol of the fertile flood waters and the mythical source of the Nile in the cataract area.

Of all the structures in the northern part of the island, only the Roman town gate was moved to the new island. Charming reliefs can be seen on the columns in the forecourt of the small **Temple of Hathor** (second century B.C.) on the east bank: monkeys playing instruments and the god Bes playing the tambourine. Next to this is the **Trajan Kiosk**, a stone baldequin with wonderful plant pillars which may have served as a shrine for the divine barque during the time of the Roman emperors.

From New Kalâbsha to Abû Simbel

From the crown of the Sadd al-'âlî, the great **Kalâbsha Temple** of the Nubian god Mandulis can be seen to the south.

Above: One of the four impressive 20-meter-high Colossi of Abû Simbel.

Even though approach roads to the temples have been under construction for some time now, at present the only way of visiting them is by taking a three-day cruise on Lake Nasser from Aswan to Abû Simbel. In **New Sabû'a** there are three impressive structures to be seen: a Temple of Ramses II, which was transported from the sunken Wâdî as-Sabû'a, four kilometers away; the late-Roman

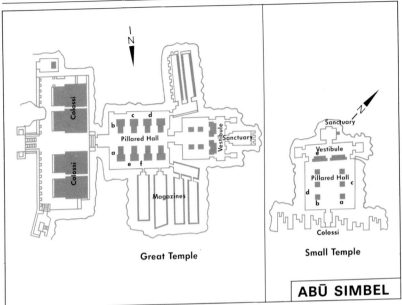

Great Temple

Small Temple

ABŪ SIMBEL

Temple of Serapis from Al-Maharraqa; and a Ptolemaic-Roman temple from Ad-Dakka, work on whose complex was begun under the Nubian king Ergamenes in the third century B.C.

Forty kilometers south of New-Sebû'a, in **New 'Amâda**, three further monuments were re-erected: the Rock Temple of Ad-Derr from the days of Ramses II; the Rock Tomb of Pennut from Aniba, where the administrators of Lower Nubia served during the Twentieth Dynasty; and the Temple of Thutmose III from 'Amâda, which, in a unique project, was moved along a 2.6-kilometer track to a new site, 65 meters high.

The Miracle of Abû Simbel

Those who do not come to Abû Simbel by cruise ship or plane can take the asphalt highway that was opened in 1985 further south to Sudan. It cuts its way straight through the desert, parallel to the caravan route along which Sudanese camels are driven to the market held every weekend in Darâw. Fine sand dunes alternate with rocky fields of rubble along the way, and the closer you get to Abû Simbel, the more the scenery is marked by the pyramid-shaped cones of rock which seem to tower up like mirages from the shimmering heat rays, looking like mountains rising from the sea. Only from the air can the fjord of the lake be seen, which branches for kilometers deep into the desert in some places.

The rescue of the two rock temples of **Abû Simbel** was a project of the superlative. The sacred mountains were moved 180 meters further inland and 64 meters higher up. They were sawn into more than a thousand blocks, weighing up to 30 tons each, and were rebuilt on an east-west axis, exactly as before.

Today a gigantic concrete cupola arches over both of the "inner" rock chambers and supports the artificial mountain built over the top (this can be seen in the Great Temple). The work took three years to complete (1965-68) and cost a total of US $42 million.

203

god is part of a "pictorial puzzle" symbolizing the throne name of the king.

The interior rooms of the temple begin with the **Pillared Hall**. Its central aisle is flanked by eight 10-meter-high statues of the king. The colorful wall reliefs once again celebrate the courage of the great Ramses. Besides the traditional reliefs which depict the slaying of the enemies, portrayed as Asians on the right (a) and Nubians on the left (b), you can see the king storming a Syrian fortress, lancing a Libyan, in a triumphal procession with Nubian prisoners (c-d), and in the various phases of the famed Battle of Qadesh against the Hittites (e-f).

The side chambers served as storerooms for the instruments of worship and the temple treasures. You pass through a small hall with four pillars showing scenes of offering before the divine barque, and then into the vestibule and the **Holy of Holies**. Here you will find the large sculptures of Ptah (left), of Amen wearing the high feathered crown, of the king, and of the sun falcon Ra-Harakhti.

The **Lesser Temple** was dedicated by Ramses II to his favorite wife, Nefertari, and to the goddess Hathor, with whom the queen is particularly identified in this temple. In the colossal figures on the façade where she is surrounded by statues of her husband, for example, the beautiful Nefertari is shown with the horned crown of the goddess.

The interior room is divided by six pillars decorated with Hathoric heads. In the center of the fine, well-preserved reliefs are scenes of sacrifice (c), the coronation of the king (d) and of the triumph over his enemies (a and b). The crowning of Nefertari by the goddesses Isis and Hathor is particularly interesting (e).

Although somewhat weathered, the statue in the sanctuary can just about be made out. It is a raised relief of the cow goddess Hathor-Nefertari, protecting a statuette of Ramses II.

Like a petrified demonstration of power, the 20-meter-high seated statues of Ramses II tower majestically in front of the rock pylons of the **Great Temple**. The standing figures of the royal women and children are also larger than life. High above you will see a frieze with 22 baboons praying with arms raised to the sun. Twice a year – around February 20 and October 20 – the rays of the sun reach right into the sanctuary 64 meters down into the rock, in order to "join with the statues of the great gods": Amen, Ra and Ptah, and in their midst apears the king himself!

In Nubia, Ramses appears as a god amongst the gods – a form of existence which was otherwise only attributed to the dead Pharaoh. And so Ramses is worshipping himself in the niche above the portal, where he is shown bringing the falcon-headed sun god Ra-Harakhti an offering. For the giant sculpture of the

Above: The Lesser Temple of Abû Simbel, dedicated to Nefertari.

BETWEEN LUXOR AND ASWAN
Arrival
Esna, Al-Ka'b, Edfu and Kôm Ombo are usually visited as part of the Luxor to Aswan trip. Organized day tours by bus or taxi to the temples can be booked in Luxor, as well as in Aswân. Al-Mahamîd is the train station for the monuments of Al-Ka'b (closed to the public at present).

Accommodation
EDFU: *BASIC:* **Dar al-Salam**, next to Edfu Temple; **El-Medina**, at the bus station.

ASWAN
Area Code (also for Abû Simbel) 097
Arrival / Transportation
Egypt Air operates several flights a day from Cairo/Luxor to Aswan. The *Upper Egypt Bus Company* runs buses from all larger Nile Valley towns to Aswan. International trains with sleeping compartments are a very comfortable way of traveling, additional regular night and day trains serve the Cairo – Aswan route (see page 239).
Ferry boats to Elephantine Island land opposite the Egypt Air office (Sh. Abtâl at-Tahrîr); boats to the Rock Tombs and to Gharb-Aswan land more or less parallel to the tourist market.

Accommodation
LUXURY: **Aswan Oberoi**, Elephantine Island, tel. 314667/8, fax. 323485; **Isis Island Aswan Resort**, Isis Island, 317400, fax. 317405; **New Cataract & Sofitel Old Cataract**, Sh. Abtâl at-Tahrîr, tel. 316000, fax. 316011; **Amun Tourist Village**, Sahara City (past High Dam), tel. 480439, 480440. *MODERATE:* **Amun Island**, Club Mediterranée, Amun Island, tel. 313800, fax. 317190; **Basma Swiss Inn**, Sh. Al-Fanâdîq, tel. 310901, fax. 310907; **Isis**, Corniche an-Nîl, tel. 315100, fax. 315500; **Kalabsha**, Sh. Abtâl at-Tahrîr, tel. 322999, fax. 325974; **Cleopatra**, Sh. Sa'd Zaghlûl, tel. 324001, fax. 324002. *BUDGET:* **Abu Simbel**, Corniche an-Nîl, tel. 322888; **Happi**, Sh. Abtâl at-Tahrîr, tel. 314115; **Mena**, Atlas Area, tel. 324388; **Philae**, Corniche en-Nil, tel. 312089; **Ramses**, Sh. Abtâl at-Tahrîr, tel. 324000; **Abu Shelib**, Sh. 'Abbâs Farîd (bazaar street), tel. 323051; **Hathur**, Corniche an-Nîl, tel. 314580. *YOUTH HOSTEL:* **Youth Hostel**, Sh. Abtâl at- Tahrîr, tel. 322313.

Restaurants
The restaurants of the luxury hotels offer good Oriental and international cuisine, whereby the buffet in the restaurant of the **New Cataract** deserves special mention. Don't miss the romantic *Candlelight Dinner* with classical music in the dining room of the **Old Cataract Hotel**, known to Agatha Christie fans from the film *Death on the Nile*. Along the Nile promenade a number of smaller, reasonably-priced but still good-quality restaurants can be found. Tasty, well-cooked meals are also served at the **Hotel Abu Shelib**.

Museums
Elephantine Museum, Elephantine Island. Open daily from 8:30 am to 6 pm (in winter 8 am to 5 pm); **Nubian Museum**, across from the Old Cataract Hotel, open 9 am to 1 pm and 5 to 9 pm (in summer 6 to 10 pm).

Aswân by Night
At the **Temple of Philae** two light-and-sound shows take place every day in various languages at 6 pm (in summer at 6:30 pm) and 7:30 pm (in summer at 8 pm) in the following order: Monday – English then Italian; Tuesday – French then English; Wednesday – English then Spanish; Thursday – Arabic then French; Friday – English then French; Saturday – English then French; Sunday – French then German.

Travel agents offer package tours to these sound-and-light shows, which generally include transportation by taxi/bus, a boat transfer to the island of Philae and the entrance fee.

Belly dancing and Nubian folklore shows can be enjoyed in the **nightclubs** of the Aswan Oberoi Hotels and in the New Cataract. The Ramses Hotel runs a **discotheque**. The Culture Palace (*Qasr as-saqâfa* in Egyptian) of Aswan offers less tourist-orientated attractions. During the winter months the flat-roofed concrete building (at the tourist market) shows remarkable performances of Nubian **folklore**, daily except Fridays from 9:30 to 11 pm.

Tourist Information
State Tourist Office, Tourist Market (near Hotel Abu Simbel), tel. 323297. At train station, tel. 312811.

NUBIAN TEMPLES
Arrival
Half-day tours to **Philae** and **Kalâbasha** can be combined with a visit to the Aswan Dam. As there is no public transportation, you should either hire a taxi or book a tour through a travel agent in Aswan. Travel agents can also provide you with information regarding the three-day cruise from Aswan to Abû Simbel via **New Sabû'a** and **New 'Amada**. Between Aswan and Abû Simbel there are several daily shuttle flight connections with a limited duration of stay (two hours). The shuttle flight may be combined with a flight from/to Cairo or Luxor.

This trip is not possible overland at the present time! The erection of security control stations is planned; inquire about current conditions when you are in the region.

Accommodation
ABÛ SIMBEL: **Nefertari**, tel. 316402, fax. 316404. **Nobaleh Ramses**, tel./fax. 400381.

CORAL REEFS AND WONDROUS MOUNTAINS

THE RED SEA
THE DESERT MONASTERIES
THE SUEZ CANAL ZONE
THE SINAI PENINSULA
ST. CATHERINE'S MONASTERY

THE RED SEA

The Red Sea is a 2,240-kilometer-long "bay" of the northwestern Indian Ocean. In sharp contrast to its name it is in reality deep blue in color, changing from azure to turquoise in coastal regions. It is thought by some that the name comes from a form of algae common to its waters, *Trichodesmium erythraeum*, which colors the water red in places.

It is also possible that the ancient Egyptians called it the Red Sea, as in their language it bordered on the Red Land; the desert. This strip of the Arabian Desert, which is approximately 1,000 kilometers long and 250 kilometers wide, has virtually no vegetation. The gravel plains of the Jalâla Plateau mark its northern border, and from Ra's Za'farâna it towers up through the northern foothills of the impressive Red Sea Mountains to an incredible edifice of shimmering red primary rock.

The Red Sea was formed more than 20 million years ago when the Arabian Peninsula separated from the eastern African continent, and the trench which branches out around the wedge of the Sinai Peninsula disappeared under the flow of water from the ocean.

Left: Riding the wind on the Red Sea.

Whereas the granite mountains along the Gulf of 'Aqaba drop as much as 1,800 meters in an escarpment to the seabed, the coral reefs in the relatively shallow (100-meter-deep) Gulf of Suez extend to the south of Hurghada. These reefs were formed by limestone deposits that were built up over many thousands of years from the coral that can only flourish in the light-drenched shallows of tropical waters such as these.

Four hundred kilometers south of Suez, **Hurghada** (Arabic: *Al-Ghardaqa*), on the west coast, is a popular center for swimming and diving. This is a faceless place with a not very attractive concentration of low concrete buildings of recent construction, and numerous small hotels and restaurants. Hurghada's attraction lies in its beaches of fine-grained sand, and in its offshore banks of coral, which can also be viewed by those who are neither divers nor snorklers in glass-bottom boats.

The beaches to the south of Hurghada make up the main tourist area. Here, next to the tower of the **Sheraton Hotel**, the uniform, but by no means unattractive, bungalows of the **Giftûn**, **Magawîsh** (Club Mediterranée) and **Jasmine Holiday Village** hotel complexes line up cheek-by-jowl for kilometers. Every year new complexes are added, so that public

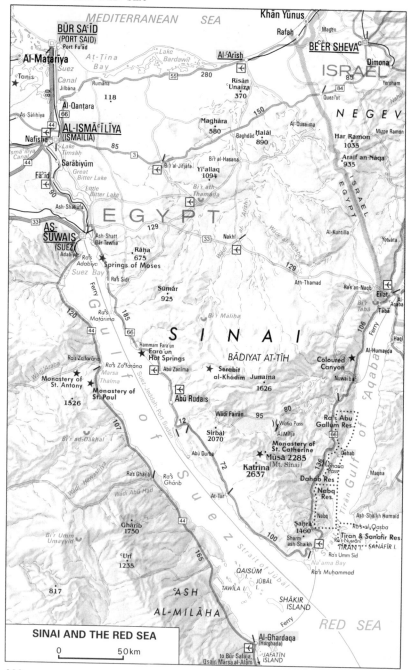

SINAI AND THE RED SEA

0   50km

beaches outside of the holiday villages have become scarce. Isolated coves, however attractive they may be, should be avoided, as there is still a danger from mines along the whole coast. Fenced-off areas and warning signs should be heeded at all times!

The next large town to the south of Hurghada is **Port Safâga** (Arabic: *Bûr Safâja*), located 60 kilometers away. This is an uninteresting harbor town where phosphate extracted in the area is loaded onto ships. In the north of the town there is the **Menaville Village**, which boasts a small beach and a diving school. A little further away lies the **Sea Land Village Tourist Camp**, situated on a beautiful bay with a coral reef.

The remaining 230 kilometers down to the village of **Marsâ al-'Alâm**, where the open road officially ends, offer attractive coastal scenery and beautiful places to dive, but, with the exception of the drab harbor town of **Qusair**, virtually no accommodation.

Despite a few nice areas, the coast north of Hurghada up to Suez is not really suitable for swimming or diving, as offshore drilling has been taking place along the Gulf for years now to exploit the region's rich oil reserves.

THE DESERT MONASTERIES

The monasteries of St. Anthony and St. Paul, near the oil harbor of **Ra's Za'farâna**, are interesting places to visit. Both monasteries came into existence in the mountains of the eastern desert, where Anthony and Paul had led their lives as hermits at the end of the third century A.D. The **Monastery of St. Paul** can be reached by a marked road which branches off from the coastal road 25 kilometers to the south of Ra's Za'farâna and ends at the monastery 12 kilometers further on. The buildings, established in the fifth century on the site of the saint's cave and grave, are located like a fortress at the bottom of a valley basin. Surrounded by a garden, the monks' quarters and a guest house, the five-story **keep tower** and the domed **church** form the center. A staircase connects the 11th-century upper church with the much older lower church, of which St. Paul's grotto and its sepulchral chapel form a part. The frescos, which were touched up in the 18th century, date as far back as the sixth and seventh centuries. The one-day journey by foot through the mountains to the **Monastery of St. Anthony** is an impressive experience, but it should not be undertaken without a guide who knows the area. The route normally followed is along the 14-kilometer-long road which branches off from the connecting road to the Nile Valley about 30 kilometers to the west of Ra's Za'farâna.

Surrounded by a 12-meter-high and two-kilometer-long wall, the monastery is situated in a picturesque palmery at the foot of a rocky slope containing the saint's hermitage. The "father of monasticism" lived here, teaching a colony of hermits, until his death in the year 356. There has been a church at his grave from the early fifth century at the latest. Around which the monastery developed. As with the monastery of St. Paul, it was plundered in the 15th century and abandoned for a time. Most of the monastery buildings therefore only date back to the time of its restoration in the 16th century.

The **keep tower** offers a beautiful panoramic view over the spacious site, with its farm buildings, living quarters, seventh-century refectory and gardens. In all, there are six churches, of which the **Titular Church** (10th/11th century), is significant for its frescos. The oldest depictions on the interior of the arcade in front of the sanctuary are from the 10th century; others date back to the 11th to 13th centuries. In the **side chapel** next to the narthex, the paintings depicting the enthroned Christ surrounded by four angels are well preserved.

THE SUEZ CANAL ZONE

Since the reopening of the Suez Canal and the return of the Sinai, Egypt has directed its efforts toward economic and infrastructural development in the Canal Zone. The former "wallflowers" – Suez, Ismailia and Port Said – are developing into attractive centers through efforts to bind the Sinai to Egypt.

The **Suez Canal** was not the first link between the Red Sea and the Mediterranean. As early as around 600 B.C., Pharaoh Nekho II began to build a canal that was supposed to link the Nile, through Lake Timsâh and the Bitter Lakes, with the Red Sea. But it was the Persian ruler Darius I who, 100 years later, first completed the ambitious project. He celebrated this event by having a series of commemorative stelai erected on the banks of the canal inscribed in a number of languages.

The canal silted up, was cleared, and silted up again. Finally, it was destroyed by the Arabs in the eighth century and was forgotten. When Vasco da Gama discovered the sea route to India, the Venetians, fearing for their trade monopoly, were the first to think about a canal between the two seas. However, more than 350 years passed before the Suez Canal was finally opened in 1869, after a 10 year construction period.

Right from the very start this strategically and economically important waterway was at the center of international conflicts. The canal was closed during the Six Day War in 1967, and was not reopened until 1975. Its channel is 195 kilometers long, between 140 and 365 meters wide and 18 meters deep. Ships of up to 150,000 tons capacity and up to 450,000 tons in ballast can pass through the canal fully laden. Three convoys pass through it every day in a journey of

around 15 hours duration, and there are a number of bypasses which allow passage in both directions. Almost 30,000 ships use the canal each year, bringing the country an annual income of over US $1 billion.

Together with the harbor of **Port Tawfîq**, **Suez** (Arabib: *As-Suways*) marks the southern end of the canal. The history of this city, founded in the 15th century, is intimately linked with that of the canal. It was almost completely destroyed in the Yom Kippur War of October 1973. Since the reopening of the canal and the discovery of rich oil deposits in the Gulf of Suez in the late 1970s it has, however, experienced a tremendous boom as an oil port and center of an expanding petrochemical industry.

Seventeen kilometers to the north of Suez, the **Ahmad Hamdî Tunnel** is the first of three planned road links under the Suez Canal to have been opened.

The queen of the canal cities is **Ismailia** (Arabic: *Ismâ'îlîya*) on Lake Timsâh. It is a well maintained garden-city planned on a grand scale. Many buildings in the colonial style have been preserved from the time of its founding in 1863. The well situated **Hotel PLM Azur**, right beside the lake, and the **Beach Club**, which is also open to visitors, attract many excursionists from Cairo on weekends. A few hundred meters to the north of the ferry to the Sinai (free of charge), there is an observation platform which commands a good view of the ship convoys. In the city center there is a small **Archeological Museum** with finds from the area around Ismailia, including the canal stelai of Darius I.

Port Said (Arabic: *Bûr Sa'îd*) is Egypt's second-largest seaport and, as a free trade zone, a favorite port of call for Egyptians who can buy foreign goods here, especially electrical and electronic items which are otherwise difficult to obtain. Opposite, **Port Fu'âd** is essentially a "commuter town" for Port Said.

Right: Fascinating and beautiful mountain landscape of the Sinai Peninsula.

THE SINAI PENINSULA

The Sinai Peninsula, with its approximately 60,000-square-kilometer surface area, is not only one of the most famous desert areas in the world, it is also one of the most fascinating. To the south of the Mediterranean coast, the lime and sandstone plains rise up to the high plateau of **Bâdiyat at-Tîh**, the "Desert of Straying," which breaks off at its southern edge in impressive limestone precipices. This is where the mountainous world of the southern Sinai begins, with bizarre cleft giants of granite, porphyry, gneiss and other magmatic plutons rich in form and color, often threaded by black strips; the cooled lava streams that seeped through crevasses in the earth's crust from its interior millions of years ago.

As a land bridge between Asia and Africa, the northern Sinai has been an important trade and military route since ancient times, while the southern Sinai was valued for its treasures and mineral resources. The turquoise mines and copper beds of the ancient Egyptians have long since been exhausted, but the oil fields of **Abû Rudais** are today of no lesser importance.

The history of the peninsula begins long before the Pharaohs, when nomads got their flint from the area about 20,000 years ago. Permanent cultures can be traced back to the fifth millenium B.C. to the Eilat culture (around 4500-3500 B.C.), and to the Timna people who were absorbed around 250 B.C. by the immigrant Egyptian population. Ancient tunnels and slag heaps, inscriptions on rocks and the ruins of a temple to Hathor are evidence of the Pharaohs' mining activities here. The rulers of the New Kingdom built their temple for Hathor, the "Queen of the Turquoise Land," in a pathless area on the high plateau of **Serabit al-Khâdim** near Abû Zanîma.

It is, however, the Second Book of Moses which made the Sinai famous. In it, the Exodus, the departure of the Israelites from Egypt, is described. The climax of the many years of wandering over

the Sinai Peninsula was the proclamation of the Ten Commandments on Mount Sinai, which is traditionally identified with Jabal Mûsâ, the 2,285-meter-high Moses Mountain, at the foot of which lies St. Catherine's Monastery.

Recently, researchers have begun to favor another theory which states that the "Red Sea" in the Bible is actually Lake Bardawîl in the north of the peninsula, and that the mountain where the Ten Commandments appeared can therefore only be Jabal Halâl (892 meters), the only prominently elevated point in the area.

Even today, nomads still travel through the Sinai, but of about 70,000 Bedouins on the peninsula (of a total population of 180,000) many have become settled, or semi-settled, over the last few decades. A directed policy of settlement, the chance to earn money in mining and tourism, were the reasons for

Above: A hospitable Bedouin profers an invitation to tea. Right: St. Catherine's Monastery.

exchanging the black Bedouin tent for a house of concrete or a corrugated iron shack. The old habits, customs and tribal structures remain, however. As always, the sheikh is considered the highest authority in the tribe, which is the most important social grouping for the Bedouin. Supported by a judge, the Kadi (Arabic: *qâdî*) and a council of elders, the sheikh judges everyday disputes according to customary law developed over hundreds of years. It is a law that has grown from the requirements of the desert, and in which hospitality still today counts as one of the highest rules.

The Suez-Tâbâ road forms the borderline between the provinces of **North Sinai**, with its capital Al-'Arîsh and **South Sinai**, with its capital At-Tûr. The untouched, white palm beaches of **Al-'Arîsh** are the main attraction in the north of the peninsula, and have helped to turn the provincial capital (population 40,000) into a favorite swimming resort in recent years. But most tourists from home and abroad are drawn to the fascinating mountain regions and underwater wonders of the coral reefs of South Sinai, which are uniquely combined on the Gulf of 'Aqaba.

Tâbâ, which has just recently been returned to Egypt, **Nuwaiba'**, **Dahab** and **Sharm ash-Shaikh** are the four tourist centers along the 180-kilometer-long gulf coast. They all offer nice bays for swimming and excellent areas for diving, along with hotel complexes and diving schools. While Nuwaiba' and Dahab offer mainly bargain hotels for backpackers, **Na'ama Bay** near Sharm ash-Shaikh boasts a wide seaside promenade lined with the very tasteful flat-roofed and dome-shaped buildings of various elegant hotels. Very close by, at **Ra's Muhammad**, **Ra's Umm Sid** and **Ra's Nusrânî**, the most famous diving areas in the Sinai are to be found.

In all of these resorts excursions are offered to places of note along the coast or

into the hinterland, be it a camel trip to the mountains lasting several days, a starlight dinner in the desert, a trip in a glass-bottom boat or an expedition to some of the more remote valleys. But whatever other sights might be visited, St. Catherine's Monastery and Moses Mountain still remain at the top of the list.

ST. CATHERINE'S MONASTERY

Depending on one's point of departure, there are two routes to the monastery: over the breath-takingly beautiful stretch which branches off into the interior between Nuwaibâ and Dahab – or over the rather monotonous coastal road along the Gulf of Suez, which at least has the bonus of passing through the Fairân Oasis.

Taking the latter route, south of the oil towns of Abû Zanîma and Abû Rudais, turn toward Wâdî Fairân. After about 30 kilometers you will reach the picturesque palm groves of the oasis. There was a substantial Christian settlement here until the seventh century, with a bishopric.

The mountainsides are riddled with caves which were inhabited in the third century by Christian hermits. They considered **Jabal Sirbâl** (2,070 meters), in the south of the oasis, to be the site where Moses received the Ten Commandments. In the center of the oasis are remains of a Christian basilica which was destroyed by Arab invaders in the seventh century.

After about 30 kilometers the oasis road over Fairân and the main road to Dahab and Nuwaibâ join together and continue in a southerly direction for another 20 kilometers to **St. Catherine's Monastery**. The monastery fortress stands at an elevation of 1,570 meters in a narrow valley between Jabal Mûsâ and Jabal Katarîna. Hermits had already settled here around 300 A.D., in the place where the legend of the holy thornbush originated. Empress Helena had a church built on this site around 330, and Emperor Justinian incorporated it into a fortified monastery citadel with a 12- to 15-meter-high granite rampart. The monks of the Byzantine and Greek Orthodox

churches have kept the faith alive ever since. Saint Catherine, an Alexandrian martyr from the fourth century whose mortal remains were found in a miraculous way high up on Jabal Katrîna, has only been the patron saint of the Sinai monastery since the Middle Ages.

The **Justinian Basilica**, from the sixth century, rises in the center of the monastery. Most of its splendid interior decoration is, however, from the 17th and 18th centuries. The beautiful Byzantine mosaics (sixth century) in the apse are famous. At their center they depict the transfiguration of Christ on Mount Tabor, on the upper left of the front wall, Moses removing his shoes before the burning bush, and, to the right, Moses receiving the tablets of the Commandments.

Right behind the chancel is the **Chapel of the Burning Bush**, which was built over the roots of the holy thorn bush. A thriving green shoot of the bush can still be seen on the rear side of the front outer wall of the basilica.

The whole of the southwest front of the monastery is taken up by an arched building which houses a valuable **collection of icons** and the world-renowned **library**, which is surpassed only by the Vatican library in its collection of writings (it is, unfortunately, not open to visitors at the present time).

The three- to four-hour walk over **Jabal Mûsâ** (2,285 meters) offers an unforgettable panorama. A comfortable winding path and the 3,000 Pilgrim Steps (very high and steep) lead up it. The nightly ascent to the top has become a regular feature on tourists' schedules. When the weather is clear, you can experience the unique natural spectacle of sunrise – although, these days, rarely peace and solitude. For that you must climb **Jabal Katrîna** opposite. At 2,639 meters it is the Sinai's highest mountain. The chapel at the summit commemorates the spot where the relics of St. Catherine were discovered.

Above: Watching the sunrise from the rocks of Jabal Mûsâ.

RED SEA
Arrival

The *Upper Egypt Bus Company* runs buses daily from Cairo (Mîdân Ahmad Hilmî Bus Station) to Hurghada; the *Travco Sharq ad-Delta Company* has one bus daily (except Friday; from Sinai Bus Station in 'Abbâsîya). There are buses (in military convoys) daily from Luxor (from behind the temple) to Hurghada via Port Safâga. **Group taxis** to the Red Sea leave Cairo from the Mîdân Ramsis (Main Station) and from Mîdân Gîza; from Luxor depart from the Shâri' Abu Gûd (behind the Luxor Museum); at present these only travel with military convoys. There are regular flights to Hurghada with **Egypt Air**, **Air Sinai** and **ZAS Passenger Service**.

Accommodation

HURGHADA (area code 065): *Beach: LUXURY:* **Hilton Resort**, tel. 442116-7, fax. 442113; **Magawîsh Village**, tel. 442446, fax. 442759; **Sonesta Beach Resort**, tel. 443660, fax. 441665. *MODERATE:* **Giftun Tourist Village**, tel./fax. 442666; **Jasmine Holiday Village**, tel. 442442. *Center: BUDGET:* **Moon Valley**, tel. 442811. **QUSEIR** (area code 065): *LUXURY:* **Mövenpick Hotel**, El Qadim Bay, Quseir, Red Sea, tel. 432100, fax. 432128. **PORT SAFÂGA** (area code 065): **Menaville Village**, tel. 451761, fax. 451764; **Sea Land Village**, 3545756, fax. 3545060.

Tourist Information

State Tourist Office, Hurghada, Sh. al-Mahafza, tel. 446513.

DESERT MONASTERIES

The monasteries cannot be reached by public transportation. The overland buses from Cairo to Hurghada stop on request at the junctions to the monasteries. The monasteries have guest houses for overnight stays; reservations can be made at the Patriarchate in Cairo, Sh.Ramsîs (St. Mark's Cathedral). Visits by car from Ismailia or Suez (from Suez ca. 400 km round-trip). Hurghada – St. Paul's Monastery: ca. 525 (long!) km return journey. Monasteries are closed on all Coptic holidays.

SUEZ CANAL ZONE

The *East Delta Bus Company* has hourly buses from 6:30 am to 6 pm from Cairo (Md. al-Qulâlî) to Ismailia and Port Said, and half hourly to Suez.

Accommodation

SUEZ (area code: 062): *BUDGET:* **Red Sea**, Port Tawfîq, tel. 223334, fax. 227761; **Summer Palace**, Port Tawfîq, tel. 224475, fax. 321944. **ISMAILIA** (area code 064): *MODERATE:* **Mercure Forsan Island**, Forsan Island, tel. 765322, fax. 338043. *BUDGET:* **Crocodile Inn**, 179 Sh. Sa'd Zaghlûl, tel. 222724; **El-Salam Touristic**, Sh. al-Geish, tel. 324401.

PORT SAID (area code 066): *LUXURY:* **Helnan Port Said**, Sh. al-Corniche, tel. 320890, fax. 323762. *MODERATE:* **Holiday**, Sh. al-Gumhûrîya, tel. 220711, fax. 220710; **New Regent**, 27 Sh. al-Gumhûrîya, tel. 223802, fax. 224891. *BUDGET:* **Abu Simbel**, 15 Sh al-Gumhûrîya, tel. 221595; **Riviera**, 30, Sh. Ramsîs, tel. 228836.

SINAI
Transportation

The buses of the *East Delta Bus Company* (tel. 4824753) run several times daily to Al-'Arîsh, Tâbâ, Nuwayba' and Sharm ash-Shaikh; there is service once daily to Dahab via St. Catherine. The buses leave from the Sinai Bus Station in 'Abbâsîya (northwest Cairo). Group taxi stand to Sinai at the Al-Qulâlî station.

Egypt Air flies from Cairo to Al-'Arîsh, At-Tûr, Sharm ash-Shaikh and to St. Catherine's Monastery. There are also seasonal flights from Hurghada to the monastery. Booking in Cairo only: Md. at-Tahrîr, tel. 760948. The airport of Sharm ash-Shaikh is served by a number of international charter companies. There is ship service three times a week between Hurghada and Sharm ash-Shaikh.

Accommodation

'AL-ARÎSH (area code 068): *LUXURY:* **Egoth Oberoi**, Sh. Al-Fariq Abû Zikrî, tel. 351321, fax. 352352. *MODERATE:* **Sinai Beach**, Sh. Fu'âd Zikrî, tel. 341713; **Sinai Sun**, 23 Sh. 26th July, tel. 341855. **TÂBÂ** (area code 062): *LUXURY:* **Tâbâ Hilton**, Tâbâ Beach, tel. 530140, fax. 5787044. *BUDGET:* **Salah el-Deen**, tel. 530340, fax. 530343. **NUWAIBA'** (area code 062): *LUXURY:* **Noweiba Hilton Coral Resort**, tel. 520320, fax. 520027. *MODERATE:* **El-Sayadeen Tourist Village**, tel. 520340; **Barracuda**, Nuwaiba' Harbor, tel. 520300, fax. 762298. **DAHAB** (area code 062): *MODERATE:* **Novotel Dahab Holiday Village**, tel. 640304, fax. 640305; **Helnan Dahab Hotel**, Tourist Center, tel. 640425, fax. 640428. *BUDGET:* **Gulf Hotel**, Tourist Center, tel. 640147. **SHARM ASH-SHAIKH** (area code 062): *LUXURY:* **Mövenpick Jolie Ville**, Na'ama Bay, tel. 600100, fax. 600111; **Fairouz Hilton Resort**, Na'ama Bay, tel. 600136, fax. 770726. *MODERATE:* **Sanafir**, Na'ama Bay, tel. 600197, fax. 600196. **ST. CATHERINE'S MONASTERY:** **St. Catherine Tourist Village**, Wâdî ar-Râha, tel./fax. 770221; **El-Salam**, St. Catherine Airport, tel. 771409, fax. 2476535.

Tourist Information / Excursions

'AL-ARÎSH: Fouad Zikry St. tel. 340569. **SHARM ASH-SHAIKH**: Tel. 762704.

St. Catherine's Monastery is open daily (except Fri, Sun, Orthodox holidays) from 9:30 am to 12:30 pm.

RESEARCHING ANCIENT EGYPT

The pyramids, the Valley of the Kings, the beautiful Nefertiti and the treasures of Tutankhamen – for many people these are magic words, the very mention of which evokes images of mystery and adventure. And not only in our days: the land which, in the words of the Greek historian Herodotus (fifth century B.C.), "contained more wonderful things and astonishing works than all other lands" was the quintessence of high culture, even in earliest times.

The pyramids were considered to occupy the first place among the Seven Wonders of the World, and scholars and philosophers traveled often and gladly to the Nile to visit the monuments of the Pharaohs. One encounters such famous names as Plato, Strabo and Diodorus alongside that of Herodotus. Their re-

Preceding pages: In the festival tent. Above: Historic painting by G. J. Poyntner (1867).

ports became a rich source of information for later generations of researchers, because the ancient authors still experienced the world of the ancient Egyptians with their own eyes.

In the Christian era, when monks, fearing the magical power of pagan Egypt, destroyed many buildings and sculptures in their iconoclastic fanaticism, knowledge of ancient Egyptian culture was lost. It wasn't until the arrival of Islam that a growing interest in ancient Egypt, in the mystical, mysterious aura which surrounded everything to do with the Pharaohs, came about. The descriptions of journeys by Arab writers who reported the wonders of the Land of the Nile helped to spread the pyramids' fame far into the Orient, just as much as the Tales of the Thousand and One Nights.

However, this did not stop the Mameluke sultans from using these revered ancient burial monuments, together with many other structures from the time of the Pharaohs, as stone quarries for Islamic Cairo.

The roots of Western Egyptology go back to the Renaissance, when the works of the ancient writers began to be translated first into Latin, and later into other languages. Once the favorite souvenirs of the Roman emperors, the obelisks in Italy were to become the first objects of study for those who wished to unravel the secret of the hieroglyphs. But despite some noteworthy results, the understanding of Egyptian culture remained in that realm of speculation where mysteries and occult rites were the favored areas of interest. As the European aristocracy of the 17th and 18th centuries became more and more drawn by the exotic, painters and architects feasted on Egyptian themes and styles; at the same time, the first great collections of Egyptian art began to appear.

Even in the sphere of classical studies, the Enlightenment, with its encyclopedic strivings, led in the end to a sober and systematic presentation of the subject matter. The foundations of modern scientific study of the country were not laid down, however, until Napoleon's Egyptian campaign. A large staff of scholars accompanied the army on its journey to the Nile and wrote up their assessment of the country in the 24-volume *Description de l'Égypte*. The fantastic, true-to-detail drawings and engravings by Vivant Denon, who copied Egypt's ancient monuments along the Nile all the way to Philae, became one of the pillars of nascent Egyptology. It celebrated its first great triumph, indeed the first hour of its very birth, in 1822, when Jean-François Champollion announced that he had deciphered hieroglyphics.

Pioneers of Egyptology

The unusually gifted Champollion – he was a professor of history in Grenoble at the age of 18 – was the first to come up with the idea that hieroglyphics was not a pure system of symbols in which one picture or one group of signs represents one word. The key to his discovery was the *Rosetta Stone*, a black basalt slab bearing a text inscribed in hieroglyphic, demotic and Greek characters. It had been discovered by French soldiers near Rosetta in 1799.

Another important step on the way to this encryption was the realization that the Coptic language, well known through Christian literature written in the Greek alphabet, must be related to the language of the hieroglyphs. The English physicist Thomas Young, who is primarily known today as the founder of the wave theory of light, was the first to make some progress in this direction. He managed to identify the names of Ptolemy and Berenice contained in royal cartouches in the hieroglyphic version of the Rosetta Stone.

Champollion's hour of glory arrived with the realization that what he had before him must be a combined system of word symbols and letters. With the help of other hieroglyphic texts, and by making a comparison with the Coptic, he was soon able to decipher the names of 79 kings, and in 1824 – only two years after he made his brilliant discovery – he presented an extensive report on his findings. It was now possible to unlock the door to the mysteries of Egypt's past, and detailed study of its millenia-old culture could finally begin.

Until the middle of the 18th century, the main concern of scientific expeditions to the Land of the Nile had been to draw and describe the accessible sights of the Nile Valley in order to make further material available for study in scholars' rooms back home. At that time, excavations were mainly the concern of rich art collectors, above all of accredited diplomats in Egypt, who carried out a lively trade in Egyptian antiquities.

The Italian Giovanni Battista Belzoni (1778-1823) also belong to the first generation of archeologists. This giant of

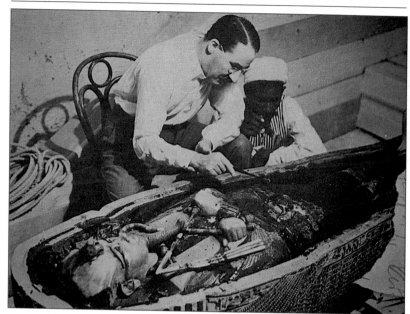

a man with the strength of an ox already had a career as a circus performer behind him when he came to Egypt to try to sell his new irrigation system to the viceroy, Muhammad 'Alî.

Although his water wheel was not a particular hit with the viceroy, the English consul general, Henry Salt, engaged the Italian Hercules for the transport of a colossal seven-ton head of Ramses II. Belzoni's attention was soon drawn to the ancient monuments and, after a short intermezzo in Abû Simbel, he started to excavate in Thebes West. His most important discovery was one of the most beautiful tombs in the Valley of the Kings, that of Seti I, which is today known as "Belzoni's Tomb."

In the garden of the Egyptian Museum in Cairo there is a white marble sarcophagus which is clearly not from the time of the Pharaohs. It is the tomb of

Above: Howard Carter and Tutankhamen's mummy. Right: A golden lion from the treasure of Tutankhamun.

Mariette-Pasha, the founder of the museum. Auguste Édouard Mariette (1821-81) arrived in Alexandria by ship on October 2, 1850. He had been given the task of acquiring Coptic manuscripts for the Louvre, but a visit to the Citadel changed his whole life. Faced with the overpowering panorama that spread out before him, he made the following entry in his diary: "This dream that I have dreamt all my life suddenly took on real form. Within my grasp lay a world of tombs, stelai, inscriptions and statues. What more can I say? The next day I hired two or three mules..."

On October 27, he began to explore the necropolis of Saqqâra. The unparalleled discoveries of the Avenue of the Sphinxes and the Serapeum were to be the prelude to his further successes as an archeologist; he later found 115 tombs from the Old Kingdom there. These included some that are now among Egypt's most famous attractions. Appointed director of the newly founded *Service des Antiquités*, the Egyptian department for the administration of antiquities, in 1858, all excavations in the country, as well as the building and control of the Egyptian Museum, came under his charge.

One of the most charming Egyptian films, which can nowadays sometimes be seen in English-speaking countries under the title *The Mummy*, has as its theme an occurrence which concerned Mariette's successor, Gaston Maspero.

In the 1870s, a number of pieces that must quite clearly have come from a royal tomb in Thebes suddenly began showing up on the art market. Investigations led to Qurna, and to the 'Abd ar-Rasûl brothers. After several interrogations and a few months of imprisonment, one of the brothers confessed: deep in the valley basin of Dair al-Bahrî they had found a hidden burial chamber full of royal coffins. As was soon ascertained, among them were the coffins of the greatest Pharaohs of Egyptian history, such as Ahmose, Thutmose III and Ramses II. As a precaution against graverobbing, which also went on in ancient times, priests of the Twenty-first Dynasty (about 1000 B.C.) had the royal mummies brought to this hiding place.

When the mummies were brought to Cairo by ship soon thereafter, the fellahs honored their ancestors with a ghastly escort. Along the entire route, women stood on the banks of the Nile, tearing their hair in mourning and shrilly crying out while the men fired salutes.

To record the deeds of the Egyptologists, their spectacular discoveries and the results of their research, would require many volumes. One of the most famous of all of them is the Englishman Howard Carter, who, in 1922, discovered the tomb of Tutankhamen in the Valley of the Kings.

Carter was already a renowned excavator when, in 1914, his countryman Lord Carnavon became his patron in the search for Tutankhamen's tomb. Since the time when he had discovered, among other

things, the tomb of King Horemheb in the Valley of the Kings, he was convinced that he would also find Tutankhamen's tomb there. Among experts in the field heads were shaken, since most considered that the Valley of the Kings had already been thoroughly investigated.

Howard Carter began excavation work in 1917, but fate did not seem to favor him: he missed the entrance to the tomb by a hair's breadth. It was covered by the rubble of ancient workmen's huts. Years of painstaking and disappointing searching followed, but Carter – obsessed by his idea – did not give up. He was to prove right. In November 1922, the news of his sensational discovery traveled the world like wildfire.

Overnight the "Boy King," who was, in fact, a rather unimportant Pharaoh, became the most famous ruler in Egyptian history. Later discoveries, regardless of how spectacular they might have been, never again had the effect on the public that Howard Carter's discovery of the "Golden Pharaoh" did.

THE MYSTERY OF THE HIEROGLYPHS

Unlike almost any other writing system, the signs of the ancient Egyptians arouse the curiosity of anyone who examines them closely. They look like reduced individual figures in a relief or painting, and completely agree in coloration and form with their great archetypes which appeared at the same time (around 3000 B. C.). But the 700 symbols – there were 1,000 in Ptolemaic time – are too few for a pure system of picture symbols. On the other hand, there are far too many for an alphabetic script. Champollion's great achievement was to realize that hieroglyphics are actually a complex combination of both systems: of picture symbols (ideographs) and phonetic symbols (phonograms).

We speak of ideographs when the meaning of the word is symbolized by a symbol: so that a rudimentary outline of a house stands for the word "house," a palette and brush for "scribe," two legs walking for "go." Phonograms are understood to be letters or combinations of letters which no longer have any connection whatsoever with the content of a symbol: so that an owl can have the phonetic value "m," a hare "w + n," and a beetle "kh + p + r."

Since the vowels were not written out, a polysyllabic phonetic symbol could be used in spelling a variety of words which had entirely different meanings. In order to define the specific meaning of a word, an ideograph would be added to it, which in this case, however, would only be read as a mute symbol. The direction of the writing can easily be variable, though it is not difficult at all to distinguish: the figures always face toward the beginning of the line.

As with the picture cycles in a temple or tomb, the symbols of religious writings gained a magical power. So much did the Egyptians believe in the efficacy of these "words of god" that they wished to counteract the threatening danger of hieroglyphs by means of a protective spell. This is why there is sometimes a knife drawn through the body of the desert viper, the ancient Egyptian letter "f." But pictures and objects in the sacral world depended on the magical power of the written word: only with the naming of a statue or by fixing a sacrificial formula in writing could a cult be guaranteed to last for eternity.

The Greeks called these sacral writings "Holy Symbols" (from the Greek *hieros*, meaning "holy") and distinguished two types: the beautiful **hieroglyphs** cut into the stone of temples, tomb walls, stelai and statues, and **hieratic writing**, written with reed and ink. The starkly-abstracted cursive writing used since the eighth century for mostly profane texts was called **demotic** – "people's writing" (Greek: *demos*, or "people").

Above: Vertical rows of hieroglyphs. Right: A minaret.

ALLAHU AKBAR

Five times daily the muezzin's call to prayer rings out from minarets all over the land. It always begins with the words *Allahu akbar*, in order to remind the people, whatever they might be doing at the moment, that "God is great." "Devotion" to this all-embracing knowledge – that is what the Arabic word *Islâm* means. It comes from the same root as *Salâm*, "peace." The faithful Muslim finds this peace in his devotion to the will of God in Islam.

The fundamental articles of faith of Islam, proclaimed by the prophet Muhammad, are: faith in the kind and merciful God, the one and only, who has created the world and given it his universal law; faith in his angels, his prophets, the revealed writings, the resurrection and day of judgment.

A system of rules of behavior and commandments together make Islam into an all-pervading way of life. Not only does it give a meaningful order to everyday living, but it also prescribes foods, regulates social relations, sets down solidarity and social welfare as fundamental values of society, and encompasses a complete legal system, the *Sharî'a*.

The Koran (*Qur'ân*), the Holy Book of the Muslims, revealed to the prophet Muhammad by God, is the most important source of Islam's code of law and behavior. In addition to the *Suras*, the Koran's 114 chapters of varying length, the traditions of the *Hadîth* (records of the life of Muhammad handed down from generation to generation) are also authoritative. They consist of an important collection of the prophet's sayings and conduct, the so-called *Sunna*, which helps to interpret the often very difficult to understand Koran.

The main tenets of Islamic practice are succinctly expressed in what is known as the "Five Pillars." The First Pillar: The creed, the *Shahâda*, which is spoken at

the beginning of each prayer and which the muezzin often repeats in his call to prayer: "I bear witness that there is no god other than the one God, and that Muhammad is the Prophet of God." The Second Pillar: This is the prayer (*Salâh*) performed by every Muslim, according to strict rules, five times daily while facing in the direction of Mecca. The Third Pillar: The annual giving of alms (*Zakâh*), a social duty, according to which everyone should give 2.5 percent of his wealth to the poor and needy once each year. In Egypt the Zakâh is a voluntary donation which may also take a form other than money. At the same time, the Koran also speaks of the *Sadaqa*, the giving of alms, which one is always and everywhere called upon to do. The Fourth Pillar: The fast (*Sawm*) in the month of Ramadân, when all pleasures of the flesh are forbidden between sunrise and sundown. And, finally, the Fifth Pillar: The journey of pilgrimage to Mecca (*Hajj*) which every Muslim should undertake once in his life.

THE RENAISSANCE OF ISLAM

For quite a few years now, the actions of militant Islamic groups have been occupying the headlines of the international press, and the calls for Islamic social order have become increasingly loud from Morocco to Mindanao. This is a political vision that, for Westerners at any rate, conjures horrifying images of terror, violence, and fanaticism. Even on the Nile, Islam is playing an ever larger role: the extremist Jamî'at al-Islâmîya ("Islamic Society") is causing serious problems for the secular government of President Mubarak.

Just how should this phenomenon be interpreted? Is Egypt going the same way as Iran? Or will it soon find itself in the same situation as Algeria? Is this return to Islam in every case tantamount to terror and violence? The West is confused by and somewhat helpless at what is going on in the whole of the Islamic East at the moment, and by something that, in its radical outgrowths, also appears to be quite threatening.

The roots of re-Islamization, the resurrection of Islamic concepts and values, go back to the 19th century, when the Orient, at the time under colonial – mainly British – rule was searching for its lost national identity. For many of those actively involved in this search for national identity, it soon became clear that the way forward should not only bring political independence, but also a reorientation of social and political values. The answer was a return to the country's locally-developed culture, which was in danger of fading away under superimposed Western thinking. A return to Islam was the answer.

One of the spiritual fathers of the new movement was the poet Muhammad Iqbâl (1875-1938), who incisively for-

mulated the fundamental ideas of the Islamic revival in his book *The Reconstruction of Religious Thought in Islam*. In this work he suggests: "It is religion alone, soley and exclusively, that can ethically prepare modern man for the burden of responsibility which the progress of the modern natural sciences necessarily entails. ... Only by raising his understanding of his origins and his future, his wherefrom and where to, to a new vision can man finally triumph over a society that is driven by inhuman competition, and claim victory over a civilization which has, as a result of its inner conflict of religious and political values, lost its unity."

In Egypt, none other than the grand mufti himself, Muhammad 'Abduh (1849-1905), was among the leading Muslim reformers. His philosophy of a rationally-oriented Islam became a central idea in modern Islamic awareness, and it still points the way for millions of Muslims today. And, contrary to the deep-rooted prejudices of many people in the West, it also sees no contradiction whatsoever between progress and technology on the one hand, and a religious life on the other.

Along with the liberal modernists around Muhammad 'Abduh, however, there were also fundamentalist groupings being formed, such as the Muslim Brotherhood, founded in 1928 by Hasan al-Bannâ, which was more than willing to resort to violence and terror, if their aim of creating an Islamic state so required. In general, though, the Brotherhood played only a relatively minor role in Egyptian affairs.

That the spirit of Islam once again pervades all areas of Egyptian daily life is the result of a process of fundamental change. The search for a new national awareness has brought with it, at the same time, a separation from the modern Western lifestyle which was always a second-hand culture for the East.

Right: Today the veil is again a part of Egypt's Islamic culture.

Recent events, although they may not have caused this reflection on native cultural and religious values, have certainly speeded it up: for one thing, there was a definite reaction to the failure of Nasser's pan-Arab ideology, which was demonstrated in the catastrophe of the Six Day War in June 1967 and, for another, to the influx of Western consumer goods and customs under Sadat's policy of opening up the country.

Curiously, it was Sadat himself who sponsored the re-Islamization of the country. The president liked to portray himself – and often did – as a devout, practicing Muslim. However, the spirits he called forth soon turned out to spell disaster for him.

The separate peace treaty he concluded with Israel resulted in Egypt being banished from the brotherhood of Arab nations. This, in turn, ignited a flammable situation in which a growing number of Egyptians saw his profession of adherence to the faith as being nothing more than empty words. Indeed, his

economic policies had not only flooded the country with Western goods, but had also brought unemployment, inflation, and social injustice in their wake. This laid the groundwork, even in liberal Eygpt, for militant Islamic activities, including, among other things, the 1981 assassination of President Sadat, violent assaults against the Coptic minority, and the occasional terrorist attack on foreign tourists. The vast majority of Egytians, though, are decisively opposed to such fanatical excesses.

Besides the political effects of re-Islamization, Egypt is also witnessing a movement of religious revival that is being felt at all levels of society, and which therefore includes the Coptic Christians. This revival is fundamentally apolitical and, in its deep devoutness, tends much more towards a mystical search for god. Its principal intent is to return to the values of a religion-oriented life in which the secular ideas and interests of Western consumer society have only peripheral significance.

NASSER'S PYRAMID STANDS IN ASWAN

"Nasser's Pyramid" is what the people call the Sadd al-ʿâlî, the gigantic High Dam of Aswan, the main body of which has 16 times the volume of the Pyramid of Cheops. And, just like the pyramids of the Pharaohs, the dam was supposed to be a guarantee and symbol of a prosperous Egypt which had entered into a new, better age with the revolution of the "Free Officers."

Today the euphoria has long since disappeared and, even in Egypt, the critical voices are increasing. In the international press Nasser's pyramid has become the main target of a brand of environmental journalism which never ceases to paint what it sees as an impending ecological catastrophe in the blackest of colors – apparently completely unaware of the latest scientific findings which prove, among

other things, that the High Dam has been made the scapegoat for any number of environmental problems whose origins can be traced back to the time before its construction.

The Nile has always been Egypt's vital artery. It had to sustain seven million people in ancient times, and 26 million when work on the dam began. Now that number has grown to more than 60 million; within the next few years it is expected to climb to 70 million. Intensive use of water was the main concern at the time when Nasser's revolutionary regime decided to build the dam.

Unlike the Old Aswan Dam, which had let most of the water flow into the sea unused, the new dam was to close off the Nile completely and release regulated amounts of water all year round from its massive reservoir. The High Dam was built between 1960 and 1971, according to German plans which, after the West's about-face, were modified somewhat by Soviet engineers – primarily for reasons of costs.

Above: Under construction. Right: View of the power plant from the High Dam.

Without doubt, a project of this dimension represents a large-scale interference with nature. In addition to the calculated drawbacks, it brings with it a whole series of unforseen consequences. For example, the water's rate of evaporation is surprisingly high, and its influence on the climate is not the least of its effects. The water of the Nile is faster flowing, as it now contains very little mud. This means that it not only hollows out the riverbed, but also washes away embankments, bridges and weirs.

As has been determined in the meantime, the lack of nutrient-rich Nile mud has had only a minor effect on soil fertility, whereas it has led to a drastic decline in sardine catches along the Mediterranean coast. But vermin such as rats and mice, which used to be decimated by annual floods, now have ideal conditions for surviving and even thriving.

Most of these problems can be dealt with providing the proper measures are taken. Today, the elevation of the ground water level and the salination of the nearby arable land are being dealt with with a great deal of success. This is being accomplished in part through selective educational programs for the fellahs, and in part through the accelerated expansion of the drainage system used for the irrigation of the valley floor.

There are powerful arguments for viewing the High Dam in a positive light, which even pessimists cannot refute: the amount of land available for cultivation has up to now increased by about 15 percent thanks to land reclamation, and with two to three guaranteed harvests per year, yields have doubled. And current from the power station at Sadd al-'âlî has not only helped to speed up industrialization, it has also brought the comfort of electricity to thousands of villages.

The African drought in the 1980s, furthermore, demonstrated in a dramatic way how vitally important this dam is for Egypt; for without the massive water reserve in the gigantic reservoir, those "eight lean years" would have been an unavoidable catastrophe.

LITTLE SPACE FOR MANY CHILDREN

In Egypt a child is born every 26 seconds. This means that the population of the country grows by about one million every 10 months. Sixty-two million people live along the Nile today. In the next few years that number will have risen to 65 million. These figures do not appear to be very spectacular at first glance, as Egypt is almost twice as large as France. But in light of the country's particular geographic circumstances they are worrying: only 3.5 percent of the country's land area is arable or habitable, the vast expanse that is left is made up of inhospitable desert.

One of the main problems in Egypt is that increases in agricultural output cannot keep pace with the enormous growth in population. Despite the favorable conditions offered by extremely fertile soil and the possibility of year-round irrigation, the dream of self-sufficiency in food production has long since faded away. Ambitious projects of land reclamation and for progressively increasing agricultural productivity will make little difference under the circumstances. Since the mid-1970s, Egypt has imported more agricultural products than it has exported. Today fully 36 percent of foodstuffs have to be be imported.

Agriculture and fishing, which together with trade were once among the most important branches of the nation's economy, today play only a minor role. As a proportion of gross national product they have dropped from 40 to 18 percent over the last three decades. The change in the number of farmers, the fellahs, has been even more drastic. Almost half of them have migrated to the cities in order to try their luck in industry, as construc-

tion workers or working in the service sector. Unlike other developing countries, in Egypt, migration from the countryside has not created rings of slums around the cities, as fertile land here is far too valuable. The "immigrants" are therefore concentrated in the poorer old town quarters of the city centers. The lure especially of Cairo, which, in addition to offering the hope of finding a job has the prestige a capital city, means, above all, that it seems to be bursting at the seams in places.

The results of this are an unparalleled shortage of housing and urban sprawl, which increasingly devours valuable farmland. The catastrophic earthquake of October 1992 has illustrated the severity of this situation quite clearly. Victims came primarily from the overcrowded poor quarters, where, in their need to create additional housing, extra stories were often added – illegally – atop the flat roofs of existing houses.

The desert is the solution to this dilemma. Hundreds of thousands of people will find a new home in a place where once only Bedouins could survive, thanks to modern technology and construction techniques. In order to relieve the overburdened centers of population, in the mid-1970s work was begun to construct six satellite towns with industrial zones on the other side of the agricultural region, and to develop them into attractive places for settlement. Favorable land prices and a 10-year tax exemption provide the attraction for industry, in which about 40,000 people are now employed. But many of them must commute a long distance to work, as not everyone can afford the much sought-after apartments in these towns.

Today more than a third of all Egyptians are under 15 years of age. Two new schools would have to be opened every day just to guarantee them and their future brothers and sisters an adequate elementary school education. Where this

Right: Two children are enough, according to the state – but who will guarantee their parents' retirement.

is not possible, efforts are made to counteract the deficit with large classes and by teaching in shifts. In this way most of the children in even the more remote areas can now read and write – which is still not the case with their parents; for although school has officially been obligatory since 1923, it is only since the government of Presient Nasser (1952) that it has effectively become widespread. That is why there is still an illiteracy rate in Egypt of around 38 percent. At the same time, the Egyptian standard of education is a model for other Arab states, which recruit predominantly Eyptian teachers for their schools and universities.

Many dream of a job in one of the other Arab nations – and not just university granduates. The oil-rich states of the Persian Gulf offer attractive salaries which at home could not even be earned with the customary second job. Millions of Egyptian migrant workers, from university professors to fellahs, have moved in the last 20 years, mainly to the Gulf countries. Their money transfers have earned the Land of the Nile so much in foreign currency (between two and four billion US dollars annually) that they are described as one of the "four pillars of the Egyptian economy."

The other three pillars of the economy are income from oil exports, tolls from the Suez Canal and tourism. As the recent past has shown once again, tourism and money transfers from migrant workers are both highly crisis-prone sources of income. Terrorist attacks, the Gulf War and recession in the oil-producing countries showed their effects immediately. Tolls from the Suez Canal, earning a yearly revenue of around US $1 billion, and earnings from oil exports are stable sources of income.

With an output of 47 million tons a year, Egypt nowadays belongs to the middle rank of oil-producing countries. Offshore oil discoveries in the Gulf of Suez and in the Libyan Desert have noticeably increased the importance of "black gold" in Egypt; so much so, in

fact, that it has now become the country's most important export product.

The Land of the Nile does not only have rich natural resources at its disposal (in addition to oil and natural gas there is also phosphate, iron, manganese and salt, for example), it also has a realtively good infrastructure in the industrial centers of the north. Of Egypts's industries, the food industry tops the list today, but chemical and petrochemical plants, together with machine-building and the electronics industry, are also experiencing a large rate of growth. To the south of Cairo, near Heluan, is Africa's largest steelworks, and near Naj' Hammâdî in Upper Egypt is the continent's largest aluminum smelting works.

Now as before, the famous Egyptian cotton is of significant economic importance – especially in the export market. The once-flourishing textile industry has

Above: Watching TV can be a community activity. Right: Ahlan wa-sahlan – a hearty welcome!

been in the red for years now, as have so many other state-run industries that left over from the socialistic Nasser era.

Privatization and decentralization were and still are, therefore, the cornerstones of President Mubarak's economic policies. Tax reform, liberalization of prices and import trade, and the introduction of a unified exchange rate are a few of the significant elements of his comprehensive reform plan. To this came cuts in subsidies for numerous goods and service industries, long demanded by the International Monetary Fund.

The upswing which all these measures brought about can clearly be seen: the country has managed to sink its foreign debt from US $50 billion to US $30 billion in less than 10 years. Still, these reforms mask a number of potentially explosive social problems, since the common man has rarely if ever profited from increased industrial growth. This will change, though – or so promise those in charge at any rate. Only the future will show just how earnestly they mean it.

A JASMINE MORNING

It is possible to get by in English almost everywhere in Egypt, but a few words in the native language have a magical effect. They not only show that you are interested in the people of the country, but also allow a small glimpse into the Arab soul.

The Egyptians enjoy a laugh above all else and always have time for telling a funny joke, pulling a prank or making fun of a situation. But this does not mean any lack of politeness or mutual respect on their part. Nowhere is that more vividly evident than in the playful poetry of ritual greetings which rise to ever more fragrant wishes in predetermined dialogue. So that in answering a simple "Good Morning" – *Sabâh al-khair* – a typical reply might be "Morning of Light" – *Sabâh an-nûr*, which the other speaker elevates into a "Morning of Jasmine" – *Sabâh al-full* – and which the first speaker in turn can only surpass with a "Morning of Whipped Cream" – *Sabâh al-qishta.*

After this, questions are exchanged about each other's well-being – *kaif al-hâl?* – and that of one's children and family. The reply is *Al-hamdu lillah* – "Praise be to God" – a pious phrase which is suitable for all circumstances and situations. To equate it with the rather mechanical and empty phrase "Thank God" is just as inaccurate as putting down the oft-cited *In schâ' Allah* – "If God wishes" – to a careless attitude to life. Only when the formal but heartfelt greeting ends does the actual conversation get underway.

The greeting *Salemaleikum* sometimes playfully uttered by Westerners is, in fact, understood by no one in Egypt. In Arabic this peace greeting, used mainly among Muslims, is actually *As-salâmu 'alaikum.* Christians usually greet one another with *Sa'îda* or *Nahârak sa'îd* – "May your day be a happy one." But

most often you will hear *Ahlan wa-sahlan* or *Marhaban*, which both mean "welcome." And one is truly always welcome in Egypt.

One of the most important words is *mumkin* – "possible." And just about everything in Egypt is possible; people at least try as hard as they can to make it possible. But should it not be possible in the end, then the word is *mâlîsh* – "don't take it too badly; it's not serious; it doesn't matter!" And perhaps there is always another chance: *In schâ' Allah bukra* – "If God wishes, tomorrow."

It is not just consolation that is expressed in these words, but also a cool attitude to time which reaches its height in that most elastic of Egyptian words *shuwayyah* – "a little." If this is used to refer to a period of time, it can actually mean anything from "five minutes" to "tomorrow." Repetition of the word, shuwayya shuwayya simply means "Take it easy!" That now just leaves one of the most important expressions in any language: "Thank you" – *Shukran!*

NOBEL PRIZE FOR NAGUIB MAHFOUZ

Cairo's winding old town and the alleys around the famous Khân al-Khalîlî bazaar are the backdrop for Naguib Mahfouz' novels. That is where little Uncle Kamil, the fat candy-seller, lives and where he spends almost all of his day dozing on a chair in front of his store in the Midaq Alley. A few houses further along the beautiful, dark-eyed Hamida dreams of the rich husband who will satisfy her every desire. And one of the cafés is the "famous Kirsha Coffee House, with its walls covered in arabesques from a long-forgotten time, now crumbling and decayed, and with the strong odor of ancient medicinal herbs which have become fragrant perfumes in the meantime."

Naguib Mahfouz is himself a son of this world of cafés, small alleyways and narrow lanes which he portrays in his novel *Midaq Alley* with such insight and sensitivity. He was born on December 11, 1912, the son of a minor government official in Gamalîya – the medieval old quarter of Cairo which stretches between Mîdân al-Husein and Khân al-Khalîlî to the Fatimid city gates of Bâb an-Nasr and Bâb al-Futûh.

This is the quarter where the author spent his childhood – among the tall, ancient houses, playing in the streets with little greenery and in the homey surroundings of the alleys which were "isolated from the hustle and bustle... preserving and hiding the secrets of the old, past world in itself." In touching short stories he evokes memories time and again of those childhood days, which also came under the strong influence of political events and upheavals.

After completing his studies in philosophy, the young Naguib Mahfouz first went to work for a few years in the university's administration department and, from 1939 on, had a position as an official in the Ministry for Religious Institutions. During this period he wrote his first novels – works in which he projected contemporary problems back into the world of the Pharaohs. But it was through his realistic novels about contemporary Egypt that he was first to become famous. *Midaq Alley*, published in 1947, was one of these works.

Mahfouz portrays his protagonists with love and a faithful recreation of reality. There are no heroes in his books, just ordinary people from working-class backgrounds. Their hopes and dreams, their conflicts and failures are all the stuff of his novels, which are at the same time an expression of those events in history which leave their indelible mark on man. With few words he creates an atmosphere the gravity of which is sometimes almost painful, and through which the fatefulness of existence runs as a central theme. In an unsentimental though committed manner he describes how people try to get along in the modern world and to discover new points of orientation – and how some fail helplessly.

Between 1951 and 1957 his famous 1,200-page work *The Cairo Trilogy* was written, by which Naguib Mahfouz would finally come to be recognized as one of the leading writers of the Arab world. Each of the three volumes has the name of a street or square in Cairo's old town as its title: *Palace Walk, Palace of Desire* and *Sugar Street*. The progress of a merchant family in the eventful years between 1919 and 1944 is the theme of this three-part novel of the generations. It describes the hopes and disappointments of the nationalist movement, the dissolution of the old social order and the search for new meaning and values.

Naguib Mahfouz also won the official recognition of his country with *The Cairo Trilogy*. President Nasser awarded him

Right: A candidate for being a hero in a novel by Naguib Mahfouz.

with the Egyptian State Prize for Literature and had him promoted to ever higher positions within Egypt's cultural administration. During the years 1966-68 he was appointed director of the State Film Society and, after that, was made an advisor to the Minister for Culture.

But Naguib Mahfouz' career never led him to write literary propaganda in support of Nasser's policies – quite the contrary: in 1961, with the publication of his novel *The Thief and the Dogs*, he had his first confrontation with the regime over social affairs. And in novels and novellas of later years, such as *Adrift on the Nile*, for example, he showed the ever more acute disillusion of many people who felt betrayed by the unfulfilled promises of the revolution.

The quest for the right way of life and social order, and the vision of living in an atmosphere of social justice and human dignity are core themes which appear again and again throughout the extensive body of his work. This is also the concern of the mystical and symbolic works of

the 1980s, which were already presaged in his novel *The Children of Gebelawi*, published in 1959.

In this book Mahfouz uses a parable to project the history of the salvation of the Jews, Christians and Muslims onto a section of Cairo's old town, and after the failure of the founders of the three great religions he has another deliverer of hope appear. But the modern scientist, who attempts to usher in a just New Age, inadvertently causes the death of God. Alone the realization that the ethical norms set by God can still be followed remains as hope for the future.

In the Arabic-speaking world, Naguib Mahfouz has for many years had a broad reading public. By awarding him the 1988 Nobel Prize for literature, the Stockholm Acadamy of Sciences showed that Mahfouz also has something to say to the Western world.

In 1994, Naguib Mahfouz was stabbed in the neck and seriously wounded in an assassination attempt by an Islamic radical.

CULINARY DELIGHTS

The menus in most hotel restaurants offer both international and Egyptian dishes that one should make a point of trying at least once. Turkish or Arabic influences can be recognized in many Egyptian dishes; they usually require a long preparation time and a large variety of ingredients. But even the simplest dishes may be turned into culinary delights by adding fresh herbs and exotic spices. Favorite seasonings are coriander, cumin, chili, pepper, turmeric, cloves, ginger and sesame. Of the herbs, dill, parsley and mint are widely used.

Most everday dishes do not have meat in them, but this does not mean they are lacking in substance. *Fûl* form the basis of many local dishes. These are thick brown beans which can be bought for a few piasters as *fûl mudammas* – a bean stew – in the small eating houses where voluminous tin pots simmer away all day over a low flame. Enriched with oil, garlic, lemon and a hard-boiled egg, they are eaten together with round flatbread – *'aish baladî*. Another of the thousand and one tasty *fûl* dishes is *ta'mîya* (also called *filafil*) – spiced balls made from bean purée and herbs. Stuffed into an open round flatbread with onions and tomatoes, they make a hearty meal. *Kûsharî* is a speciality of the colorful mobile kitchens. It is a dish made from rice, maccaroni and lentils with tomato sauce and fried onions.

On special occasions, holidays, and for guests, Egyptians will put on a lavish spread and make you feel at home. As with Italian food, the various delicacies can be divided up into entrée, first course, main course and dessert, but with the noticeable difference that in Egypt individual dishes are served more or less at the same time.

Right: Would you care for a helping of basbûsa?

234

In Egypt the **entrée** comes in the form of delicious savories known as *mâzza*, and salads, *salatât*, which usually have little in common with salads as they are generally known in the West. The main exceptions are *salata baladî* (a mixed salad of finely-diced tomatoes, cucumbers, parsley and onions) and *salata tomâtim* (tomato slices with a fiery herb and garlic sauce).

Other "salads" are *bâtingân* (marinated fried eggplant), *bâbâ ghanûg* (sesame paste with grilled eggplant pieces), *bîsâra* (bean purée with garlic and fried onions), *hummus* (sesame and chick pea sauce), *tahîna* (sesame paste with cumin and garlic) and *turshî* (pickled cucumbers, carrots and turnips). In addition, fresh round flatbread is used to dunk into the sauces.

The **first course** could be soup, or else a rice or vegetable dish, as with the following examples: *shurbat 'ads* (finely-puréed lentil soup with cumin and lemon), *mulûkhîya* (a slightly bitter oily soup made from the spinach-like edible jute), *mahshî* (vegetables – zucchini, tomatoes, peppers, eggplant, and so on, depending on the season – filled with rice and herbs), *waraq 'ainab* (vine leaves, stuffed with rice and sometimes also minced meat, and eaten warm), *bâmîya* (okra pods in tomato sauce), *mussâqa* (a casserole of eggplant and minced meat in tomato and béchamel sauce).

For the **main course** there is meat, fowl or fish, including such delicacies as *shîsh kabâb* (skewered pieces of mutton, liver and onions grilled over a charcoal fire; sometimes also prepared with chicken – *firâkh*), *kabâb halla* (mutton goulash with cumin), *kufta* (small grilled balls of minced meat), *fatta* (mutton served on round flatbread in a spicy broth), *hamâm mahshî* (stuffed pigeon) and *shâwirma* (mutton grilled in thin layers on a revolving spit).

Alexandria and the Red Sea coast are the places where you will find many

good seafood restaurants where all sorts of fish (*samak*) and seafood, such as prawns (*gambarî*), are prepared in varied and exquisite ways.

Egyptian **desserts** are sweet and substantial, and anyone with a sweet tooth will have great trouble resisting them. A few after dinner favorites are *baqlâwa* (a strudel made with nuts, almonds and honey), *basbûsa* (a sugar cake), *kunâfa* (a pie of wafer-thin, crisply baked pastry strips with honey and nuts), *umm 'âlî* (a hot delicacy of puff pastry, raisins, nuts, cinnamon and vanilla baked with milk and cream).

A good meal should be rounded off with a cup of *ahwa* (coffee). This is Turkish mocha which can be drunk either *mazbût* (medium sweet), *ziyâda* (very sweet) or *sâda* (without sugar). In good restaurants it is often improved by adding some cardamom and a pinch of nutmeg, following Bedouin tradition. A glass of hot *shay* (tea), perhaps with a fresh leaf of peppermint, *bi-na'na'*, also tastes wonderful.

Muslim Egyptians drink water with their meal, but in most of the restaurants (but not all!) which are used by foreigners alcoholic drinks are served. The local *Stella* is a good light beer, and the state wineries in the Delta have good wines in their cellars: *Omar Khayyam* (a strong, dry red wine), *Château Gianaclis* (a velvety, dry red wine), *Rubis d'Égypte* (a refreshing dry rosé which can, however, turn to a kind of sherry if it is stored incorrectly), *Cru de Ptolemées* (a delightful medium dry white wine), *Village Gianaclis* (a dry white wine).

There are delicious non-alcoholic drinks, such as freshly-pressed fruit juices (orange, lemon, guava and mango, according to the time of year). These are good quality drinks and are also available in cans. There is also *karkade* (a fruity sweet mallow tea which can be drunk hot or cold), *tamarhindî* (the sweetened juice of the tamarind).

Contrary to Western custom, in the Orient you wish *bon appetit – hanî' an!* – after the meal.

235

METRIC CONVERSION

Metric Unit	US Equivalent
Meter (m)	39.37 in.
Kilometer (km)	0.6241 mi.
Square Meter (sq m)	10.76 sq. ft.
Hectare (ha)	2.471 acres
Square Kilometer (sq km)	0.386 sq. mi.
Kilogram (kg)	2.2 lbs.
Liter (l)	1.05 qt.

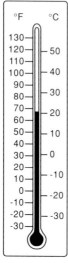

PREPARATIONS

Climate / Travel Season

Egypt is situated between 22° and 32° latitude in North Africa's subtropical dry belt. As a result, a dry desert climate with mild winters and hot summers is characteristic. Changes in temperature between day and night can be as much as 17°C.

To the south of Cairo it hardly ever rains, but since the building of the Aswan High Dam higher air humidity and increased cloud formation have been recorded. The Delta and northern coast are part ot the Mediterranean climatic zone with abundant rainfall in winter. Between November and April precipitation in the Sinai is rare but heavy. When it occurs, it causes dangerous flash floods in the *wadis* (dried out river valleys). Almost every winter snow falls in the mountains.

Spring is the time of the *khamsîn,* a hot dry desert wind which usually lasts many hours, and sometimes even many days.

As far as climate is concerned, the months from October to April are the best time to travel to Cairo and Upper Egypt. But Christmas and Easter vacations are peak periods for tourists. Between November and April you should be prepared for more frequent rain and cool days in Alexandria and the Delta. The same is also true of the Sinai and the Red Sea, although its water temperature never drops below 21°C.

In the hot summer months temperatures in the south of the country can often climb to over 40°C, but because of the relatively low humidity (approximately 30%) they are usually easily bearable. It is the ideal time to travel, if you can stand the heat, as tour organizers and hotels offer discounts, and temples and tombs are left in peaceful tranquility. But in Alexandria it is then the peak season.

Clothing

It is advisable to take light cotton clothes, comfortable shoes and some kind of head covering. You should also pack some warm things for the winter months, as it can sometimes get noticeably chilly, even during the day. Neither too informal nor too scanty clothing is suitable – even when the barometer climbs to unaccustomed heights.

But Egyptians have now, unfortunately, had to get used to the fact that Western visitors would rather undress than dress in the summer heat. In a time of a resurgence of traditional values, it is good to keep in mind that bare arms and legs are unseemly for both women and men in Egypt. Sleeveless shirts, shorts and tight-fitting trousers should therefore be avoided – and not only in mosques and churches.

Entry Requirements / Visas

To enter the country you need a passport which is valid for at least six months and an Egyptian visa. You can obtain a one-month visa on arrival in Egypt at any airport or harbor. A three-month visa can be obtained from Egyptian consulates. Even if you have a South African visa stamped in your passport, you can once again travel to Egypt. No visas are issued at border stations on land routes, with the exception of Eilat/Tâbâ (see below).

Tourist visas are issued for a period of one month. The maximum duration of stay in Egypt is three months, but this can be lengthened to six. If you plan to make an excursion into any neighboring country, you must apply for a multiple-entry visa. There are special regulations for tourists who wish to cross the border at Eilat/Tâbâ without a visa. They can obtain a short-stay visa for the South Sinai, but this only allows them to spend 14 days on the Gulf of 'Aqaba and around St. Catherine's Monastery. They are not allowed to travel farther on toward the Nile Valley. For those who decide on the spur of the moment to travel here, a visa can be obtained at the Egyptian embassy in Tel Aviv.

You should not overstay your visa by more than two weeks. For an extension you need a passport photo and a lot of patience. In Cairo the authority responsible for the registration of passports and extension of visas is located in the Mugamma' in the city center at Mîdân at-Tahrîr. In Alexandria it is in Sh. Tal' at Harb 28. In other towns and cities it is located in local police stations.

Entering the Country by Car

You will need an international driver's license, an international vehicle registration, and a *Carnet de Passage*, allowing for the temporary tax-free import of a vehicle. Rental cars are not allowed to be brought into the country. Four-wheel-drive and diesel powered vehicles can enter the country at all border crossings except Tâbâ.

The *Carnet de Passage* can be obtained at most auto clubs for a hefty deposit, which is refunded when your car is once again in your home country. The Carnet is valid for a maximum of six months, though its validity expires with that of your visa. The name and address in the Carnet must be identical to those on your driver's license. The vehicle's information will be entered in your passport. You will receive Egyptian license plates, which will be fastened onto your own. Before you travel out of the country, the return of these plates must be arrange with the border officials in advance. Customs taxes are based on engine size.

Regulations regarding the bringing of vehicles into Egypt are strictly adhered to as a means of hindering the illegal import of cars. If you should have any problems with customs clearance, the English-speaking tourist service of the Egyptian Automobile Club (ATCE) can help you. Call them in Alexandria at (03) 548-1494/95, and in Cairo at (02) 574-3355 or 574-3176.

As the international green insurance card is not valid in Egypt, supplementary auto insurance must be purchased upon arrival in the country.

Customs and Import Regulations

All travelers recieve a customs declaration form on arrival, which have only been infrequently inspected as of late. However, for your own good you should fill it out and have it stamped (!), in the event you will be taking more than US $500 in currency or checks with you when you leave the country. Video cameras must be declared and entered into your passport.

Egyptian currency may be taken into or out of the country up to a maximum of only LE 20. Import of the following items are tax free up to the amount given:

200 cigarettes or 25 cigars or 200 grams of tobacco; one liter of spirits; items intended for person use. Toll-free goods can be bought at Cairo International Airport even after arrival in the country.

Currency / Foreign Exchange

The Egyptian Pound (abbreviated LE for *Livre Égyptienne*) is the country's unit of currency. It is divided up into 100 *piasters* – abbreviated PT. In Egyptian Arabic the pound is called the *Ginéh* and the piaster *Qirsh* (pronounced "irsh" in Cairo).

The usual credit cards and travelers' checks are accepted just about everywhere, unlike Eurocheques, which are only accepted in a few banks and at the airport. Bank branches in hotels, unlike regular banks, usually have a 24-hour service. You should keep your exchange receipts until you leave for re-exchanging Egyptian pounds. Egyptian pounds are only converted into US dollars when re-exchanged. Stays in international hotels must be paid for in foreign currency.

Always keep plenty of small bills on hand (50 piaster and one-pound notes) for baksheesh and taxi fare. The Duty Free Shops at the airports do not accept Egyptian currency!

Health Care

Vaccinations are not needed to travel to Egypt. But people traveling from infected areas, or who have passed through an infected area in the previous six days, must have yellow fever and cholera vaccinations. Inquire at the appropriate health office before you travel.

A gamma globulin injection is recommended, as this gives a certain amount of protection against hepatitis A lasting for about six weeks. For the summer months it is advisable to take precautions against malaria. Private medical travel insurance is strongly recommended.

A medical kit for the journey should contain medicine against all kinds of colds (the most common illnesses which you will catch in Egypt), fever, flu, digestive and circulatory problems. A disinfectant salve for wounds, adhesive bandages and dressings are just as important as sun cream with a high blocking factor and insect sprays or lotions (for preventing and treating bites).

The most common cause of those unpleasant, but mostly harmless, digestive tract disorders is drinking beverages which are too cold. The great difference in temperature between day and night, and excessively air-conditioned hotel rooms and buses can often bring on colds. Because of the danger of contracting bilharziasis, you should only swim in chlorinated water or the sea; never in the Nile, fresh-water lakes or canals.

ROUTES TO EGYPT

By Air

Cairo International Airport is the hub of international air traffic between Europe, Africa and Asia. It is used by numerous international airlines. The state-owned Egyptian carrier Egypt Air runs regular flights from New York, Los Angeles, Copenhagen, Helsinki, Stockholm, Bangkok, Bombay and Manila, among other cities. Otherwise you can catch a plane to a European capital and take a regular flight from there.

A number of charter airlines offer year-round bargain tickets and package arrangements. The direct flights to Hurghada, Luxor-Sharm ash-Shaikh or Aswan are very attractive.

By Ship

A charming, and until not long ago traditional, way to travel to Egypt is by passenger ship. Since the passenger service from Venice to Alexandria was discontinued in 1993, the only maritime alternative is to make the trip by freighter. Naturally, this is only advisable for those who aren't on a tight schedule, as routes and departure times can only be determined at the last minute, depending on cargo and loading conditions. By this method you can usually take your car; in fact, for some companies the transport of a car is a precondition. Information can be obtained from special travel agents for cargo-ship journeys. For cargo journeys from England, write to: *Weider Travel,* Charing Cross Shopping Concourse, The Strand, London WC2N 4HZ.

By Road

The land route to Egypt is only recommended for those who have a sense of adventure and a lot of time on their hands. Over the 4,000- kilometer stretch through Austria, Bulgaria or Greece, Turkey, Syria and Jordan you will "experience," in the truest sense of the word, the change in country, climate, people and culture. Most of the roads are good, but you can also go by train and/or bus. Before traveling, check with your country's Foreign Affairs Office.

The ferry from 'Aqaba (Jordan) to Nuwaiba' (Sinai) sails daily (around three hours journey time), and the 'Aqaba to Suez route is served four times a week. From 'Ammân there are direct buses to Cairo, which also use the 'Aqaba-Nuwaiba' ferry. Since Camp David you can also travel through Israel to Egypt. There are daily buses between Tel Aviv and Cairo, and you can also enter Egypt at the Eilat/Tâbâ border crossing. The Libyan-Egyptian border near Musâha'id and As-Salûm was reopened several years ago, making it possible to travel through a number of North African countries. Because of the civil war in Algeria, a trip across the continent from Morocco to Egypt should not even be considered.

TRAVEL WITHIN EGYPT

A Few Words before You Travel

Terrorist attacks carried out in recent years against tourists have created a feeling of anxiety for those traveling to Egypt. Official agencies do not necessarily advise against visiting Egypt, but they do point out that throughout the country – and especially in central Egypt – there is always the risk of terrorist attack.

While there are no travel restrictions per se on tourists, certain routes and places, including sometimes larger regions, may be subject to temporary closure to tourists, showing that the Egyptian government is very concerned about the safety of visitors to the country. Foreigners heading south, therefore, must travel with a military escort. On trips in the Nile Valley between Dandara and Abû Simbel, private vehicles and tourist buses travel with a police escort.

If you are traveling with an organized tour, your tour operator will take care of all organizational problems. If you are traveling on your own, find out well in advance what the current safety regulations are for specific regions. Information can be obtained through travel agents, tourist offices and hotel staff.

By Train

The railroad is a good and very cheap means of transportation in the Delta and Nile Valley. There are two daytime and several night trains of the Egyptian State Railroad with sleeping cars which travel the Cairo-Luxor-Aswan route. In addition, there are two of the international *Wagon Lits* trains per night. Journey time is approximatively 11 hours to Luxor and 15 hours to Aswan. Tickets should be purchased at least a week before departure from a travel agency or train station.

Trains shuttle between Cairo and Alexandria almost hourly, and several times a day there is an express train (journey time 2.5 hours). Every other day a night train with sleeping cars travels to Matrûh, for which tickets and seats should be reserved at least one day before departure. Reservations are especially necessary during the peak season.

By Air

Internal flights in Egypt are no longer as cheap as they once were, but apart from problems with sandstorms in the spring they are usually punctual and reliable. Egypt Air flies the Cairo-Alexandria, Cairo-Luxor and Cairo-Aswan-Abû Simbel routes several times a day, as well as the Cairo-Hurghada, Cairo-Khârga routes several times a week, and the Cairo-Matrûh route once a week.

Air Sinai regularly shuttles between Cairo, Luxor, Hurghada and the Sinai. Main airports in the Sinai are Sharm ash-Shaîkh, At-Tûr, St. Catherine's Monastery and Al-'Arîsh. You can get flight details in the Air Sinai office in the arcades of the Nile Hilton Hotel at Mîdân at-Tahrîr in Cairo, tel. 760948. All Air Sinai flights must be booked there, even if you are flying to the Sinai from Hurghada or Luxor.

By Ship

A cruise along the Nile has always been considered the classical Egyptian journey. Of the approximately 400 luxury hotel ships that ply the river, only a few travel the entire stretch between Cairo and Aswan: all the others travel only the standard route between Dandara and Aswan. In addition, there are a few ships offering three-day cruises to the temples of New 'Amâda and New Sabû'a, as well as Abû Simbel. These cruises are usually sold as part of a package tour, which includes full board and guided tours of regional sights. Bookings can be made at almost any travel agency or at the reservation office of most of the major hotels.

A trip of several days from Luxor to Aswan, or vice versa, on board a *feluka,* a large sailboat, is a unique experience. You sleep on deck in the open air, the sailor is responsible for providing blakets and board – he shops en route and cooks for his guests. The price is agreed upon beforehand.

By Bus or Group Taxi

Egypt's large cities are connected with each other and the hub of the traffic system, Cairo, by an excellent, value-for-money bus network. It is advisable to buy tickets in advance if you can; normally, they are available at the bus station or office of the bus company two days before departure.

There are buses with or without air-conditioning; normal or deluxe. A few of the Upper Egypt Bus Company's vehicles, as well as the *Flying Eagles* and *Golden Arrows* of the Super Jet company, are luxury buses with toilets, video films and a drinks service. A small supplement is charged for air-conditioned buses and night services.

As an alternative to the cross-country buses you can use group taxis which run parallel to the buses on pre-determined, somewhat shorter, routes. That means you have to change more often. Their stands are located near bus stations. They leave as soon as the car is full, but you can also hire a group taxi just for yourself, if you are willing to pay the full fare for all passengers.

By Car

In the last few years the Egyptian road network has been well expanded and repaired. Although four-lane highways are only found in the Delta, the main roads in the Nile Valley, the Sinai and along the Red Sea, as well as their connecting roads, are now all easily passable. But minor roads are often only dirt tracks. On desert roads you must reckon with sand drifts. As a rule, you should travel desert routes with at least one other car and make inquiries at the *Automobile Club of Egypt* (you should also ask about possible restricted areas): 10 Sh. Qasr an-Nil Cairo, tel. (02) 574-3355.

Egyptians drive on the right side of the road. All important road signs are bilingual. Outside built-up areas and villages the speed limit for cars is 90 kmh; within built-up areas it is 30 kmh. There is no lead-free gasoline in Egypt. Be prepared to encounter often chaotic driving styles in cities. Also, be careful and alert when driving at night: vehicles with little or no light, horse-drawn carts, people riding donkeys, animals and passers-by can easily turn an otherwise relaxing drive into a risky enterprise.

If you break down, you will always find people ready to help. Garages are cheap and Egyptians are masters of improvisation. If you have a seemingly insoluble problem, the Egyptian automobile club ATCE in Alexandria has set up an English-speaking service for tourists: Tel. (03) 548-1494.

Note: Don't refuse any offer to wash or keep an eye on your car and always remember to reward this with a suitable tip. This service is a veritable business in Egypt.

Car Rental and City Taxis

Car rental firms, such as Avis, Bita, Budget and Hertz, are represented in all the large hotels and at the airport. To hire a car you must be over 21 years old and have a driver's license issued to you no less than one year ago, plus an international driver's license. The price of rental cars is considerably lower than in Europe; credit card users usually do not have to pay a deposit.

If you do not want to drive yourself, you can get a car and driver at a reasonable price at most travel agents or the state hire company *Misr Limousine*, tel. 259-9813. Taxi drivers often offer to take people on tours of the sights and surroundings. The fare should be agreed upon in advance.

In Egypt taxis are very good value. Group taxis can be flagged down, though it is simpler for foreigners to find a taxi at stands in front of the hotels (these are somewhat more expensive). The fare is agreed upon as you get inside. It is best to find out from the hotel reception desk what the maximum fare for a specific route should be (and have the amount written out in Arabic).

The horse-drawn cabs which can be seen everywhere in Egypt are not really a tourist attraction, but are genuine "taxis." Like their motorized colleagues, they also offer sightseeing tours, which can be very enjoyable.

Tours

Organized tours – from a day's excursion to trips lasting several days, with or without a guide – can be booked at all of the larger Egyptian travel agencies. The state travel agent *Misr Travel*, which has a branch in all the interesting tourist towns, has even got a set route guide for daily tours and visits.

PRACTICAL TIPS FROM A TO Z

Accommodation

The official system of classification of Egyptian hotels, from one to five stars, does not always correspond to European divisions – especially in the lower categories. Prices of hotels in the luxury class (four- and five-star) are between approximately US $65 and 200 per double-room. In the middle category (three-star) prices differ greatly. In Alexandria you only pay about US $25 for a double room which would cost US $45-65 in Cairo and the rest of Egypt. In the more rudimentary hotels (two-star and clean boarding houses) you usually have to pay LE 25-80 for a double-room. In addition to the cost of the room there is usually a 10 percent service and 12 percent tax charge.

If you're willing to lower your standards of hygiene and comfort a little, you will always find small bargain hotels. At the height of the season, i.e., Christmas and Easter vacations, individual travelers should certainly book rooms in advance! Even the smaller hotels are fully booked then.

Up until now camping has not been very common in Egypt. Although there are a small number of camp sites, they don't come up to standard. There are youth hostels, for which you need an international youth hostel card, in most of the large cities.

Alcohol

In Egypt, Islam is the state religion and alcohol is therefore restricted in its availability. International hotels, large restaurants and a few licensed businesses offer Egyptian wine and local beer.

Baksheesh

Service tips of 10 to 15 perent are usually expected in hotels (no matter how lowly) and restaurants. In addition to that, a little baksheesh is expected for every small service.

This is not only true of hotel staff, taxi-drivers, boat owners, carriage and camel drivers, but also of attendants at mosques, temples and tombs, who usually try to "earn" their baksheesh by pointing out particularly beautiful camera shots. Amounts equivalent to US $0.50 to $1.50 are usually suitable, and it is therefore advisable to keep enough spare change on hand. Ball-point pens and brightly colored lighters are treasured items, which no traveler should be without! Children who beg should not be given any money.

Baksheesh is a social obligation which must be met by those who can afford it. All small services, naturally including those outside of the tourist sector, are paid off in this way. This creates socially acceptable employment opportunities and extra income for many people for whom, given their low wages, it is of vital importance.

Banks

In the international hotels in Cairo, and at the airport, the banks are open around the clock. All other banks are open from 9:30 a.m. to 12:30 p.m. Monday through Thursday, and on Sunday from 9:30 a.m. to noon.

Electricity

The voltage is 220V, but you need an adapter for plugs with a ground. In Egypt a small flashlight is also an absolute necessity, be it for power cuts in the hotel or when visiting temples and tombs which are sometimes badly, or not at all, illuminated. A small voltage stabilizer is recommended for running electronic appliances.

Festivals / Calender / Holidays

In Egypt there are three different calenders which are simultaneously in use: the Islamic lunar calender, which begins in the year of *Hijra*, the time of Muhammad's emigration to Medina in A.D. 622; the Julian calender used by the Coptic Church, which begins with the year A.D. 284, the coronation year of Emperor Diocletian, the persecutor of the Christians; and, of course, the official Gregorian calender.

The dates of the great **Islamic festivals** are determined by the lunar calender: at the end of the month of fasting, *Ramadân*, the three-day festival of breaking the fast, *'Id al-Fitr* or *Small Bairam*, takes place. It is celebrated by giving presents, visiting relatives and putting on lavish feasts.

Seventy days later, in the month of pilgrimage, *'Id al-Adhâ* (Festival of Sacrifice) or *Great Bairam* is celebrated for three days with the slaughtering of a lamb, the exchange of presents and feasting. *Mûlid an-Nabbî* (Birthday of the Prophet), in the third month of the Islamic calender, falls together with the festivals of birth for local holy men in many towns and villages. Communal prayers and recitations of the Koran, as well as a rich feast and fair with stands of colorful sweet things, are characteristic of these festivals.

Coptic festivals correspond to those of the Christian year, but they are celebrated on different, mostly fixed dates: so Christmas falls on January 6/7; Easter is celebrated only after April 5, the beginning of spring for the Eastern Church, and Whitsun on July 12.

Coptic Easter Monday falls on the same day as the commmunal spring festival *Shamm an-Nasîm* (literally: Fragrance of the Spring Breeze), when Muslims and Copts fill their picnic baskets with delicious food and travel out into the countryside for the day.

Other **official holidays** are:

January 1 . . . . New Year's Day
February 22 . . . . Day of Unity
April 25 . . . . Return of the Sinai
May 1 . . . International Worker's Day
June 18 . Withdrawal of British Troops
July 23 . Anniversary of the Revolution
October 6 . . . . . Invasion of the Sinai
October 24 . . . . Suez Day
December 23 . . . . Victory Day

Filming and Photography

Egypt is a photographer's paradise, but a few written – and unwritten – rules should be observed: You are not allowed to photograph military installations, bridges or harbors. In most ancient Egyptian tombs, temples and museums, taking photographs or making videos is allowed after payment of a fee, but without flashbulbs. You can buy tickets allowing you to take photographs at the entrance booths, except for the west bank of Thebes (see *Guidepost: Luxor / Thebes West*, pp. 180-181).

If you wish to take a photograph of someone, you should always be sure to ask their permission first. One simple gesture can overcome any language barrier! A little baksheesh is also suitable, if it is requested.

Slums or poverty should not be photographed, as you may insult peoples' feelings and they may also on occasion react in an extreme manner.

Good quality film material is available in tourist centers, and especially in Cairo, but you should buy sufficient amounts before the journey in order to avoid possible shortages.

Food and Drink

Hygiene in the large cities and tourist centers is very good. However, care should be taken with unpeeled fruit and raw vegetables, mayonnaise and icecream. Tap water is on the whole clean, but so strongly chlorinated that you will not want to drink it for that reason. Mineral water is the safest bet.

Guides

You can get a guide through any of the local travel offices and agencies in all the larger cities. In Cairo you will also find guides in front of the Egyptian Museum who have a license for the whole city. Most of them speak good English.

Opening Times

Friday is the legal day of rest, but that is only for offices, official organizations and banks. Most shops are open from 2 p.m. at the latest (after Friday prayers). Many business people, international companies and entrepreneurs of the Coptic faith, on the other hand, shut up shop on Sunday. Even the bazaar is dead on Sundays (not Fridays!). Being between the two, Saturday can form a weekend with either the Islamic Friday or Christian Sunday.

Business hours are relatively regular from Monday to Thursday: 9 a.m. to 7 p.m. in the winter (until 8 p.m on Thursdays), 9 a.m. to 1:30 p.m. and 5 to 8 p.m. in the summer (until 9 p.m. on Mondays and Thursdays). Grocery stores are allowed to remain open until late in the evening.

Most mosques, temples and tombs can be visited from 7 a.m. to 4 p.m. in winter, and in summer from 6 a.m. to 5 p.m. The large museums are usually open daily from 9 a.m. to 4 p.m., the smaller ones from 9 a.m. to 1 p.m. On Fridays some, but not all, shut at 11:15 a.m. for two hours during prayer time.

During the month of Ramadân other opening times are in operation. The Egyptian Museum in Cairo closes at 3 p.m., the museum in Luxor at 3:30 p.m., and most excavation sites at 5 p.m., whereby tickets are only sold until 3:30 p.m. So you should check again before undertaking anything.

Pharmacies

There are pharmacies with a comprehensive selection on almost every street corner. As the international pharmaceutical concerns also produce in and for Egypt, you can get the usual medications – generally without a prescription. If you need a certain medicine, you should, however, be able to name its active substances, as trade names may differ.

Post

Letters and postcards are best mailed from hotels. Stamps can usually be bought at shops selling postcards. Public mailboxes are blue for foreign airmail and red for internal Egyptian mail. The main Post Office in Cairo at Mîdân 'Ataba 15 is open daily from 6 a.m. to 8 p.m.

Prices

Favorable exchange rates make Egypt a reasonably cheap country to travel to on the whole. The most notable exception to this rule are the entrance prices charged at tourist attractions. You will have to reckon on paying up to about US $14 per person for tickets.

This measure is to be welcomed, however, as the money is needed for the maintenance and restoration of the monuments. By showing an International Student Identity Card students can receive discounts. The Egyptian State Railroad (but not the Wagon Lits company)

also gives reductions, but these can only be applied for in Cairo and you have to go through an extremely bureaucratic and time-consuming procedure.

Print Media

The Egyptian daily newspapers *Al-Ahrâm* and *Akhbâr al-yaum* only report in Arabic. But the English-language *Egyptian Gazette* and the French *Le Progrès Ègyptien* are on sale daily in Cairo. In only a few pages they both give a brief account of the day's political events, sport and culture. There is also the more extensive and very informative *Middle East Times Egypt*.

Interesting articles on art and culture, together with a calender of events and an address section, can be found in the English-language monthly magazine *Cairo Today*. International papers and magazines are available in all the large hotels. There is sometimes an even greater selection at the newsstand at Mîdân Tal'at Harb in Cairo.

Shopping

Egypt is regarded as a true paradise for souvenir-hunters – with the positive and negative aspects that go along with that. As is the custom in the Orient, you have to haggle about prices. The first rule of this game is: Take your time! Everything else is a question of intuition and your own business talent.

Classic mementos from Egypt include: copper and brass goods, such as salvers with ornamental engravings or inlaid work, candlesticks, lamps, pots and dishes; fine woodwork with mother-of-pearl inlay which can be bought as boxes, playing boards or wall plates – sometimes you can also find wonderful intricate *mashrabîya* lattice-works of a transportable size (e.g., elegant mirror frames or folding screens); woven carpets with beautiful geometric patterns or the well-known pictorial carpets with naive depictions of nature and life in the country – traditionally they used to come from Harranîya and Kirdâsa (near Gîza), but now you find them everywhere, even in the Sinai; leather goods of all kinds made from camel and buffalo hide, such as belts, bags, shoes, cushions, etc., which are very good value (though you should be sure to check the quality of the work); gold and silver jewelry in various forms and price categories; ancient Egyptian motifs, such as scarabs, ankhs – the Egyptian symbol of life – and cartouches into which you can have your name worked in hieroglyphics are original and attractive.

Then there is Egyptian clothing, such as the *gallâbîya*, the traditional ankle-length gown worn by men, which you can have made within a day. Especially imaginative creations have been thought up mainly for the tourist market: cotton sweatshirts and T-shirts with hieroglyphic or other Egyptian motifs, and summer clothes and housewear in the *gallâbîya* style; the colorful glittering belly-dancing costumes are a good idea for carnival time.

Perfume essences and oils which are offered by veritable masters of ceremony in their seductively fragrant plush grottos are a pleasure not to be missed! There are spices, of which there are a great variety; papyri painted with Pharaonic motifs which vary in quality and size, and can be bought everywhere – in many papyrus shops (especially those near to the Gîza pyramids) there are demonstrations showing how the papyri are made from the papyrus plant according to ancient Egyptian tradition.

So-called "antique" items (which are guaranteed to be at least three days old) are on offer everywhere. A few licensed dealers in Cairo and Luxor do sell real antique items now and again, along with well-made replicas. But trade in, and export of, genuine antique goods, that is, items over one hundred years old, is forbidden by law.

Sports

Soccer is the Egyptians' favorite sport. If you also have a passion for the game, go and have the thoroughly enjoyable experience of watching one of the great Cairo teams – Ahly or Zamalek – play in their stadium.

Many luxury hotels are fitted out with their own tennis courts, and in Cairo there is a public golf course right at the foot of the pyramids. You can also go horseback riding in Cairo and Luxor. Those interested in water sports or diving get value for their money in Egypt. The necessary equipment can be hired from diving clubs.

Telecommunications

The telephone and postal services are separate in Egypt. National and international card phones can be found in all larger "Telecommunication Centers," which now connect long-distance calls without those previously notorious waiting times. They also offer a telegram and fax service (faxes are only available in the larger cities). Their main offices in the center of Cairo operate around the clock: Sh. Adlî, Sh. Ramsîs and Sh. al-Alfî.

In addition, you can also use direct telephone and fax services to all parts of the world from all the large hotels, but they charge more for their services than the public operators.

To call Egypt from abroad, dial +20 plus the area code (without the first "0") plus the number. To place a call to the U.S. or Canada from Egypt, dial country code 001; for the U.K. 0044; for Ireland 00353; for Australia 0061.

Time

Egyptian time is Greenwich Mean Time plus two hours; Eastern Standard Time plus seven hours. As Daylight Savings Time has also been introduced in Egypt recently, the difference remains in effect throughout the year.

EGYPT IN STATISTICS

Area: One million square kilometers.
Population (1997): 62 million.
Population Density: 62 per square kilometer, but in the actual inhabited and cultivated areas closer to 1,700.
Form of Government: Presidential Republic with a multi-party system.
Administrative Areas: 25 provinces (governorates) and eight economic zones.
Religion: 90 percent Sunni Muslim, 10 percent Christian.

ADDRESSES

Airline Offices

The main offices of all the large airlines are located in Cairo's city center around the Mîdân at-Tâhîr.
Air Canada: 26 Sh. Mohamed Bassiouni. **Air France:** 2 Sh. Talaat Harb, tel. 574-3300/465/479/516. **Air India:** 1 Sh. Talaat Harb, tel. 392-7467. **Air Malta:** 2 Sh. Talaat Harb, tel. 574-7420. **Air Sinai:** Nile Hilton Hotel, tel. 760948. **Al Italia:** Nile Hilton Commercial Center, tel. 574-0984 (airport: 665143). **American Airlines:** 20 Sh. El Gehad, Mohandessin, tel. 345-5707. **British Airways:** 1 Sh. Abdel Salam Aref, tel. 762852 (airport: 671741). **Delta:** 17 Sh. Ismail Mohamed, Zamalek, tel. 342-0861. **El Al:** 5 El Maqrizi, Zamalek, tel. 340-8912, 341-1429. **Egypt Air:** Nile Hilton, Md. Tahrir, tel. 575-9703; Sheraton Gîza, tel. 348-8630, 348-9122; 9 Md. Talaat Harb, tel. 392-2835, 393-0381; Sheraton Hotel, Md. Galaa, tel. 348-8630. **TWA:** 1 Sh. Kasr El Nil, tel. 574-9904/08/10/17. **United:** 42 Sh. Abdel Khalek Tharwat, tel. 3908099/5090.

Automobile Club

Automobile et Touring Club d' Egypt (ATCE), 10 Sh. Qasr an-Nil, Cairo, tel. (2) 574-3176/3355; 15 Sh. Salah Salem, Alexandria, tel. (3) 481494/5.

Embassies and Consulates

In Egypt: *AUSTRALIA:* World Trade Center, Corniche El Nil, Boulak, tel. 575-0444, fax. 5781638. *CANADA:* 6 Sh. Mohamed Fahmy El Sayed, Garden City, tel. 354-3110, fax. 3563548. *IRELAND:* 3 Sh. Abu El Feda, Zamalek, tel. 340-8264, fax. 356-2495. *UK:* 7 Sh. Ahmed Ragheb, Garden City, tel. 354-0852. *US:* 3 Sh. Lazoughli, Garden City, tel. 355-7371. **Abroad:** *AUSTRALIA:* 1 Darwin Ave., Yarralumla, Canberra ACT 2600, tel. (62) 273-4437/8 (embassy); 124 Exhibition St., 9th fl., Melbourne, Victoria 3000, tel. (3) 654-8869/8634 (consulate); 335 New South Head Rd., Double Bay, Sydney NSW 2028, tel. (2) 362-3482/8, 327-5538 (consulate). *CANADA:* 454 Laurier Ave. East, Ottowa, Ontario K1N 6R3, tel. (613) 234-4931/35/58 (embassy); 3754 Cote des Neiges, Montreal, Quebec H3H 7V6, tel. (514) 937-7781/2 (consulate). *IRELAND:* 12 Clyde Rd., Dublin 4, tel. (1) 606566/718 (embassy). *UK:* 26 South St., London W1Y 6DD, tel. (171) 499-2401 (embassy); 2 Lowndes St., London SW1, tel. (171) 235-9777 (consulate). *US:* 3521 International CTM. W., Washington, DC 20008, tel. (202) 895-5400, fax. (202) 224-4319/5131 (embassy); 1110 2nd Ave. New York, NY 10022, tel. (212) 759-7120/1/2 (consulate); 3001 Pacific Ave., San Francisco, CA 94115, tel. (415) 346-9700/2 (consulate).

Egyptian Tourism Authority (ETA) Offices

In Egypt: Misr Travel Tower, Md. Abassia, Cairo (Headquarters), tel. (2) 285-4509, 284-1970, fax. 285-4363. **Abroad:** *CANADA:* 1253 McGill College Avenue, Suite 250, **Montreal**, Quebec H3B 2Y5, tel. (514) 861-4420, fax. 861-8071. *UK:* Egyptian House, 170 Picadilly, **London** W1V 9DD, tel. (171) 493-5282, fax. 408-0295. *US:* 645 N. Michigan Ave., Suite 829, **Chicago**, IL 60611, tel. (312) 280-4666, fax. 280-

4788; 8383 Wilshire Blvd., Suite 215, **Beverly Hills**, CA 90211, tel. (213) 653-8815, fax. 653-8961; 630 Fifth Ave., Suite 1706, **New York**, NY 10111, tel. (212) 336-3570, fax. 956-6439.

BASIC GUIDE TO THE EGYPTIAN LANGUAGE

High Arabic is the official language of Egypt; though it is really only used in broadcasting and in the church. The commonly used language is Egyptian-Arabic dialect. The Arabic article is *al* (pronounced "el" or "il" in dialect). When the following word begins with d, n, r, s, t or z, the article is assimilated to form *ad*, *an*, *ar*, *as*, *at* or *az*.

Useful Words and Phrases

In Arabic, conversations are different between men (m) and women (f). If conversation is formal, the word *hadritak* (m) or *hadritik* (f) is added at the beginning of sentences and questions.

The most important every-day expressions and greetings are mentioned on page 231. A selection of useful words and phrases follows:

What is your name? . . . *ismak ê? (m)*
ismik ê?(f)
My name is... . . . . *ismi ...*
Where are you from? . . . . . *inta (m)/*
inti (f) minên?
I am from... . . . . *ana min ...*
Are you married? . *inta mitgawwis (m)?*
inti mitgawwisa (f)?
Yes, I am... . . *Na'am* (or *aiwa*), *ana...*
No, I am not... . . . . . *la, ana mish...*
How many children have you got? . .
'andak (m)/'andik (f) kam aulâd?
I have... . . . . *'andi...*
a daughter . . . . *bint*
a son . . . . *ibn*
two daughters . . . . *bintên*
two sons . . . . *ibnên*
I haven't got any children (yet). . . . .
ma'andîsh aulâd (lissa).

How old are you? . . . .
'andak (m)/'andik (f) kam sana?
I am ... years old. . . . . *'andi ... sana.*
I don't understand. . . . .
ana mish fâhim (m),
ana mish fahma (f).
How do you say that in...? . . . .
ê ma'na da bi-l- ...?
Arabic . . . . *'arabi*
English . . . . *inglîzi*
You speak well... . . . .
inta kuwayyis fi-l-... (m),
inti kuwayyisa fi-l-... (f)
Where did you learn Arabic? . . . . .
ta'allamt (m)/
ta'allamti al-'arabî fên?
at school . . . . *fi-l-madrasa*
at university . . . . *fi-l-gâm'a*
from friends . . . . *ma'a ashâbi*
Do you like Egypt? . . . *Misr gamîla?*
Yes, Egypt is beautiful! . . . .
aiwa, Misr gamîla awi!

In the Hotel

hotel . . . . *funduq*
room . . . . *ôda, ghurfa*
with bath . . . . *bi-hammâm*
with breakfast . . . . *bi-l-fitâr*
with half board . . . . *ma'a nuss iqâma*
with full board . . . *ma'a iqâma kamla*
how much is a room? . *kam igâr il-ôda/*
il-ghurfa?
by the day . . . . *fi-l-yôm*
by the week . . . . *fi-l-usbû'*
suitcase . . . . *shanta*, pl. *shunat*
Where is the restaurant? . . . .
al-mat'am fên?

Traveling

taxi . . . . *taks*
car . . . . *'arabiyya*
bus . . . . *bâs*
subway . . . . *metro*
train . . . . *qatr*
plane . . . . *tayyâra*
train station . . . . *mahatta*
airport . . . . *matâr*
street . . . . *shâri'* (abbr. Sh.)
square . . . . *mîdân* (abbr. Md.)

left	'ash-shimâl
right	'al-yimîn
straight	'ala tûl
fast	bi-sur'a, yalla
slow	'ala mahlak (m)/mahlik (f)
pyramid/pyramids	haram/ahrâm
temple	ma'bad
tomb	maqbara
museum	mathaf
church	kinîsa
mosque	masgid oder gâmi'
with	bi
to	ila/li
in	fî
Where is/are...?	fên...?

What time is the bus to...?
imta fîh bâs li...?

A ticket to ... please. / A ticket to...?
tazkara li ..., min fadlak (m)
/min fadlik (f).

At the Market

market	sûq
vegetables	khudâr
tomatoes	tamâtim
cucumber	khiyâr
salad	salata
grapes	'ainab
apples	tuffâh
apricots	mishmish
bananas	môs
strawberries	faraula
dates	balâh
bread	'aish
butter	zibda
cheese	gibna
eggs	bêd
yoghurt	zabâdi
meat	lahma
fish	samak
oil	zêt
salt	malh
sugar	sukkar
milk	laban
coffee	qahwa
tea	shai
one kilogram	wâhid kîlû
one pound	nuss kîlû
one hundred grams	mît grâm

good	kuwayyis/tamâm
expensive	ghali
Do you have...?	fîh?
No, we don't have...	la, mafîsh

How much does that cost?
bi-kam da?

Thanks, that's plenty.
shukrân, kifâya kida.

A description of Eyptian dishes can be found on pages 234-235.

Time and the Days of the Week

hour	sa'a
day	nahâr
week	usbû'
month	shahr
year	sana
in the morning	fî-s-sabâkh
in the evening	bi-l-lêl
today	al-yôm
tomorrow	bukra
yesterday	ams
Monday	yôm l-itnên
Tuesday	yôm at-talât
Wednesday	yôm al-arba'
Thursday	yôm al-khamîs
Friday	yôm al-gum'a
Saturday	yôm as-sabt
Sunday	yôm al-had
What time is it?	as-sa'a kam?

Numbers

Although in the West we use Arabic numerals, true Arabic numerals look quite a bit different to those that we are used to:

0	٠	sifr
1	١	wâhid
2	٢	itnên
3	٣	talâta
4	٤	arba'a
5	٥	khamsa
6	٦	sitta
7	٧	sab'a
8	٨	tamanya
9	٩	tis'a
10	١٠	'ashara
11	١١	hidâshar
12	١٢	itnâshar

13	١٣	talatâshar
14	١٤	arba'tâshar
15	١٥	khamastâshar
16	١٦	sittâshar
17	١٧	sab'atâshar
18	١٨	tamantâshar
19	١٩	tis'atâshar
20	٢٠	'îshrîn
21	٢١	wâhid wa-'ishrîn
30	٣٠	talatîn
50	٥٠	khamsîn
100	١٠٠	miyya
1,000	١٠٠٠	alf

Regarding Pronunciation

â, ê, î, ô, û are pronounced as long vowels. The letter *h* is aspirated from the back of the throat, whether at the beginning or the end of a word. The combination *sh* is pronounced as in English. *Kh* is similar to *h*, but is more heavily aspirated; more of a throat-clearing sound. The letter *z* is pronounced as "s."

' is actually an apostrophe, used to mark a break in pronunciation between two vowels. ' is a typical Arabic throat sound, always used in association with a vowel.

The *gh* combination is a rasping sound produced at the back of the tongue and resembling the French "r."

The letter *q* is a gutteral "k" (not "kw"!), which is generally not pronounced in Egyptian. There are exceptions, however, such as Al-Qâhira (Cairo), for example. *Y* is pronounced as in "yet."

AUTHOR

Eva Ambros, project editor and author of Nelles Guide Egypt, studied Egyptology, classical Arabic and the languages of Christian cultures in the Orient. She spent a great deal of time in Egypt refining her knowledge of Arabic and taking part in archeological expeditions.

Furthermore, she spent twelve years working as a guide for study tours in Egypt. She currently lives in Munich, where she works as a free-lance writer and editor.

PHOTOGRAPHERS

Fischer, Peter — 37, 81, 96, 163

Kunert, Rainer — 85

Legde, Benjamin — cover, 10-11, 14, 15, 17, 19, 20, 21, 23, 25, 26, 27, 29, 30, 31, 32, 33, 35L, 35R, 39, 40, 41, 42, 44, 45, 46, 47, 49L, 49R, 50, 51, 56-57, 58, 63, 64, 65, 66, 67, 69, 74, 77, 83L, 83R, 84, 89, 90, 91, 92, 93, 97, 102, 104, 107, 109, 11, 112, 113L, 113R, 116-117, 118, 122, 125, 126, 129, 133, 135, 137, 140-141, 142, 148, 149, 153, 154, 155, 156, 157, 161, 162, 165, 166, 167, 169, 170, 171, 173L, 173R, 175, 177, 179, 184, 189L, 189R, 195, 197, 199, 201, 202, 204, 206, 211, 212, 213, 218-219, 220, 222, 223, 224, 225, 227, 228, 229, 231, 233, back cover

Nelles, Günter — 193

Skupy, Jitka — 72-73, 100, 108, 168, 192

Spring, Anselm — 8-9, 12-13, 16, 53, 54-55, 87, 88, 95, 98, 123, 127, 131, 147, 172, 190, 214, 216-217, 232, 235, 237

Thiele, Klaus — 182-183.

Explore the World

NELLES MAPS

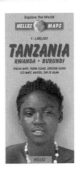

AVAILABLE TITELS

Afghanistan 1 : 1 500 000
Australia 1 : 4 000 000
Bangkok - *and Greater Bangkok*
  1 : 75 000 / 1 : 15 000
Burma → *Myanmar*
Caribbean - **Bermuda, Bahamas,**
  Greater Antilles 1 : 2 500 000
Caribbean - **Lesser Antilles**
  1 : 2 500 000
Central America 1 : 1 750 000
Central Asia 1 : 1 750 000
China - *Northeastern*
  1 : 1 500 000
China - *Northern* 1 : 1 500 000
China - *Central* 1 : 1 500 000
China - *Southern* 1 : 1 500 000
Colombia - Ecuador 1 : 2 500 000
Crete - Kreta 1 : 200 000
Dominican Republic - Haiti
  1 : 600 000
Egypt 1 : 2 500 000 / 1 : 750 000
Hawaiian Islands
  1 : 330 000 / 1 : 125 000
Hawaiian Islands – **Kaua'i**
  1 : 150 000 / 1 : 35 000
Hawaiian Islands – **Honolulu**
  - **O'ahu** 1 : 35 000 / 1 : 150 000
Hawaiian Islands – **Maui - Moloka'i**
  - **Lāna'i** 1 : 150 000 / 1 : 35 000

Hawaiian Islands – **Hawai'i, The Big**
  Island 1 : 330 000 / 1 : 125 000
Himalaya 1 : 1 500 000
Hong Kong 1 : 22 500
Indian Subcontinent 1 : 4 000 000
India - *Northern* 1 : 1 500 000
India - *Western* 1 : 1 500 000
India - *Eastern* 1 : 1 500 000
India - *Southern* 1 : 1 500 000
India - *Northeastern - Bangladesh*
  1 : 1 500 000
Indonesia 1 : 4 000 000
Indonesia **Sumatra** 1 : 1 500 000
Indonesia **Java - Nusa Tenggara**
  1 : 1 500 000
Indonesia **Bali - Lombok**
  1 : 180 000
Indonesia **Kalimantan**
  1 : 1 500 000
Indonesia **Java - Bali** 1 : 650 000
Indonesia **Sulawesi** 1 : 1 500 000
Indonesia **Irian Jaya - Maluku**
  1 : 1 500 000
Jakarta 1 : 22 500
Japan 1 : 1 500 000
Kenya 1 : 1 100 000
Korea 1 : 1 500 000
Malaysia 1 : 1 500 000
West Malaysia 1 : 650 000
Manila 1 : 17 500
Mexico 1 : 2 500 000

Myanmar (Burma) 1 : 1 500 000
Nepal 1 : 500 000 / 1 : 1 500 000
Trekking Map **Khumbu Himal -**
  Solu Khumbu 1 : 75 000
New Zealand 1 : 1 250 000
Pakistan 1 : 1 500 000
Peru - Ecuador 1 : 2 500 000
Philippines 1 : 1 500 000
Singapore 1 : 22 500
Southeast Asia 1 : 4 000 000
South Pacific Islands 1 : 13 000 000
Sri Lanka 1 : 450 000
Taiwan 1 : 400 000
Tanzania - Rwanda, Burundi
  1 : 1 500 000
Thailand 1 : 1 500 000
Uganda 1 : 700 000
Venezuela - Guyana, Suriname,
  French Guiana 1 : 2 500 000
Vietnam, Laos, Cambodia
  1 : 1 500 000

FORTHCOMING

Argentina *(Northern)*, **Uruguay**
  1 : 2 500 000
Argentina *(Southern)*, **Patagonia**
  1 : 2 500 000

Nelles Maps are top quality cartography!
Relief mapping, kilometer charts and tourist attractions.
Always up-to-date!

Explore the World

NELLES GUIDES

GREEK ISLANDS

CYPRUS

TUSCANY

AVAILABLE TITLES

Australia
Bali / Lombok
Berlin and Potsdam
Brazil
Brittany
Burma → *Myanmar*
California
Las Vegas, Reno,
Baja California
Cambodia / Laos
Canada
Ontario, Québec,
Atlantic Provinces
Canada
Pacific Coast, the Rockies,
Prairie Provinces, and
the Territories
Canary Islands
Caribbean
The Greater Antilles,
Bermuda, Bahamas
Caribbean
The Lesser Antilles
China – Hong Kong
Corsica
Costa Rica
Crete
Croatia – *Adriatic Coast*
Cyprus
Egypt
Florida

Greece – *The Mainland*
Greek Islands
Hawai'i
Hungary
India
Northern, Northeastern
and Central India
India – *Southern India*
Indonesia
Sumatra, Java, Bali,
Lombok, Sulawesi
Ireland
Israel - *with Excursions*
to Jordan
Kenya
London, England and
Wales
Malaysia - Singapore
- Brunei
Maldives
Mexico
Morocco
Moscow / St. Petersburg
Munich
Excursions to Castles,
Lakes & Mountains
Myanmar (Burma)
Nepal
New York – *City and State*
New Zealand
Norway

Paris
Philippines
Portugal
Prague / Czech Republic
Provence
Rome
Scotland
South Africa
South Pacific Islands
Spain – *Pyrenees, Atlantic*
Coast, Central Spain
Spain
Mediterranean Coast,
Southern Spain,
Balearic Islands
Sri Lanka
Syria – *Lebanon*
Tanzania
Thailand
Turkey
Tuscany
U.S.A.
The East, Midwest and South
U.S.A.
The West, Rockies and Texas
Vietnam

FORTHCOMING

Poland
Sweden

Nelles Guides – authoritative, informed and informative.
Always up-to-date, extensively illustrated, and with first-rate relief maps.
256 pages, approx. 150 color photos, approx. 25 maps.